Sweet Talk

by the same author

Platform Souls
The Trainspotter as Twentieth-Century Hero

Blue Period
Notes from a Life in the Titillation Trade

Sweet Talk

The Secret History of Confectionery

Nicholas Whittaker

Victor Gollancz
London

First published in Great Britain 1998
by Victor Gollancz
An imprint of the Cassell Group
Wellington House, 125 Strand, London WC2R 0BB

The right of Nicholas Whittaker to be identified
as author of this work has been asserted by him in accordance
with the Copyright, Designs and Patents Act, 1988.

A catalogue record for this book is available
from the British Library.

ISBN 0 575 06555 9

Typeset by Production Line, Minster Lovell, Oxford
Printed in Great Britain by St Edmundsbury Press Ltd,
Bury St Edmunds, Suffolk

98 99 10 9 8 7 6 5 4 3 2 1

Contents

For Oliver and Robin*

*This dedication is null and void if either party
forgets a daily brushing and flossing!*

Taking the Wrapper off

'What happened to Aztecs?'

Whether drunkenly sentimental or prematurely nostalgic (or smugly bursting with an answer), those who ask this question are nearly always of a certain age – 35 to 50, say, and more often than not male. What troubles them is not the fate of Mexico's indigenous Indians but the extinction of a chunky nougat and caramel choc bar. Introduced in 1968, Aztec was Cadbury's ill-starred attempt to knock a hole in sales of the mighty Mars Bar, then taking the lion's share of a choc-bar market worth £72 million.

Ad budgets were enormous. Actors were flown out to Mexico to make a TV commercial. But why? Little green men had never been employed to gee up sales of Mars Bars. Britain's famous holey mints were not advertised by chaps playing polo. What was all this Aztec nonsense about?

Oh, yes, Aztecs invented chocolate, so we're told.

And we were supposed to be impressed? Using the heritage angle can boost sales no end – viz. Hovis, Yorkshire Tea and Mr Kipling – but foreign history doesn't soften us up so easily. Polite interest soon turns to resentment: 'Let me get this straight. Fourteenth century, right? While we were dropping from Black Death, these guys were sitting around sipping cocoa?'

Some might say that Aztec was a doomed idea from the outset. When it comes to credibility, actors poncing around in Montezuma headgear are no match for earthy vox pop. If a Cockney barrow boy could get through his day on a Mars Bar, it had to be good. 'A Mars a day helps you work, rest and play,' they told us – a mantra we dutifully repeated and then remembered for the rest of our lives.

Aztec lasted ten years. Mars has clocked up sixty-five. Still, despite its commercial failure, everyone over 35 seems to remember the Aztec. Its disappearance left a loose thread in Britain's cultural tapestry: tiny, hardly noticeable, but unmendable. Obsolescence hurts.

People get very attached to their confectionery. Similar plaintive questions are asked about Loot, Prize and Amazin' Raisin. Who today recalls Glees, lime-flavoured Aero and penny Arrow bars?

Well, someone does. Trivial footnotes in history, perhaps, but every brand, every wrapper, every taste, is the touchstone of someone's childhood. Rolos, Polos, Bubblies, Jubblies, Chix, Twix, Kix and Kliks – our sweets are as peculiar and joky as our language. As a set of cultural references, they form part of a common past, a source of pride. Sweets, if not the first gift a child receives, are certainly the first things they buy for themselves. Exchanging coin for candy is Lesson One in the Child's Guide to Consumerism.

The choc bar I miss most is the Nutty, Rowntree's answer to the Georges Pompidou Centre in Paris: defiant, modern, challenging, its peanut insides proudly exposed for all to see.

Does anyone now give two hoots for the fate of Lord Toffingham? Curiously omitted from Burke's Peerage, one might suspect some kind of establishment cover-up. Genealogists anxious to check his pedigree might find a clue in Wall's product list for 1973. There he is – Lord Toffingham – the ice lolly with a toffee centre.

Cornetto is still with us three decades after Walls first rallied shopkeepers with the cry 'Profitissimo Italiano!' But who recalls Wiz and Woppa, Dude and Totem Pole, Heart, Rev and Squeeze? What memorial exists for 2-Stix, the 1960s lolly with, yes, two sticks. A great wheeze, but, it has to be admitted, of limited practical use, except in cases of disputed ownership.

Toddler, child, teenager, adult, pensioner – the ages of Man are flagged not just by dummies, toy guns and Zimmer frames, but by an individual's progress from one sweet stage to the next. Just as dolly mixtures were tailor-made for chubby little fingers, and chewing gum ideal for surly teenagers, so the herbal lozenge was designed to clatter around an OAP's dentures, providing its sucker with a suitable smell. These things are expected; the coded signals of social status. Deep suspicion would greet any granny who exhaled the sickly pink scent of Hubba Bubba.

It's a senior-citizen thing, fondly recalling vanished child-hoods. And each personal set of Blue Remembered Hills comes complete with its own sweetshop, run by some paragon of cheeriness and wisdom and offering more choice than any wide-eyed child could cope with. 'In my day ...' they love to tell us. We know, we know, we know: humbugs were as big as cricket balls, sweets were ten a penny, and a halfpenny bag had to last all week. And don't we take just as much delight in shocking them with today's obscene inversions ...

'It's not ten a penny now, Nan. It's ten pence for one single sweet!'

Pointless jibes. Shake out that box of Roses, count the chocs, divide them into the price. Still feel smug?

But it's more than olde worlde prices. Their toffees were so much creamier, their humbugs mintier, their fruit drops fruitier, their kali fizzier. Could they have been so blessed? Were their sweets really so superlatively delicious? Butter substitutes, colourings and artificial flavourings had been widely used since Edwardian times. Nostalgia for 'Victorian values' toffee had started by the time of World War One. Ice-cream, at least according to grousers in the 1920s, was scarcely worth the name. A ready market has always existed for sweets purporting to be Old English Bullseyes, Ye Olde Barley Sugars and Old Time Favourites – but no one has ever specified the old time they are supposed to date from ...

Heck! Everyone's entitled to their memories, false or otherwise. We'll never really know how good or bad those old sweets were, and it scarcely matters now. Of one thing we can be pretty sure: the shop displays of today – clean, corporately branded, as neatly stacked as Lego bricks – look virtually identical from one store to the next. Yesterday's sweetshop may not have been the epitome of bonhomie, daintiness and value we like to imagine, but, good or bad, it had character. Where else but in your grandad's childhood would you find a cat dozing in the window, its bum comfortably cushioned on a box of liquorice novelties?

At the beginning, as an incorrigible trainspotter, I had the idea of compiling a definitive alphabetical list of every sweet, ice-lolly, chocolate bar and bubblegum that ever existed in Britain. Just for the fun of it. I started off with my own memories. Old schoolmates and people on the bus, all were happy to chip in. I was doing well, but I knew there was more. Early research was promising. I came across names I'd never heard of – Voice Gums, Oh Henry, Radio Toffee, Ogo Pogo Eyes, Ainsdale Smilers, Kiro Assorted, Cats' Tails – and rubbed my hands with glee. Hundreds of cops, to use an old trainspotting term. I'd unlocked confectionery's secret history – not concealed, merely neglected: damson fruit pastilles, chocolate bars with greengage cream filling, chewing gum flavoured with blood-oranges. But it was a short-lived triumph and it soon became clear that I'd set myself an impossible task. Dozens became hundreds, then thousands. Disturbing dreams followed. It was as if someone had turned up at my house with a dumper truck full of hundreds 'n' thousands. Answering the doorbell,

I'm deluged. As the truck drives off, a coarse proletarian laugh cracks the air: 'Count that lot, mate!'

One look at Needler's 1900 price list would be quite enough to discourage anyone with half a brain. Its 17 pages included 38 kinds of boiled sweets, 40 toffees, 35 'health' sweets, 15 sticks of rock, and more – 200 lines in all. From one year alone, 1933, I was able to glean the names of scores of chocolates. Liquorice, too, came in dozens of formations. What on earth were Japanese Screws, Dr Jim's Rifles and Spanish Juice? I couldn't even guess. Books, dictionaries and trade journals – all were searched without success – and the only ones who could explain were sitting on the wrong side of a Ouija board.

Some I did find out about. Motto Nuts, for instance, were hazelnuts with their ends sawn off and the kernel replaced by a tiny scroll of tissue paper printed with a motto. The remaining space was primed with a thimbleful of hundred and thousands – and the whole sealed with a smear of nut paste which set hard. This was surely the work of elves, not men. Each one must have taken ten minutes to make and would have sold for less than a farthing. No one would ever become known as the Motto Nut Millionaire ...

Bung Carraways, Sixes, Ching Changs, Horehound Tablets, Bandstrings, Diabalones – the names just kept on accumulating. Together they made an oddball poetry, fun-sounding words for sure, and with a spooky effect, too: memories that seemed so real, but couldn't possibly be mine – rambling through woods, skipping on summer evenings, chasing the organ grinder, trudging to school. But names were all they were, no more meaningful than words discerned on neglected tombstones. I began to have doubts. What use would it have been, anyway: a list of ten thousand sweets, gums, chocolates and ice-lollies?

Who knows? But, quite apart from the dubious fun of trainspotting, I had another agenda. For as well as the ten thousand kinds of sweets, what happened to the thousands of firms who made them and the hundred thousand shops that sold them? By 1956 Britain's 10,000 sweet makers had been reduced to 580 – and today to a mere 80, dominated by Cadbury, Nestlé and Mars. All those who survive and make millions from sweets owe much to the Unknown Confectioner – and yet they so rarely pay their respects. It bugged me to see so many of confectionery's pioneering spirits having their names erased from the roll of honour, in much the same way as Marconi and Baird are given increasingly scant regard. When I saw my children tucking into a pack of Nestlé Smarties I felt that someone was trying to rewrite history.

Let us not forget that it was Fry's who invented Crunchie and Picnic, nor that the glory of Rolo and Toffee Crisp belongs to Mr Mackintosh. MacDonalds (John not Ronald) gave us Penguin, and to Rowntree's we owe thanks for our beloved Smarties and those wonderfully snobby After Eights. To those of a certain age it will always be Rowntree's Fruit Pastilles, Fry's Turkish Delight, Duncan's Walnut Whip. Nestlé Smarties? Nestlé Polo? Cadbury's Crunchie? It just doesn't sound right. Nor is it fair.

Perhaps the most ruthless rebrander of all, Nestlé applies its corporate monicker to everything it acquires.

The light chocolate bubbles in Aero are part of Nestlé's proud chocolate heritage.

But, hang on, Nessie. If you have to blow a trumpet, shouldn't it be your own? Rowntree's invented Aero, thought up the name, spent years building up the brand. Nestlé had bugger all to do with it. Doubtless they are within their legal rights but taking credit for someone else's ideas leaves a very bad smell. Ideally, every sweet and choc bar ought to carry the name of its inventor, its authorship, somewhere on the wrapper, as compulsory as the credits for a pop song have to be.

*

Few books end up fulfilling their original vision and this one is no exception. Even now I'm unsure what kind of book it has ended up as. Claims to a definitive history would be pretentious. It is not a company history, a recipe book or biography of eminent Victorians. The Cadburys and Rowntrees have had their eulogies. If the book has heroes, they are the factory workers, the poor doomed sweetshop owners and us, the people who have chewed, sucked, crunched and licked our way through a trillion tons of sugar and cocoa sweets.

Nor is it particularly serious. Apart from dental do-gooders, dieticians and EU rule-makers, who wants to take the subject seriously? It would be too much like analysing comedy.

Let's just call the book one man's reading of sweets, chocolate and ice-lollies as part of British culture. A previously unwritten history, *Sweet Talk* contains facts and stories buried for years, and is, I hope, simply entertaining and informative. If readers still discern now and then the bare bones of my original lists poking through the prose, I can only apologize ...

An advert for Rocket Rinking Toffee: Edwardian lovers discuss the only sticky
moments they're likely to enjoy prior to their wedding day *(British Library)*

Sugar Sugar

1900–1919

By 1912 Needler's price list had expanded to nearly 600 items: 106 caramels and toffees, 79 pastilles and lozenges, 74 chocolate lines, 34 tinned assortments, 33 rocks and cracknels – and a staggering 224 kinds of boiled sweet. All from one firm – and Britain had hundreds more. Visitors to 1914's trade show, the last before war broke out, when company reps still wore top hats, would have blinked at the sparkling glass: rank after rank of sweet jars, packed with colours and corners, like so many kaleidoscopes frozen in mid-tumble. Floral Tablets, Pear Drops, Clove Cushions, Army Rock, Lime Juice Pastilles, French Almond Rock, Bon Bon Kali, Hothouse Grapes – every conceivable combination of fruit, nuts, sugar, herbs and spices, boiled up and turned into sweets. Wonder at these names, barely discerned in faded photographs: Moonstone Assorted, Cocoa Scotch Cubes, Trinidad Candy, Alabama Coons, Town Hall Gums, Berlin Mixture … Lovely names, but as baffling as hieroglyphics. Flavours, shapes, colours – all lost. Everton Mints and Lemon Sherbets are still with us; Caramel Bullets, Choc Cream Dots and Dolly Pears we might make an educated guess at. But what on earth were Tom Tit Mix, Little Yorkshire Girls and San Toy Mixture, all 2oz a penny from Horn's? Hard to say, but they sound delightful.

Why so many? Why the need for such restless invention? Because sweets have always been more than sweets. Used for medication, meditation, resuscitation, as dummies, bribes, tokens of love – confectionery had an all-embracing agenda. Breath freshening, too, with tiny cachous, perfumed and delicately tinted. Who could resist these jars, crystal minarets with queer and exotic labels: Opoponax, Heliotrope and Pink Aromatics, Tsfani-Ihang, Phul-Nana and Shem el Nessim? Or, saucy and upfront: Sweet Lips and Kiss Call.

Who could resist? Men could. Breath freshening today is a unisex imperative, but Edwardian chaps would rather carry the hum of stale ready-rubbed – bear it with pride! – than be overheard asking for, 'An ounce of Sweet Lips, please.'

With sweets widely regarded as effeminate and childish, sales to males demanded a knack for diplomacy. This helps explain Batger's Jockey Club, an odd name for sweetly scented cachous but a perfect face-saver. It may well have been this same cleverly marketed brand that accounted for the considerable amount of cachous purchased by MPs from the House of Commons shop.

Confectionery was already surrounding itself with guilt and humbug. Fibs came easy. Call your sweets cough drops and perhaps you'd get away with it. No one could accuse a man of sissiness while he sucked on a mouth-sized brick that could include anything – peppermint, ginger, cayenne pepper, sassafras, even wintergreen – with fusions so fearsome and macho as to risk spontaneous combustion. People even wrote to newspapers, asking for mints to be segregated from other sweets since the smell and taste contaminated anything within six feet. Jokes about the effect of mints on the digestive system were numerous and coarse. 'Take some when you go yachting,' advised one wit, 'just in case the wind drops. We gave our captain peppermints and he was able to bring us home in record time!'

Others looking for excuses could always claim the goodness angle. A spin on the name was all it took: Grapejuice Caramels, for instance, or All Fruit Nutlets. Children were unlikely to share a taste for Keiller's Lactor Chocolate: 'Guaranteed to contain highly active bacillus,' proclaimed the wrapper. The magic ingredient was Bulgarian sour milk – as recommended by the serious-sounding Professor Metchnikoff. Inspired by the longevity of Balkan peasants, Prof. M's formula was touted as a perfect answer to rheumatism, neuritis, indigestion, not to mention the tactfully termed auto-intoxication.

But, surely, confectionery ought to be fun: like Rocket Rinking Toffee, all the rage in 1910, the perfect chew for that Edwardian pick-up joint, the rollerskating hall. Looking cool couldn't have been too easy, though. There must have been many an awkward moment when the toffee – not nicknamed stickjaw for nothing – was at its tooth-clamping stickiest.

He: 'Do you come here often?'

She: 'Mmmmnrrgggggg ...'

For younger kids, fizz was the biz. Teasdale's 1911 New Season Kali,[1] for instance, was announced with as big a fanfare as the latest Beaujolais. Could it really have been that much different to 1910's kali? It may well have been. Sweet-makers were bold, innovative and perhaps slightly crazy. Kids waiting at the sweetshop door never quite knew what would turn up next – sweet tobacco, candy confetti, liquorice chains, boiled sweets in the guise of gooseberries and lemons. Whatever it was, they'd always be tickled,

---

1 It wasn't crack cocaine, but kali could have fatal side-effects, especially when taken dry. Fizzing like billy-o, it could easily affect the heart of a weak child, claimed a doctor who signed the death certificate for a Huddersfield girl who died just hours after shovelling in a whole bagful. Kali was intended for making drinks and the craze for eating it wholesale ought to be sternly discouraged, he said.

could count on a fair exchange for their precious pennies. The time when new products would only appear after surveys, committee debates and banking advice was still a long way off. Factory owners were more than happy to leave things to the eccentric genius of their sugar-boilers ...

When Fred Needler set up in Hull in 1886 his staff comprised two – a sugar-boiler and a lad named Watson. The 'man and a boy' set-up was something of a joke even then. One of history's unsung menials, Watson's tasks would have included anything Needler and his boiler disdained. They had a horse and cart, so it's probable that Watson, as well as sweeping floors and humping boxes, did the deliveries, too.

A year previously Fred had been the junior, at Buckton's Confectionery just across the road from Hull station. His mother had secured him the post, ostensibly as a bookkeeper, but everyone was expected to muck in, high collars or not. Hours were long, conditions filthy, and the boss a drunken bully who disappeared for days on end – a lot to suffer for five shillings a week. But Buckton's benders gave Fred the chance to pick up valuable knowledge. When the old soak finally went under and his business came up for sale, the two stoves, slabs, rollers and sundry utensils necessary for making boiled sweets, listed at £100, were bought for 22-year-old Fred by his mother.

Money and business brains were provided by Fred, but the main man was his sugar-boiler, one of the alchemists behind all sweet-making. Sugar turns liquid at 100° Celsius, but it has to get hotter before work starts. A finger, licked and crack-nailed, was the dipstick of choice for many old hands.[2] Old hands gauged temperatures by sight, using a variety of tests. Between 107° and 110° the syrup gets tacky, forming threads when pressed between finger and thumb. At around

---

2 It's not as painful as it sounds, not if you first wet your finger – the vapourized water forms a protective vacuum.

112° comes the 'blow' state: dip the round end of a skewer in the syrup and you can blow a sad bubble. At feather stage (115°) the bubble bursts, leaving flossy threads floating in the air (which gives us the simple principle behind candy-floss). And soon we're in business. At 118° is soft ball; 121° hard ball, when a pea-sized blob moulded between finger and thumb and thrown on the floor should bounce – perfect for caramels and butterscotch – and, no doubt, some great fun when the boss wasn't watching. At around 137° comes soft crack, when syrup dropped into cold water hardens immediately, cracking and sticking to the teeth when chewed. Another 17° (between 154° and 160°) and it becomes hard crack, as brittle and translucent as glass, perfect for boiled sweets. Well, you and I call them sweets, the trade prefers 'deposited boilings' – technically correct but hardly suitable for the soft sell.

Control is vital. At 161° the syrup yellows, turning into barley sugar. A spot of bleach would be sufficient to fix that, though a drop of colouring could easily suffice to hide any defects. But any more boiling and the stuff becomes black jack – useless for anything.

Turned out on to a slab (greased by lard, olive oil or petroleum jelly), colours and flavourings were added and the molten gunge was kneaded, turned, folded and thumped a hundred times while it cooled. After being rolled out into an elongated sausage – or 'rope', as they called it – pieces were snipped off with oiled scissors, the flattened ends giving a sharp-cornered pillow shape to the sweets.

By pressing two or three or more lumps of molten sugar together prior to rolling out, all kinds of patterns could be obtained. Stripes and chequerboards were kids' stuff. And even a Union Jack didn't take much planning. With a good eye and a sense of humour, arty sugar-boilers could make all kinds of novelties – miniature slices of orange, for instance, formed with half a dozen roughly triangular lumps wrapped around by a sheet of 'peel' and then extruded and sliced.

Genuine Acid Drops [3]

8lb sugar
2oz powdered tartaric acid
2 qts water
24 drops lemon oil

Boil the sugar, roll out on to slab. When cool enough, start turning, adding the acid and lemon oil and working in well. Don't add acid until the sugar is cool or it will burn and discolour. Roll into a rope. When cold, break up and dust with icing sugar. Use as light a sugar as possible and add a pin's head of non-poisonous blue for each pound of sugar. By substituting citric for tartaric acid and adding the appropriate flavourings, good raspberry or lime drops can be made.

Most sweets and toffees were made to order. Apart from gums and pastilles, which might take up to a week to dry, little stock was kept in reserve. But, even in small batches, weekly output soon amounted to around ten tons. Turnover was healthy, the money rolled in. By the turn of the century, with Watson and the boiler joined by ten girls and twenty-three men, Needler's humble workshops were getting crowded. In 1905 they all decamped to bigger premises, where the workforce soon grew to hundreds.

Ingredients arrived daily, by the cartload – barrels of glucose, boxes of starch, bottles of acids, wooden crates packed with oranges, lemons and grapes. All the men were rallied to help, unloading the supplies along a human chain. Sugar loaves – conical sticks of moulded crystals weighing anything up to 14lb – were the main form in which

3 Or, to use the trade's own precise terminology, acidulated drops – 'a first-class and time-honoured confection'.

the industry's most vital resource arrived.[4] In one process oranges were grated against the rough surface of sugar loaves, the flavoured crystals then being scraped off and stored in jars for later use. The oranges, wrecked and denuded, were given away to employees, thereby providing management with waste disposal and worker welfare in one.

The scale of manpower (more accurately, womanpower) needed to run a confectionery factory was staggering. From cutting out and folding boxes, to an inspection for each chocolate soldier, every stage called for a keen eye and nimble fingers. Every chocolate was decorated by hand, by girls who'd become experts in squiggling, swirling and scoring. Fifty lasses were assigned to caramel-wrapping duty, with twenty more to weigh and box. Nuts for Needler's famous Buttered Brazils had to be cracked open one by one, a job for a team of twelve girls wielding hammers. Glass jars, which Needler's pioneered the use of, were returned empty, properly washed in soapy water and dried with a teatowel. At lunchtime Needler's high-roofed canteen hummed with the chatter of over three hundred girls. And girls they were, since most started at 14, as soon as they left school. Smartly dressed in works uniform of bow ties and starched polka-dot dresses, they were widely regarded as a credit to their employers.

'Happy as a lark, chirpy as the morning sparrow' was how one observer described girls at another firm. And lest anyone scorn them as working-class drudges, let this fan hasten to disabuse them. 'Many of the women make up in the evening into well-dressed respectable members of society. They like factory life and prefer it to the endless rope of domestic service.'

---

4 There's sugar and there's sugar. Weekly stock reports were gazeteers of geographical exotica: Dutch Crushed – the best for boiled sweets – Russian Crystals, Madras Cane Jaggery, Pale Porto Rico, Yellow Crystallized Trinidad and St Kitt's Syrup, Crystallized Demerara, right down to our own pedestrianly named Tate's No. 1 and No. 2.

But sparrows often starve. If food was short at home, work provided an ideal opportunity for free snacking. Sometimes, if caught out, they were hauled up to the manager's office for a ticking off. Now and then one got nabbed by the Grim Reaper instead – like the young almond sorter who died shortly after collapsing with agonizing gut pains. Doctors confessed themselves mystified – until her workmates spoke about the poor starving soul trying to keep body and soul together by nibbling dozens of nuts from the production line. And there, among all the sweet almonds, enough bitter ones – up to 8 per cent prussic acid – to kill her.

A girl's career as a box-folder or nut-cracker could be curtailed by other indiscretions. Like falling in love. At Needler's, rules called for Saturday's brides to leave on the preceding Friday; with a suitable send-off, of course, and a company wedding present, value dependent on length of service.

While firms like Needler's grew, many sweetshop owners still made their own goodies in a back room or shed. Some tongs and knives, a couple of saucepans and a stove were ample tackle for some entry-level sugar-boiling. A marble slab would be handsome, but for those who couldn't afford state-of-the-art, any old table might suffice. Recipes and tips were easy to come by. Here's one for sherbet:

> *All you need is a 6 parts pulverised sugar, 1 of tartaric acid and 1½ of carbonate of soda. Plus essence of lemon. Sieve all the ingredients three times. Add lemon. Spread it thinly on trays to dry. Sieve it all again and there you have it, all ready to bottle or package.*

With appearance almost as important as taste, good colours were vital to catch the eye. DIYers avidly followed the advice in trade journals, like this formula for a toothsome red:

Take 2oz each of cochineal, cream of tartar, pearl ash and ground ash. Grind down your cochineal beetles in a coffee mill or with a rolling pin. Put into a large copper pan with 2 pints of cold water and boil. Add rest of ingredients. Strain liquor through flannel bag. Restore filtrate to rinsed pan. Add 2lb of sugar and boil, stirring until a thick paste is formed.

'The young woman of today owes much to this little bug,' the writer noted. 'The roses in her cheeks, her crimson lips – not to mention the pink ices and chocolate creams which she loves to eat – all are given colour by these little insects from the Canary Islands.'[5]

Colourings were one thing, but flavourings were often beyond the amateur, however enthusiastic. Synthetic vanilla, for example, could be obtained by oxidizing glucose from the sap of conifers – a daunting task for DIYers, even those with a larch plantation down the road. Far easier to buy it in handy packs from one of the increasing number of professionals: the Confectioners Vegetable Colours and Fruit Essences Co., for instance, based in Hackney Wick:

HARMLESS COLOURS – THE LATEST TINTS
FRUIT EXTRACTS – THE CHOICEST FLAVOURS

Chlorophyll of spinach sounded yucky, but it produced a lovely green. The new products were infinitely preferable to extracts of chromium, copper, mercury and arsenic – all widely used until an outcry in the *Lancet* in the 1850s. The latest colours, though sounding just as fearsome, were quite safe. Pretty pink was obtained from hydrochlorate of

---

5 Since the cochineal beetle lives on cactus, rare in the UK, Canary Islanders found full-time work brushing them into buckets, bottling them and sending them to Britain to be roller-pinned to crimson dust.

phthalein of di-ethyl-meta-amido-phenol; cherry red came from sodium salt of tetra-iod-fluorescine. And what, pray, was sodium-benzene-napthosulphonic acid? Simply red.

What with rivalries, money worries and keeping up with developments (not to mention sugar tax at a halfpenny a pound), home-based sweet-makers were often stressed. In South Wales people still talked about the Llanelli man who prised the lid off a barrel of sugar from Cuba and found a black man's severed head staring at him. Gruesome tales lived on for years. It provided a great argument-clincher for wheedling kids. The bogeyman may not come to their bedrooms, but did they want his nasal hairs in their toffee?

Almost matching it for Gothic horror is another tale of a fellow tradesman up the road in Cardiff. One spring evening, cheesed off with kids messing around the door of his Greyhound Street workshop, he scattered them with a pan full of lukewarm water. When their mother turned up to complain about her sodden offspring (wasn't one wash a week enough?), he brandished an iron bar in her face. But Sarah Jones was a feisty sort. She refused to back off. As the row escalated the sweet-maker picked up a pan from the stove and chucked the contents at her – not water this time, but boiling sugar, half a pint of frothing crack, ruined now because of the aggro. A crowd, attracted by the screaming, found Mrs Jones with a huge blister already forming across her throat and breasts, her hair matted into a glittering cake. But this was worse than a bad hair day. Much worse. As the sugar cooled it formed a translucent mask, through which horrified onlookers could see the poor woman's countenance, burned and bubbled – 'the skin drawn in such a way as to take the face out of all resemblance to a face'. As panicky first-aiders picked off the flakes of dried sugar, large pieces of skin came away with it. Mrs Jones looked boiled, flayed and very upset.

'I thought it contained cold water,' the sugar-boiler told magistrates.

'Aha!' The prosecution swooped. 'Then why did you take off your cap to hold the handle with it?'

After being fined five pounds, 'the sugar-boiler thanked his lordship and left the court in tears – to receive the hearty congratulations of his friends'.

With hours in the kitchen followed by hours in the shop, a small-trader's life was one of hard work and hassle for modest rewards.[6] The run-up to occasions like Easter and Christmas was especially hectic. But when the clamour died down and the Closed sign went up, maybe there'd be a few minutes' peace. Time, perhaps, for a peek at the festive issue of his trade magazine, the *Sweet Shop*. Many years before Page 3 came Page 22. The headline was not 'Phwoar!' but 'Compliments of the season from Natal's new woman' – and underneath, with a winning grin, a topless African girl astride a bicycle. Quite what such blatant nudity had to do with sweets is unclear, but what the heck! Just better make sure the missis doesn't see it – you know she'd never believe it was an innocent article about the latest errand boys' bikes …

Women – always jumping to the wrong conclusions! Luckily, they were easily pacified with sweets, at least according to *Confectionery Journal*.

> *Suppose a couple of lovers have a quarrel. How are they to make it up without confectionery? Perhaps he forgot to kiss her at their last parting, or dared to speak to another girl. Apologies won't do. If he understands women he will take her to the confectioner's and when she is chock full of candy she will be a very agreeable young woman. With her pockets full, her hands full and her mouth full, she is yours for ever!*

---

6 'Heaven helps the man who helps himself, but heaven help the man found helping himself in this shop.' There are people in 1998 who believe this is cutting-edge wit, but this notice from a sweet-shop window dates from 1901. Next time you see this witticism on display, point out that it must be nigh on a hundred years old.

Xenophobia came easily to traders who felt their livelihoods threatened by imports. At a trade fair in Yarmouth a drunken sugar-boiler abused a Russian visitor for a whole fifteen minutes, much to the amusement of the public. Perhaps the British could hardly be blamed for distrusting foreigners, especially when confronted with adverts featuring cartoon Frenchmen snakily hissing: 'Vill you try mine nougat?' (Any accent would do, it seemed, even if inaccurate.) By being less up-front, other competitors could infiltrate more easily – like the German Confectionery Co., who were doing quite well until World War One broke out. The firm's Channel Mixture may have had dangerous hints of Continental ways, but their Britannia Assortment was sweet diplomacy.

Sweets they would pay any price for,
anything to moisten their sand-dried lips and tongues ...

This plaintive appeal, from a Tommy fighting the Boers, was typical of many letters sent to folks back home. Charities responded nobly, collecting enough for ten thousand packs of Invalid Toffee, to be sent out to Red Cross stations in the veld. Queen Victoria matched them, sending ten thousand tins of chocolate.[7] Sweet-makers flew the flag, too, repackaging products with all manner of topical names – like Buller's Bullets, Khaki Toffees and Kruger's Favourites. The Dewsbury Confectionery Co. offered Ladysmith sweet cigarettes and Transvaal Toffee, while Filshill's, makers of the gentle-sounding Reindeer Caramels, rushed out Real Tommy Atkins Rock. From Batger's came a series of marzipan generals – French, Buller, Roberts, Brabant and DunDonald.

Liquorice had a plasticity that was ideally suited, with twists, sticks, strips, laces and loops all taking on a wartime guise, reinvented as lifebelts, motor chains, telephones, cartridge

---

7 Some of which are still uneaten! We'll come to those later ...

belts and pneumatic tyres. Again, the names were delightful: Royal Navy Monster Screws, Military Braid, Telegraph Wires, Tommy Talkers and Dr Jim's Rifles. And, for rounding up deserters, there were even liquorice handcuffs.[8]

Celebrating war with sweets was nothing new: even the Crimean campaign had enjoyed its moment of sugar-coated glory in the shape of Alma Drops, Inkerman Balls and Sebastopol Balls. Impossible to imagine such exploitation now. Would Cadbury's cash in on our patriotism with a Gulf War Chocolate Assortment or a Falklands Creme Egg? How about a Goose Green Sherbet Dip, a bag of SAS Caramels or Scud Nougat? Buller's Bullets must have seemed perfectly normal to the Victorians, but would anyone today dare bring out sweet landmines or liquorice Kalashnikovs? For all that, there is touching honesty about those sweets with the military touch, as if war was only a game for boys, which many believed it to be.[9]

By the end of Victoria's reign, chewing gum was becoming established. Great health benefits were claimed by some brands. Pepsin Gum, for instance, boasted one grain of pepsin in each piece – 'enough to digest one thousand grains of food!' What they didn't bother to mention is that pepsin already existed in saliva and most people could slobber up enough of it to digest ten thousand grains of food.[10]

---

8 Peacetime names were no less colourful – Greyhound Juice, Little Folk's Sticks, Cutty Pipes, Monster London Twist, Peashooters, Spanish Twists, Seville Coils, Japanese Screws, Pomfret Nail Rods, Yum-Yum Twists, Long Virginia, Farthing Starlets and Jumbo's chains.

9 It wasn't only soldiers who died during wartime. Depressed by his son serving in South Africa, William Maynard, the wine gum supremo, having first pinned his will to his chest, killed himself with a crazy cocktail of peppermint, chlorodyne and beer. Verdict: suicide whilst insane.

10 Old timers, recalling impoverished childhoods before World War One, told of how they made their own gum by putting a mint leaf inside a chunk of candle wax!

Names – Dixie Liquorice, Susannah, Queen of the May, Hiawatha – were as inventive as flavourings – blood orange, lime fruits, pineapple and vanilla. Since any supposed benefits were more than offset by potential hazards, perhaps Prudence would have been more apt than Susannah. Early versions of gum comprised anything from 8 to 30 per cent paraffin wax. Little wonder that labels carried warnings – 'This must not be eaten but chewed only' – and gruesome fables were told about the fate of idiots who swallowed the stuff. Such folklore persists to this day, especially among older generations, despite modern gum being fairly harmless.[11]

Gum, in one form or another, goes back centuries. Ancient Greeks had the sap from the mastic tree (origin of our verb 'masticate'). Women used it for sticking on false eyelashes, but its major function was breath-freshening. One Turkish sultan used 125 tons a year, half the annual harvest, in his Constantinople seraglio. His girls must have had pretty bad breath, or else he had a thing about women chewing gum. In Britain, as far back as the seventeenth century, they had a kind of chewie, made with isinglass from sturgeons' guts.

The modern story starts in the 1870s, in Staten Island where Mexican dictator General Antonio de Santa Anna, most famous for his attack on the Alamo, was living in exile. Like a *Desert Island Discs* guest he'd chosen to bring with him an enormous lump of chicle, the chew of choice in Latin America. But the lump wasn't to satisfy any addiction. Santa Anna had got it into his head that chicle's rubbery properties could be exploited in some way, though he wasn't sure how. Luckily, his landlord, Tom Adams, was also a would-be inventor. At his suggestion they tried vulcanizing it – in the hope of discovering a new kind of rubber.

---

11 Urban myth-makers have kept a watching brief on chewing gum for decades. As late as May 1996, Darren Toop, a 22-year-old tennis coach, choked to death on gum.

No luck. Theory number two was that chicle would make a good setting for false teeth and a gummy friend was even persuaded to give it a test run. His verdict is not recorded. After these somewhat farcical experiments, Santa Anna gave up and moved on.

Adams decided to try selling the chicle for its original purpose – chewing – and success came immediately. Eventually sold as New York Gum No.1 – 'snapping and stretching' – it paved the way for Adams and his sons to become America's top gum company. Originally sold in balls, gum evolved into the shape of a stubby pencil and eventually flat strips. In the 1880s, in a bid to prolong its freshness and chewiness, brothers Frank and Henry Fleer hit on the idea of a candy coating. Merida, a mountain town in Venezuela, exported so much of the raw material to the USA that it became known as the city of chicle millionaires.

The key date is 1891, when chewing gum's Messiah arrived in Chicago. Unlike the original Messiah, William Wrigley Jnr was unaware of his destiny. His father, a soap-maker in Philadelphia, had given him a horse and wagon and sent him west: his mission to get Wrigley's Scouring Soap better known. To persuade shopkeepers to stock it, William offered free packets of baking powder and chewing gum. Realizing how popular gum was, he decided that the old man could sell his own soap – chewing gum was Junior's future.

His first brands were Lotta and Vassar. Juicy Fruit arrived in 1893; Spearmint a year later. Getting a foothold wasn't easy. Adams and the USA's top six had formed the Chewing Gum Trust, a cartel which meant serious competition. They offered Wrigley membership but, despite rough patches, he chose to go his own way, criss-crossing the states on a one-man sales drive, offering a whole catalogue of bribes, including razors, lamps, scales and so on. In 1906 he decided to concentrate all his efforts on his most successful brand – Spearmint. While his rivals cut back in response to a slump, Wrigley did the opposite. He wanted the big prize – New York. He'd tried before but found chewers were reluctant to change brands. This time, persistence paid off. More cities fell. By 1910 Wrigley's Spearmint was America's favourite chew. Doublemint, introduced in 1914 – and optimistically described as having 'the flavour of crème de menthe' – made it a winning double.

The Wrigley name has been writ large on Western culture ever since – and this is surely the only confectioner to have its HQ immortalized in song by Frank Sinatra: 'The Wrigley building, Chicago is …'

While the British public heeded advice to treat gum with respect, they hardly expected to find paraffin wax in their chocolate. Nor their children to be slain by it. Like poor Jessie Blake, a 12-year-old Birmingham girl, who died from peritonitis two days after eating 'chocolate chumps' from the corner shop. Described by one critic as 'half the size of a rolling pin, a nauseous thing thickly lathered with brown paraffin wax', the chocolate chump was confectionery for plebs. To kids, whose pennies normally stretched only to cheap boiled sweets, it looked a marvellous feast – but it was crap. Some reckoned that chumps were made from 'grocers' sweepings' – including soda, bits of soap, sawdust and candle wax.

Traders summoned to the coroner's court vigorously defended their recipes. One expressed so much confdence in paraffin wax that he volunteered to eat it for breakfast in a sandwich. Doctors, on the other hand, considered the stuff as beneficial to the digestive system as a plateful of cobblestones: it dissolves at a much higher temperature than the body ever achieves and digestive acids have no effect either. An outraged public – doubtless agreeing with the writer who deplored the pathos and tragedy 'in the thought of a child delightedly sucking that which turns out to be its death potion' – called for chocolate chumps to be banned from sale.

Adulteration and poisoning hit the headlines on a regular basis. Stories all followed a basic pattern. Like that of little Liza Smith, for instance. Hours after eating a pack of Margy's Toffee she started vomiting and quickly died. Rumours spread rapidly. Margy's Toffee was nothing but a witch's brew, congealed and bar-sized, for poisoning innocent tots. But mightn't it have been the pork Liza had eaten before the toffee? In Dublin, when two children died of peritonitis, analysts seized on their sweets, convinced that arsenic had been used in the colouring. In the end their deaths were pinned down to bad corned beef. Ice-cream came under suspicion when Joe Rose, a 14-year-old errand boy, vomited an egg-sized lump of green substance and was soon after carried off to the mortuary. Since thirty of his fellow townspeople were affected, the Borough Analyst sent for poor Joe's stomach, which was delivered in a sealed jar heaving with bacteria. But no concrete proof was ever found to link the illnesses with ice-cream.

While it's true that standards of hygiene left much to be desired, sweets seemed to attract more than their fair share of suspicion. Echoes of an old puritanism were not to hard to detect in people's eagerness to blame ice-cream, toffee and chocolate for illness and death. Sweets were frivolous. Death and suffering were biblical judgements on those who indulged their greed.

A certain glee also attended persistent rumours of evil practices. Wicked witches had been usurped by crooked factory owners. Fudge was made from glucose and rust. Marshmallows got their chewiness from horse glue. Grease from machinery was used to soften chocolate, and sweets were polished up with a solution of talc and washing-up water. When clocking off, workers in chocolate factories had to hand over their shoes for inspection – all the bits picked up during their shift being scraped off and thrown back into chocolate vats.

These colourful rumours were hardly more bizarre than reality, according to a report in the *Daily Express*. Sweets *were* often made with glue or size, colour being added by a dollop of coal tar. But it didn't stop there. Inferior gelatine, used in cheap gums and pastilles, teemed with tetanus germs. Liquorice was coloured with lampblack and stiffened with household starch. Flavours were synthesized from all kinds of chemicals: nitrate of ethyl for pineapple, valerienate of amyl for apple. Pear flavour sounded especially dodgy – synthesized apparently from rotten cheese mixed with sulphuric acid and bichomate of potash. But it begs the question, how were such bizarre formulae discovered? Such experiments could hardly be initiated without some specialist knowledge, help from a corrupt chemist down on his luck …

Other cases of adulteration were more clear-cut, like the fruit drops coated with powdered glass, to give an appearance of sparkling sugar. No one died, but unsuspecting buyers suffered days of severe pain. Shopkeepers were aghast. Some suppliers had been caught bulking up brown sugar with sand – but this plumbed new depths. Had it really been done on purpose? No one knew for sure. Some thought it had, but others refused to believe anyone would stoop to such cynical cost-cutting. It must have been an innocent mix-up. Maybe the powdered glass had been delivered wrongly labelled and no one had seen any reason to check. On the other hand, what reason would a grocer have for ordering packages of ground glass?

Parents were understandably concerned. People began to treat sweets – and the men who sold them – with a certain wariness. Caution was all very well, and justified, but nannyish concern could be taken to extremes, as in the case of those who fretted over the sale of sweet pebbles. 'What if a child got them mixed up with some real gravel?' they asked, citing the poor mite who'd recently choked to death on a plum stone. Shopkeepers laughed at the idea: what child outside a home for the feeble-minded would ever get his or her sweets mixed up with gravel in the first place?

Despite these all-too-frequent cases, the evil hand of adulteration was less and less in evidence. With production on a bigger scale, cutting corners for profit was much harder to get away with. Big firms valued their reputations too much.

Machinery had already begun making inroads. At Needler's fearsome-sounding machines such as the Cyclone Pulveriser were busily pounding sugar into dust, and nuts into paste. Dog-paddling mixers churned the ingredients, while clattering and clumsy guillotines cut out shapes, chopping off the occasional finger along the way. The first simple caramel-wrapping machine had arrived as far back as 1894, an adapted contraption previously used for packing shag, and by the 1900s automated wrapping was catching on, the Oliver Twister being the most wittily named of many such machines. Early results weren't too impressive: more like little parcels wrapped by drunken elves. By the end of Edward's reign the raffishly named Lightning Twister had arrived. Its adverts boasted 'Security–Regularity–Attractiveness' and at top speed this clattering Heath-Robinson device, one-man operated, could turn out fifty-eight wrapped sweets per minute, all with perfect fantail ends. But then so could one of Needler's polka-dotted lasses.

'Can be worked by a boy' proclaimed an advert for the Eureka steam-powered sugar-boiling machine (on minimal wages of course). Likewise, the Blackcurrant Strigging Device: 'does the work of thirty girls'. As, no doubt, could a Patent Gooseberry Snuffer. Yet automation seemed at odds with the industry's avuncular style. Employers who genuinely cared for their employees would surely not replace them by a strigging machine. No, they'd keep them in work, ensuring each twig received personal attention, probably equipping each girl with one of the latest Patented Artificial (Hygienic) Thumb Nails – low-tech with kindness.

Vending machines, meanwhile, were already a common sight on railway stations and in theatres. Even in 1896 a single machine at Paddington or Waterloo might take £200 a day – an awful lot of pennies for someone to count. They could also be found on buses, at the foot of the stairs. More often than not these early automats were jammed – with hair-grips, pins, nails, tin discs. People inserted anything in the hope of getting a free chocolate bar. Maybe they were merely confused by new technology; hardly surprising given the instructions affixed to some machines:

DROP PENNY, IN SLOT, ABOVE,
GRIP, HANDLE, TIGHT, TURN RIGHT,
HANDLE, SLOWLY, HAS REQUIRED

The Sweetmeat Automatic Machine Company had three thousand automats on lease. To help in the ceaseless fight against fiddling, each one had three security locks. With twenty thousand spare keys kept at head office along with the tons of carefully piled pennies, it is a wonder the floors didn't collapse.

A century before Camelot made gambling a national pastime, Britain had the Automatic Cackling Hen Company: 'The cackling is natural and continues from introduction of coin until delivery of egg in receptacle provided.' These mechanical birds could be bought outright for £7.50, or hired on a weekly basis. Each of the sixty paper eggs it held contained a cheap sweet and, for the lucky punters, a coupon entitling them to a box of chocolates, pot of jam or somesuch – a real luxury for urchins who played the mechanized laying system. Similar, but without the chickenesque charisma, were Lucky Potatoes and Sensation Balls, twopenny sweets which held an occasional prize voucher. Kids loved these games of chance, but others took a dim view of it all. 'Illegal and disgusting,' cried critics, an unholy alliance of salvationist spoilsports and shopkeepers who resented every penny that went into a rival's pocket. Killjoys also had a downer on Lucky Bags, which were blamed for leading weak souls into a lifelong gambling habit. Many were undoubtedly a rip-off, but the better ones – Clinkers Lucky Bags, for instance – contained decent little amusements, like jacks, a spinning top or a monkey on a stick.

The inventor of the cackling hens eventually appeared in court, charged with breaking the Lottery Act. Giving evidence, a policeman who'd kept watch on one shop told of numerous children placing pennies in the slot and trying their luck. They were merely seeking amusement from the hen's cackling, protested the defendant, claiming he was only trying to encourage young people to take an interest in poultry – a ludicrous excuse that failed to save him from a three-pound fine.

It wasn't until 1897 that Cadbury's were able to offer Britain's sweet-toothed any halfway decent 'milk chocolate'. Together with Fry's and half a dozen others they'd been trying for a winning formula since the 1850s, but early versions were bitter and crumbly. Those who could afford chocolate – and it was not within the budgets of children or poor folk – preferred to spend their money on the more refined Dutch, Swiss and French versions.

> *What better than a pleasant companion,*
> *a well-hung skirt and a stick of Fry's chocolate?*
> Daily Sketch testimonial, 14 October 1896

Fry's were probably first to reproduce the Continental style successfully – their Five Boys bars came out in 1902 – but Cadbury's weren't far behind, putting blocks of Café Au Lait on sale the same year. Continuing experiments at Bournville finally produced the lighter, more attractive chocolate they sought. Names suggested for it included

Jersey, Dairy Maid and Highland Milk. By splicing the last two together and introducing it, in 1905, as Dairy Milk, Cadbury's gave Britain one of its oral classics.

Chocolate assortments were becoming increasingly popular – success that owed not a little to the packaging. Asked to brighten up the hitherto plain style of Milk Tray boxes, Richard Cadbury, a dab hand with oils and water-colours, saw a perfect opportunity to satisfy his artistic leanings. Encouraged by enthusiasm shown for his first attempt – a painting of his daughter Jessica with her kitten – he rushed out a series of scenes from his holidays. It sounds like the slide show from hell – on a nationwide scale. But Richard's cheerful vignettes brought a welcome touch of colour and fresh air into ordinary lives and children eagerly cut out chocolate-box pictures to stick in scrapbooks.

In toffee history, there is BM and AM, before and after Mackintosh's. Until the crucial year – 1892 – toffee[12] had been brittle and unappealing, devoid of chewiness. John Mackintosh, a Halifax baker who sold confectionery as a sideline, had a brainwave: 'Why not combine English butterscotch with the soft caramel favoured by Americans?' The first batch was boiled up by Mrs M in a brass pan over the kitchen fire. In a precursor to modern-day super-markets' loss-leaders, the toffee was handed out free to customers. Not that they intended to make a habit of such generosity. The following week an advert appeared in the local paper:

Last Saturday you were eating Mackintosh's toffee at our expense. Next Saturday pay another visit and eat it at your own expense.

---

12 Records refer to an Everton Toffy made by Molly Bushell in the 1750s. 'Toffee' is something of a mystery word. The likeliest explanation is that it came from taffy or tuffy, northern dialect for something tough or chewy.

People did. Word spread. When Mackintosh's little shop began to get too crowded John and his wife opened a market stall selling just toffee. From then on cakes and bread took a back seat. Within a couple of years Mackintosh's toffee provided employment for a thousand workers. In 1899, when the company was floated, Mackintosh tried to borrow £3000 from his bank, but the manager just laughed at his nerve: even if Mackintosh's made every piece of toffee in the UK it could never justify such an ill-advised loan. John had to resort to begging subs from his friends, but their confidence in him and his toffee was repaid many times over.

'Early to bed, early to rise. Never get drunk – and advertise!' In keeping with the last part of his creed, Mackintosh sent a tin of toffee and a mackintosh to every MP in the 1905 Parliament. Such was the company's reputation that the Archbishop of Glasgow attributed his popularity with children to sharing the same surname as the toffee king.

Sugar seemed to sweeten everyone it made a fortune for. Was it some kind of symbiosis? A lazy analogy, on the face of it, even a cliché. Yet the evidence would certainly bear out such a theory. One glance at the sugar-barons' portraits would be enough for those who pride themselves on their intuition: no mutton-chop whiskers or flinty stares here. These are not the hard men of Victorian enterprise. Our sweet-makers have jaunty tashes and eyes with a definite twinkle. They were businessmen, of course – but you could well believe it was all just a clever ploy to finance their grand plans.

And Cadbury's were arch-exponents. Was there a hidden agenda? Quakers had been forced into trades like confectionery by being debarred from the professions. One would hesitate to call their philosophy one of revenge, but it certainly had elements of poetic justice.

Philanthropy was *noblesse oblige*. Sedition is a word that others might choose. George Cadbury subsidized the Sweating Exhibition in 1904 (not a promotion for soaps and colognes, but an exposé of the underbelly of British industry) and funded the propaganda of the delightfully named Anti-Sweating League.[13] Thirty years had already passed since the first trainload of pale and dazed Brummies arrived at Bournville,[14] Cadbury's greenfields site south of the city. For workers, this truly was Utopia, run with the benefit of every progressive policy the Victorian mind could think up. They had it all: pension schemes, punctuality bonuses, piece work, profit-sharing, sick pay, clean overalls, heated changing rooms, paid holidays, Saturdays off, a works doctor, cheap railway fares, 'music while you work'. Even by today's standards Cadbury's – and Fry's, Rowntree's and Terry's, too – would not fall short. Workers were encouraged to know their rights, to read the Social Security and Factory Acts, while Bible readings, prayers and summer camps were part of the quasi-religious cult of capitalism-cum-socialism.

While these kindnesses were welcomed by the workers, others viewed it as backdoor socialism, a threat to the status quo. Birmingham gentry, in particular, blamed Cadbury's generosity for enticing girls away from service. 'What girl won't choose a 7-hour day for 16s a week?' moaned one letter writer in the *Birmingham Argus* – as if working a seventeen-hour day for twenty pounds a year was a far better career move.

Though not quite on the same grandiose scale, Needler's employees also enjoyed welfare and pensions, as well as company-sponsored football, netball and cricket teams. Fred Needler spent at least 10 per cent of his personal income on charitable causes, such as a hall of residence for Hull University, still known as Needler Hall. Even fizzy pop bosses and jam-makers were touched by the

---

13 During the Boer War George even bought the *Daily News* in the hope of furthering the Quakers' message of pacifism through its pages.
14 A made-up name, from the nearby River Bourn, and a nod towards the Frenchified snobbery associated with good chocolate.

charity bug: Christmas in Liverpool always meant a gift of ten thousand jars of jam from the Hartley's factory. Others, though kind, were slightly crazy, too. Caley of Norwich, for instance, banned his clerks from using blotting paper in case it smudged the exquisitely handwritten invoices.

But such kindness was by no means universal. Quakers apart, many factory owners were natural Tories and in 1910 it was time for them to show their colours. To help with the election campaign, Derby confectioners were solicited for 'any old scraps of dirty or spoiled sweets' which Tory canvassers could hand out to local kids.[15]

In spite of the paternalism of the bosses, the industry had hazards aplenty. Breaking a nail with a nutshell hammer was only the gentle end of it. Girls were especially wary of toffee-cutting machinery. Missing fingers not only looked bad, but might prevent a man from giving you a wedding ring. Lads who worked in starch rooms, where moulds were dusted to ensure the cooling sugar mixes didn't stick, left work looking like white miners – 'troupes of snowmen' as one onlooker described them.

Some dangers were more insidious, with far more sinister consequences. For the poor lad from Clarnico's[16] toffee-tin department, it started with a headache. Within two days the blue lurgy had attacked his face, neck and chest. Lead poisoning was the doctor's diagnosis – almost certainly contracted through his work: soldering tins. Proof was impossible, though, and his employers flatly denied any blame. With the young man's death attributed to 'natural causes', it seems that dying in the service of capitalism was deemed no great sacrifice in those days. *Dulce et decorum est, pro patria mori* ...

---

15 Not all youngsters would be bought off so easily. Many lads preferred a drag instead and had only turned to sweets out of desperation when 'juvenile smokists' were criminalized by a 1910 law.
16 A portmanteau name from Clarke, Nicholls and Coombes.

Sweating was a problem for the women at Murray's London factory, who went on strike in protest at sweltering conditions. Their walk-out became a cause célèbre, taken up by unions and the women's movement. The girls, nicknamed Murray's White Mice, because they always left work covered in white starch dust, were a feisty lot and their strike chant (to the tune of 'Three Blind Mice') left no one in any doubt of their mood.

> *Murray's White Mice, see how they fight*
> *They collared the fish, the cheese and the bread*
> *Twas meant for the blacklegs they ate it instead*
> *And the boss was so wild he stood on his head.*

'We will crush this strike,' said Murray's bosses, adding some choice words of contempt for the 'agitating ladies' of the women's movement who scored political points by egging on their working-class sisters. But after two weeks of lost production the management caved in, agreeing to a wage rise and proper tea breaks for the women workers.

No longer content with a role as nutcrackers and box-folders, many women, especially those with family money behind them, were aiming higher. The Ladies' Confiserie Company – with a highly respectable address in Buckingham Palace Road – offered courses for women hoping to make a mark in the trade's upper echelons. Run by the delightfully named Miss Spenderel-Moody (an ideal role for Margaret Rutherford), this college offered a single private lesson for seven and six, though how much one might learn from one lesson is anyone's guess. Ten lessons came to five guineas, while a six-month course cost fifty pounds. Many, especially the trade's universally male bosses, scoffed at the students' naïve enthusiasm: 'Why pay a sugar-boiler good money when young ladies are quite willing to pay you to learn the trade? And what a pretty sight, to watch them arrive for lessons with their dainty embroidered satchels ...'

*

For sweet-toothed people, war is a real drag. Bombs and bullets are bad enough, but not nearly so tiresome as those constant demands for self-sacrifice. Denial becomes civic duty – but not everyone conforms willingly. To encourage waverers, London County Council published a list of commandments:

DON'T GO TO PICTURE PALACES
DON'T EAT SWEETS
DON'T RIDE IN TRAMS AND OMNIBUSES UNNECESSARILY
DON'T THROW AWAY EMPTY BOTTLES AND JAM POTS
DON'T WASTE BREAD
DON'T FORGET TO MEND CLOTHES WHEN THEY WEAR OUT

Girls at one school made a public pledge: for as long as the war lasted none would buy a single bullseye, pear drop, liquorice stick or sherbet dab. Poor kids. How were they to know they'd just signed up for a four-year fast? One hopes that no mean so-and-so forced them to keep their promise. Everyone agreed that it'd be a miserable life without sweets. In 'Life Without Lollipops', a guest editorial in a trade magazine, MP Spencer Leigh Hughes waxed sentimental about the 'invisible joys' of confectionery:

> *In church, in work, in class, on the tube, we can eat sweets at any time. One man I know sucks toffee on the Treasury bench. There are cross-grained critics who would pillory a man for such, eating toffee at a time of national crisis, and compare it to Nero fiddling while Rome burned.*

Those who couldn't give up could at least make a token bow to the flag. John Bull Caramels, Duchess Chocolates, Tally-Ho Mixture, Colonial Assortment – such names were stamped with Britishness. Little surprise, then, in the cool reception given to the Hindenburg Toffee sold by one Edinburgh shop. But the name was intentional – so claimed the man who made and sold it – meant as a wind-up, a jeer at the Hun. Made from treacle and best butter, his toffee was so toothsome, so melt-in-the-mouth, that those who chewed it could make it vanish in minutes – just as our soldiers would see off Hindenburg's rabble.

If sweets were considered frivolous while men died in the trenches, buying foreign confectionery was viewed as downright treason. But it wasn't always easy to be patriotic. Chocolate boxes, with their cottages, roses, cherubic children and puppy dogs, epitomized English life – yet many, so it turned out, were trimmed with ribbons made in Germany. Patriots called for a complete embargo. Even neutral countries were viewed with suspicion: calls were made for Swiss chocolate to be turned away from the docks. How could true Brits stomach the stuff when it probably contained German sugar? The Swiss protested: their supplies all came from France and they had the paperwork to prove it.

When it came to patriotism or profit, most citizens had their priorities sorted. But many firms were still willing to do business with Germans – enough of them to worry Westminster into rushing through its Trading with the Enemy Act. Rules were easily sidestepped, though. Cocoa brought in from British colonies could be legitimately re-exported to neutral companies – and if firms there chose to sell it on to the Germans, how could anyone prevent them? (A similar twisty voyage could easily explain that 'French' sugar used by the Swiss.)

The industry was in chaos. Many imported ingredients simply stopped getting through. Supplies of gum arabic, for instance, vital for the chewiness of many sweets, were cut off when Sudan fell under German rule, and remained unavailable until the country was liberated in 1918. Sugar, also in short supply, became an emotive subject. One shopkeeper, seeing a man in a cafeteria put eight lumps in his tea, had to be physically restrained from clocking him one.

Sugar had a deadly side, too. A munitions factory worker was hauled up in front of magistrates and fined two pounds

– a week's wages – for being found with two barley sugars in his pocket. A trivial offence on the face of it, but if sugar from the sweets had somehow come into contact with the acid used in bombs – even a drop of slobber could have done it – the factory could have been blown sky high.

To justify their use of sugar, milk and other essentials, manufacturers were eager to reinvent their products. Cachous were not sweets but breath fresheners. Gum was an essential aid to concentration. A serious role for ice-cream was harder to think of, but makers still protested at a threatened ban. Milk and butter were good whole-some foodstuffs, vital for public morale, everyone agreed on that – so why should their ice-cream, made with the self-same ingredients, be dismissed as a frivolous indulgence?

But it was chocolate that sparked the biggest debate. Such vital resources – 70,000 gallons of milk at one factory alone – should surely not be squandered just to keep schoolkids and shopgirls happy. Pro-chocolate lobbyists argued that it was essential soul food. Chocolate provided Britain's Tommies with energy and comfort: love by proxy. Its manufacture should be recognised as part of the war effort, as important as producing munitions. The country should make as much as possible.

Despite all these protests, by 1916 an official embargo was imposed on sales of confectionery in cinemas, theatres and music halls. All milk – fresh, condensed or powdered – was banned for use in chocolate.

A Huddersfield toffee firm which requested military exemption for their chocolate maker, on the grounds that it would mean two girls losing their jobs as well, was turned down flat.[17] Chocolate eating was unpatriotic, said the

---

17 Other requests for exemption were met with brisk and cheerful logic. Since the confectionery trade was now racked by uncertainties, a spell at the front offered the perfect chance to leave business worries behind.

Appeals Board chairman, and those who encouraged and profited from it were equally damned. Let the man go and do his duty. Two fit girls would have no difficulty finding work in a laundry or a kitchen.

With chocolate increasingly rare, those who'd sent bars to their men at the front had to fall back on cheaper sweets. The reaction of a Middlesex regiment to the arrival of a one-ton crate of bullseyes is not recorded. Doubtless meant kindly, it looked an austere gift compared to the chocolate still being sent to their Belgian allies. While poor rookies sat in their trenches rolling gobstoppers around their teeth and staring death in the face, *les copains* from Brussels and Ghent were tucking into honeyed chunks of Toblerone: 'As supplied to the Belgian Army,' Tobler proudly boasted on its adverts.

Though Wilfred Owen's poems failed to mention it, Tommies trudging across the muck of abandoned battle-fields came across one item more than any other – not bullet cases or cigarette butts, but discarded gum wrappers. Originally classed alongside chocolate as a non-essential, chewing-gum-makers had lobbied vigorously for recognition of its benefits. An invaluable aid to concentration, gum-chewing helped our soldiers think clearer, aim better, stay awake longer – and since that was exactly what army generals wanted, gum received an official OK.

Soldiers needed no convincing. Gum had already acquired its own mythology. One GI sergeant, so the story went, with his unit cut off from supply lines, had to chew the same piece for fourteen weeks and was devastated when it went missing during a retreat from an ill-timed foray over the top. He was so distraught that he had no hesitation in turning straight back to look for it. Inspired by his guts, and thinking he was leading another assault, his men followed – so many of them that when the Germans saw them coming they abandoned their trenches. The sergeant got the Military Cross. And the lost gum? Found sticking to the heel of his boot.

Whether soldiers depended on it or not, traditionalists viewed gum as an unwelcome intrusion into the British way of life. 'When the big war is over one more Americanism will have taken hold,' complained one die-hard.

Back home, Zeppelins were employed in the first-ever air attacks. Having heard clattering on the rooftiles as one passed over their house in Essex, two schoolboys got a ladder from the shed and climbed up to investigate. War souvenirs were prized possessions in the schoolyard. To their astonishment, instead of bullet cases or a lost tunic button, they found a handful of sweets caught in the guttering. Understandably wary, the boys handed over their booty to police who sent the sweets off for analysis. And, indeed, traces of arsenic were found. Chemists were aware that certain chemical changes in glucose can produce such deadly specks, so there was no concrete proof of its origin. But why let facts stand in the way of a good rumour? The dastardly Hun were trying to kill Britain's kiddies by dropping poisoned lollipops ... Odd tactics. But those sweets had got on the roof somehow. Was it really an evil plot, or a simple pathetic gesture of friendship in the midst of hostilities?

Not all the Zeppelins made it home. While Cadbury's requested exemption from service for half of their 324 male workers (denied – no way would they be excused an appointment with death for anything as useless as making choc bars), at least the family heirs were eager to do their bit. Egbert Cadbury, son of Richard, was decorated for bringing down one of the spooky dirigibles off the Norfolk coast.

Others were less worried by air raids than the increasing numbers of lady reps who'd stepped in to replace men away at the front. 'If they think that fluttering eyelashes will make a sale they are very much mistaken!' chuntered one shopkeeper.

Introduced in 1915, just before supplies dried up, Cadbury's Milk Tray was intended to complement the firm's existing Plain Tray. The 'trays' took their name from the way in which chocolates were originally delivered to shops – on a tray containing five half-pound boxes, from which customers made their own pick 'n' mix choice. Bars of Dairy Milk had become Cadbury's best-selling brand – so popular that they'd finally broken Swiss and French dominance of the chocolate market – and though they didn't yet know it, with Milk Tray they were on to another enduring winner. By the mid-1920s this 'box for the pocket' would be outselling all other chocolate assortments – no small feat considering that by that time several hundred others were competing for space on sweetshop shelves.

A year after the Armistice, Cadbury's took over Fry's. They'd always been rivals, though hardly bitter ones. There was even a mutual agreement whereby their reps would repair each other's advertisements and window-lettering, often sabotaged by less scrupulous rivals. Fry's, though, had always had an edge on Cadbury's. Established as cocoa merchants in 1822 and credited with making the first decent milk chocolate, by 1907 Fry's employed 4500 workers and had seven factories in Bristol. Notwithstanding Cadbury's successes, when people thought of chocolate Fry's was still the first name to spring to mind. They became, *ipso facto*, 'by appointment' to virtually every explorer who donned an anorak or pair of goggles. They'd supplied Captain Scott with 'cocoa and chocolate equipment' for his ill-fated Antarctic trip. Alcock and Brown were fans, too, nibbling Fry's Vinello chocolate bars during their sixteen-hour flight across the Atlantic.

But, like many firms, Fry's had been hit hard by the post-war slump and found themselves in deep financial mire. Cadbury's, by comparison, were fit and buoyant. Company policy had always been to pay in full for all purchases. Cash rich, with no debts and no creditors, they were happy to bail out Fry's by buying shares – enough of them to seize virtual control. Being Quakers, rapaciousness hardly fitted their creed and the British Cocoa and Chocolate Company was set up to oversee both companies, its brief that neither one should lose its identity.[18] But, in reality, Fry's had become a virtual subsidiary.

At the end of the war confectionery companies counted their dead. One firm alone, Rowntree's, had lost two hundred employees, not counting the scores of limbless and shellshocked who would never return to their old jobs.

---

18 To be fair, Cadbury's did allow Fry's to keep their name on all their products well into the 1970s, and few people were even aware of the connection. Even now their Turkish Delight still carries the Fry's signature, even if it's only to distinguish it from the newer Cadbury version.

Hot Chocolate

1920s

With all kinds of poisonous gunk masquerading as confectionery, the public knew a good product when they tasted it. Harvino, for instance. One of the enduring successes of the Edwardian age, this chewy toffee, produced at the splendidly named Lion Toffee Mills, was named after its creator, Harry Vincent. Har, vin, and an 'O' just for the heck of it. Loved by the people, Harvino had a reputation. It was a brand worth fighting for.

In 1920, when a rival firm launched toffees called Vyno and Vino, Vincent slapped a writ on them. The charge – 'calculation to deceive' – when argued in court seemed to hinge on class and diction. Children, as counsel observed, no doubt in fruity public-school tones, were apt to drop their aitches. Why, many dropped whole syllables! Confusion was inevitable. The 'class of persons' asking for Harvino were precisely those most in danger of being sold a dummy.

M'lud! If that argument stood, Vincent's rights would be extended, by default, to Vino, Vyno, Ino, Arvno and half a dozen mumbled permutations of Harvino. Shrugging off this logic, the judge sided with the prosecution: the working classes deserved protection from traders who would exploit their bad diction.[1]

---

1 Vincent's lawyers were indeed right. Tizer, *(continued over)*

Smaller firms, especially those which neglected official registration of trade marks, didn't fare so well. The management of Uncle Luke's Steam Confectionery Works in Lancashire, makers of Uncle Luke's Balls, took umbrage when a rival began to ply the public with Uncle Jack's Balls. A court case followed. No one disputed that Uncle Luke was first, but the world was full of uncles. Could a word be annexed by the person who first thought of using it? It appeared not: wise men in wigs decided that Uncle Jack was just as entitled to offer his balls to the public as Uncle Luke.

Not long after Vincent's victory John Mackintosh, mentor of all toffee-makers, passed away. His death came as a great shock to many. 'He was not in good health, but no fears were entertained of a fatal termination!' A firm believer in self-promotion, Old Man Mackintosh would have been delighted with the advert created by his recently appointed agents in America. Tenses apart, it would have made a perfect epitaph:

> *I am John Mackintosh, the Toffee King, Sovereign of Pleasure, Emperor of Joy. My old English candy tickles my millions of subjects. My Court Jester's name is Appetite. I was crowned by the lovers of good things to eat. My most loyal subjects are dear little children. My throne is guarded by the Imperial Unarmed Army of Candy Makers. I am the world's largest consumer of butter, my own herd of prize cattle graze the Yorkshire hills. I buy sugar by the train load. I am John Mackintosh, Toffee King of England and I rule alone. I have legations in all parts of North America. Ask your dealer. Show him this decree. If you will do this for me I will confer on you the Order of the Milk of Human Kindness.*

---

invented by Mancunian Fred Pickup, got its name in a similar way. Launched in 1924 as Pickup's Appetizer, the story has it that children's inability to pronounce the full name led to it becoming universally (and officially) known as Tizer.

A hard act to follow. But the family heirs did him proud. After complaints about waxy tastes imparted to toffees by paper wrappers, the firm, now run by the son, Harold, patented a clever solution. By adding various essences to the melted wax used for coating the paper, scents were created that would have people rushing to get the sweets in their mouths.

Coloured wrappers proved an even more profitable advance. Pretty reds, blues and greens helped catch the eye, certainly, but by happy coincidence these same tints also blocked out light, slowing the degradation of butters and oils, a natural process which, before preservatives were widely used, left toffees tasting sour and spittable.

Mackintosh's mention of cows was a little disingenuous. While modesty forbade boasting of his trophies for breeding cattle, Mackintosh was a canny marketeer and knew that cows were a selling point. After countless horror stories about disgusting sweets made in city sweatshops, words like fresh milk, Jersey cows, butter and grazing were well chosen to create public confidence.

As proof of their wholesome credentials, some company adverts even included a picture. Exaggeration was par for the course; a trait particularly noticeable with foreigners. A sketch of the Peters and Nestlé factory in Broc made the Palace of Versailles look like a modest semi. Strolling its magnificent frontage – eight thousand windows at least! – from end to end would have taken a fit man well over ten minutes. Yet, curiously, this huge temple to chocolate enterprise seemed to have but one chimney to sully the Alpine air. British firms, of course, were far less braggardly. Barker & Dobson's Liverpool factory was half the size of its Swiss counterpart – but, if the picture were to be believed, the place still dwarfed the Houses of Parliament!

Inspired by the Cadbury's model, Harry Vincent had also gone rural. Just weeks after purchasing a sizeable patch of Worcestershire and earmarking £150,000 for a dream factory, Mrs Vincent was daintily laying the foundation stone with silver trowel and mallet. By 1927 the weekly output of Harvino totalled 1700 tons. Except that, ironically, 'Britain's best toffee' was no longer called Harvino. Vincent had had a vision. After visiting the theatre to watch a Maeterlinck play, *The Blue Bird of Happiness,* he decided that henceforth his brand leader would be known as Blue Bird. A curious twist indeed, considering that our toffee tycoon had picked a name used by Boots since 1917 for branding their ginger beer and mineral waters. Legally, it didn't matter, since one was a drink, the other toffee.[2]

Three years after the Armistice, the keepers of official secrets leaked a curious story. Toffee – brand unspecified – had apparently played a small but vital role in naval tactics. Britain's admirals had a problem: how to make sure that mines, once dropped overboard, stayed down long enough for ships to get clear. Boffins in films are usually depicted sucking on unlit pipes, but the one who came up with the ingenious solution had obviously been chewing toffee ... Mines would be shackled to weights by a chain. Incorporated in specially adapted links, toffee made an ideal slow-release mechanism: forming a bond strong enough to restrain a ton weight, but dissolving within half an hour and allowing the mine to surface and score an almighty 'Gotcha!' on a passing enemy ship.

With war out of the way, the confectionery industry could look forward to an exciting future. At a Liverpool department store, curious shoppers gathered to see a special display of the Butter-Kist popcorn machine, the latest thing from across the pond. Except for being hand-packed by neatly pinafored assistants, the whole process – from

---

2 Nor had his Lion Toffee Mills been that original. No copyright existed in factory names and Vincent's was just one of several to share this rather obvious name, among them Hillaby's, the Pontefract liquorice firm, and Lion Confectionery in Bradford, makers of the famous Sports Mixture. Maybe Vincent showed a tad more originality in naming his two yachts *Estelle* and *Grey Mist.*

popping to delivery down a chute – was automatic.[3] The show proved such a crowd-puller that the machine was kept on corn-popping duty twelve hours a day.

Increasingly, the future looked like chocolate. Needler's invested £90,000 in a dedicated five-storey factory. But, despite post-war renewal, life could never be the same again and sweet makers couldn't help but reflect this mood, in lots of ways. Box designs, for instance: war had put a damper on the romantic style. Rose-covered cottages, country churchyards, village life – how could people take the same pleasure in such scenes, reminders of the self-same 'sad shires' where so many families mourned for their dead? Apart from an outburst of gaiety at Christmas, boxes were now elegant but plain. Ribbons (hopefully of British origin) were still permissible, lending a welcome touch of colour, but the formal lines and stripy style had distinct echoes of military decorations. Some assortments were named in honour of famous generals, while Albany, Carlton, County and Westminster spoke of continued deference to establishment values.

Getting a brown person to advertise a brown confection must have seemed pretty harmless at the time, hence Packer's Piccaninny Assorted with its curly-topped cherub on day release from the cotton plantation: 'Ooh, dey's nice!'

But the mood would change. As the 1920s spirit took hold, optimism was signalled by New Era Assortment, from the Liverpool Confectionery Company. Terry's still sold a Trafalgar assortment, but traditional British values were now jostling for shelf space with cosmopolitan yearnings, renewed energy and playfulness typified in assortments

---

3 Not that popcorn itself was so new: archaeologists digging on Native American sites in New Mexico recently found some in a cave – carbon dated to around 3600 BC. If you're keen to learn more, why not write to the Popcorn Institute, Wacker Drive, Chicago.

like Biarritz, Riviera, Royale, Madeira, Matterhorn, Geneva, Versailles and Lido.

But chocolates were not without critics. For one thing they were still relatively expensive and many resented them for inflating the costs of courtship. 'Girls used to be happy with bullseyes or strippet balls,' grumbled one (obviously rejected) male. 'Now it must be expensive chocolates.' Once set off, he warmed to his theme, decrying modern mores and yearning for the good old days of the 1890s and confections like Cupid's Whispers, 'conversation sweets' shyly traded by Victorian lovers, decorated with sentiments like 'Meet me when the sun goes down' – 'far more refined than some of the racy stuff that passes for wit on modern versions'. Anyway, when certain women were now brazen enough to approach men outright, it seemed as if such polite (and cheap) courtship rituals were sadly redundant.

If our miserable so-and-so had found a girl worth opening his wallet for, he'd have had no shortage of choice. The public now had hundreds of chocolate boxes to pick from. Peach O' Mine and Romance were predictable purchases for young men out a-wooing. And Dorothy would be perfect – for a date called Dorothy. Older women probably had to be content with more workaday alternatives: 'For the wife? May I suggest a box of Oak Tray, sir? No, sir, there's no wood in them, just this clever packaging simulating an oak tray. Sure to be appreciated by a lady who takes pride in the home.'

The names Geneva and Biarritz may have added a touch of glamour to the boxes, but what of the chocolates themselves? How different were they from those we know today? Not much. A time-traveller from 1998, seized with a panic attack during General Strike riots, would only have to seek refuge in the nearest sweetshop. Grab a box of chocs and there they'd be, comforting and familiar, the same old shapes and tastes – square caramels, triangular marzipans, rounded truffles, creams of orange, coffee and strawberry.

This is a little unjust. Back then they were not 'the same

old' anything but fresh creations, the oldest dating back little over ten years. It is we who are left with the copies – and not even honest ones, dressed up as they are with all kinds of flowery descriptions. Still, however modern confectioners choose to style them, strawberry, coffee and orange creams have endured for the simple reason that people like them. Yet fruit creams came in many now-vanished varieties – pear, greengage, apricot and plum, for instance. Have they been unjustly sidelined, or merely fallen victim to natural selection? Pineapple and limejuice creams were two choice temptations from Duncan's Blue & Gold, while Bond's Venture – an 'astonishingly attractive' assortment – offered exotica such as redcurrant, cokernut, wood strawberry, maple and even wallflower creams. Though this latter was described as 'pale and aromatic', it can hardly have seemed a tactful present for a lady friend.

As for hazelnut whirls[4] – a chocolate trilobite, unsquash-able, cheerful and obstinate, surviving against all odds – sometimes it feels like they've been with us for ever. But everyone loves them, apart from grumpy denture wearers (and some of them are happy to risk the no-claims bonus on their dental insurance). Methodology of consumption varies: some bite the whole thing in two, a crude section which they examine with a mad satisfied expression, as if they'd split the atom. Others bide their time, quietly sucking, slyly smiling, waiting until every trace of chocolate is cleaned from the nut before taking it out and checking with a diamond merchant's eye – then popping it back in to be pulped between the molars.

Some centres were less predictable. Jokers who weren't too bothered about long-term relationships would have loved Freak Chocolates. 'All the rage in America,' they

---

4 Though it's a deceptively basic concept – a nut wrapped in chocolate – it is not as simple as it looks. Since nuts have a tendency to leak oils, making a right mess of the chocolate, they have to be previously sealed with a thin coat of wax.

might announce, a cruel soft-sell. Unlike normal assortments, there was no little leaflet with a key, and the freaks – a mix of olives, gherkins and cheese cubes – were mixed in among more traditional centres. Shapes gave no clue: girls who homed in on the reassuringly familiar outline of a cherry were just as likely to find themselves biting into a silverskin onion. That boring square might be a caramel – but could well turn out to be a noggin of Gorgonzola. Go on, Doris, do try one …

Joke sweets were almost as old as the real thing, a practical joke with Puritan overtones. Cayenne pepper was a favourite ingredient, used in confections such as Hot Sweets. The trick was to lull victims by planting them in your own packet of fruit gums – and ensuring they didn't get mixed up. Those who liked to nibble the top off a liqueur chocolate would have been truly disgusted to suck in a spoonful of vinegar or mustard sauce! Meticulously filled with sawdust, powdered cork or clipped horsehair, chocolates were nicely boxed and ribboned, the only clue offered by the nicely scrolled name on the lid: 'Catch of the Season'.

Some failed to see the funny side. Death could easily result from such pranks if a child took a coughing fit, complained Marylebone Borough Council officials when they took one shop to court.

With £90,000 invested in chocolate, Needler's could do without any extra money worries. Company finances depended on a certain social system. It was understood: girls who washed sweet jars and folded boxes were not doing it as a career as much as for bottom-drawer money. All but a few girls would marry and leave full-time work by the age of 21, thereby avoiding the need to pay them adult rates. But marriage was no longer such a certainty. Many would-be brides had been widowed before they'd even walked up the aisle. Others had had to take over as family breadwinners. By the mid-1920s 80 per cent of Needler's staff were on full adult wages – adding a hefty £8000 to the firm's annual wage bill.

They needed all the business and all the good PR they could get, which is why royal patronage was especially welcome. Though the exact reasons are unclear, Needler's dining room, recently reopened after extensive refurbishment, had attracted the interest of Edward, Prince of Wales.[5] None of the Windsors had ever expressed a wish to see gobstoppers being made, but perhaps chocolate had a more respectable image. Or maybe, perish such cynicism, young Edward couldn't help thinking of the 1200 nubile young women in polka-dot frocks who crowded in there every lunchtime.[6] If so, the interest was mutual. Needler's girls went wild for a glimpse of Edward, something of a pin-up in his day. To celebrate his visit, Needler's brought out a Prince of Wales chocolate assortment, as did Fry's a while later – both boxes being politely, but uninspiringly decorated with the royal feathers crest. Other firms were less formal. Prize for the most blatant exploitation of Edward's charm must go to Disern's assortment, The Prince's Smile, its box lid adorned with his dimpled and sexy royal smirk, fit to make any factory girl add a reckless extra squiggle to a passing orange cream.

For Britain's poor, decent chocolate remained a luxury, something to save up for, perhaps with one of the hundreds of Christmas clubs that sprang up around the country, especially in inner-city areas. By putting away a few pence each week, members could face Yuletide with confidence –

---

5 His mother, Queen Mary, visited in 1921 and even had a go at making chocolates. Needler's, not slow in spotting a marketing opportunity, rushed out a Royal Taste Assortment, supposedly containing the Queen's efforts.

6 Some of these girls might not be so pretty for much longer. A female hand at one firm was already suing her employers, claiming that prolonged exposure to cocoa and milk had given her chocolate dermatitis. Appearing in court, her once pretty face inflamed and disfigured by yellow scaly sores, the girl won everyone's sympathy – and walked off with a handsome £10 in damages.

their houses may have been cold, but who needed heating when they got such a warm glow from watching their bairns on Christmas morning, eagerly diving into their stockings, pulling out nuts, an orange, a rag doll, a top and – impossible to disguise, its corners poking through the wool – a chocolate bar in glittering foil.

Bogus clubs were not unknown. Catherine Godfrey, a Yorkshire housewife, broke down and appealed for sympathy as magistrates jailed her for a cruel swindle. Her husband had a dicky heart. He couldn't work. They needed money. Angry and chocolate-less, her victims jeered her sob story. They were just as poorly off as she – and since she'd blown all their money and had no way of repaying it, what kind of miserable Christmas would their kiddies have now?

Times were bad, especially up north. But if every firm had been as kind as Cadbury's, there'd have been no need for chocolate clubs, or even a Welfare State. They magnanimously sent off consignments of Dairy Milk to poor children in Jarrow and Gateshead. Admirable deeds, but even charity was not immune from corruption. What about the thirty-six boxes that disappeared? 'Put to one side; surplus to requirements' was the official explanation, though the phrase, applied to chocolate, has to be oxymoronic. Or simply moronic. A couple of months later, during local elections, the chocolate mysteriously resurfaced, given out as sweeteners by one Councillor Lumley. 'Bribery!' cried opponents, a charge serious enough to merit investigation by the returning officer, nearly finishing the councillor's chances for good.

Mugs of eggs and jugs of eggs
Baskets and flaskets
and oxidized caskets.

The commercialization of Easter, already started in Victorian times, was given a whole new dimension by chocolate. Its plasticity was ideally suited to novelty lines. Experts could produce eggs as perfectly shaped and flawless as the real thing, a line of piping all that was necessary to disguise the joins. Others weren't so good at it: a few bubbles in the mix and their eggs ended up like eccentric moons, pockmarked by craters. To distract attention, some bright spark came up with the now classic crazy-paving or 'crocodile' design – queer enough to be charming, and a perfect disguise for any flaws.

Fry's had already invented the cream egg filled with 'yolk', an idea taken up by Thorne's, who offered them in six sizes of sickliness, from tuppence to five shillings. Rowntree's started a lasting tradition with Ryta-Name, an Easter egg packaged with a small tube of icing sugar, with which a name or greeting could be written on the chocolate.

Even so, despite these novelties, chocolate did not enjoy the virtual monopoly on Easter that it has today. Toffee eggs were just as common, and cheaper, as were eggs of marzipan, nougat or marshmallow.[7]

Easter in yesterday's sweetshop was an altogether rowdier affair than today: a beastly pagan carnival cleverly tricked up in chocolate, with hens, ducks, jackdaws, bulldogs, seagulls, turkeys, roosters, squirrels, lions, pigs and elephants (not to mention the odd clown and policeman). All kinds of things could be shaped in chocolate: a champagne bottle in a bucket, chocolate hot-cross buns with marshmallow filling and – surely most delightful of all – two daredevil chicks riding the wings of a chocolate aeroplane.

As for our old friend the Easter bunny, back then he looked more like a hare: with pricked ears and cocky

---

7 In 1970 I made a jelly egg, using helpful instructions from *Blue Peter*. All you needed was an empty eggshell and a sticking plaster. The greatest challenge in this exercise was getting an empty eggshell.

stance, an altogether randier beast. Could it be that the inoffensive cotton-tail we know today is merely a stand-in? How ironic that despite our sniggering obsession with all things sexual, we've chosen to turn our back on hares behaving badly and offered the Easter job to a cuddly toy.[8]

The public expected a display and shopkeepers tried to provide it. Profit was the spur, of course, but in return for their custom, kids were offered spectacle and wonderment – with marvellous backdrops of ribbons, raffia, crêpe paper, shavings, cardboard and cellophane. To add character, fluffy fowl – chicks, ducks and robins – could be bought by the dozen.

Rowntree's issued a sixteen-page catalogue of Easter lines. Eggs were sold in baskets, jugs, bowls, tumblers, basins, egg cups, on plates and in crates, even cradled in nests of wood shavings, shredded paper and cleverly woven liquorice. For children who had their own model railways, how about an Easter egg loaded on a truck, just waiting for delivery to a tin-plate station.

Planning for Easter wasn't easy. For some time the industry had lobbied Parliament to have the holiday on a fixed date each year. In a bid to win their votes, the government's Easter Bill aimed to do just that. Royal assent was granted in 1928 and, officially at least, it became an Act. Until Pope Pius XI got to hear about it. Such meddling with red-letter days was totally unacceptable. For fear of offending Catholics, the law was suspended – and for the past seventy years, apart from occasional grumblings, no one has suggested the idea again.

Today's Easter, sanitized, pre-packaged and corporately blessed, is far less of an occasion. Stack 'em high and stick

---

8 In 1962 a consignment of chocolate bunnies self-destructed on arrival in Denver, Colorado. With the city a mile above sea-level, the change in air pressure had made them explode. Disaster for Denver's kiddies, but a problem that was easily solved by a few well-judged pin-holes before future shipments were boxed.

'em for every penny is the philosophy. Scandalously overpriced, ounce for ounce, Easter eggs conceal a price hike of anything up to 500 per cent – all for the novelty of an egg shape and some packaging which is binned in seconds. Wit and diversity have been replaced by the conformity of global brands. Kids buy the box – enlivened by the Spice Girls, Teletubbies or Thomas the Tank Engine, or often merely sponsored by their own contents, so that it becomes a Snickers Easter Egg, a Mars Easter egg, a Flake Easter egg. Divested of boxes and foil, the eggs are virtually identical. Yet, for all the exploitation, perhaps we should be thankful that children are still enchanted by something as simple as an egg-shaped shell of chocolate. And since it is not the children so much as the parents who are ripped off, we probably have the Easter we deserve.

Back in the 1920s, overt profiteering was similarly resented. After being overcharged for two ounces of peppermint balls, an Isle of Wight resident – the aptly named Mr Grinder – took his local sweetshop to court.

'There is not one tittle of evidence,' protested the shopkeeper.

Nor was there. Mr Grinder's case was thrown out and the acquitted shopkeeper filed a counter suit for being made the victim of such a frivolous charge.

Under the Profiteering Act, hundreds of similar cases took place each week, hours of court time being taken up with deciding whether so-and-so had charged a penny too much for his humbugs[9] or wine gums. Intended as an early

---

[9] 'Humbug' was known for a century before ever being used to describe a sweet. First recorded around 1750, it was something of an all-purpose word. As an expletive it was a rough equivalent to today's 'bullshit', but it also meant a kind of prank or practical joke. Young men who used the word were accused of 'jabbering in the uncouth dialect of the Huns'. Its use for a peppermint-flavoured toffee seems arbitrary, an early attempt perhaps to cash in on the street lingo. And this one's strictly for anoraks – 'Humbug' was the B-side to Greg Lake's 'I Believe in Father Christmas'.

example of consumer power, the Act's only significant effect was to highlight a shameful streak of mean-spiritedness.

The Act's expiry in 1921 doubtless deprived Mr Grinder of his little pleasures, but shopkeepers still had DORA to worry about. The Lord's Day Observance Act, with its one-penny fines (or two hours in the stocks), had long fallen into disuse, but DORA – the Defence of the Realm Act – wasn't so easily flouted. Originally brought in as a defence measure during wartime, it continued to impose a strict 8 p.m. closing time on shops. A steady parade of transgressors appeared before magistrates, who imposed one-pound fines for such heinous crimes as selling threepenny-worth of chocolate at 8.15.

DORA's inspectors were the traffic wardens of their day, reviled as spiteful jobsworths. One got his come-uppance after swooping on a Sutton-in-Ashfield shop at 8.02 and nabbing a boy buying sweets. He scarpered, but as the inspector stayed to lecture the shopkeeper on her civic duties, an ugly crowd gathered and a man called Jones, more ugly than the rest, appointed himself people's champion, blacking the inspector's eye and knocking out a couple of teeth. As a *coup de grâce* Jones shoved him into a stack of biscuit boxes, causing a shelf to collapse and half a dozen sweet jars to bounce on the hapless official's head before smashing to pieces. Despite twelve pounds' worth of damage, the shopkeeper felt obliged to defend Jones at his inevitable court appearance. The inspector had no one but himself to blame, she claimed. So obsessed was he with getting her prosecuted, it was his umpteenth swoop on her shop and surely counted as harassment. DORA's men were disliked by everyone, even magistrates, but since they had to uphold the law they felt obliged to impose a modest fine on Jones.

Sweetshop owners felt besieged on every side. While they had no objection to sweets being consumed in theatres, it was unfair of managements to exploit their captive audience. If punters knew they could get sweets and choco-late inside, who would bother calling in at a sweetshop on the way? It wouldn't have been so bad if DORA's rules applied to theatres, but many had machines and magis-trates had decided that automats were excluded from DORA's remit. To celebrate, Moss Empires, Britain's biggest music-hall group, fixed machines to the back of every theatre seat, putting ciggies and chocolates in reach of all. One theatre alone had two thousand machines, according to the grandly named London Confectionery Protection Association, who recruited a force of sandwich-board men to march outside Parliament. 'WHY GIVE THEATRES A MONOPOLY? IT IS NOT JUST!'

Competition also came from hundreds of demobbed servicemen – recognizable by their uniform of white hat and coats – who scraped a living on the streets selling chocolate and toffee from trays.[10] For those too shell-shocked to speak, a scrawled message on a piece of card was designed to tug at the heart: 'BY BUYING THE CHOCOLATE OFFERED, YOU WILL BE DOING YOUR BIT, AS THEY HAVE DONE THEIRS'.

Such emotional blackmail cut little ice with hard-headed shopkeepers, especially those who were war widows, strug-gling with family businesses and just as deserving of patronage as any disabled man with a tray of chocolate bars.[11]

Despite claims to martyrdom, sweetshop owners were hardly saints. Many were shameless skinflints. 'Miss no opportunity to remind your customers of the goodness in sugar' they were advised, during 1922's flu epidemic. Concern was voiced about shabby practices by those who

---

10 They had a point: one glance at the *London Gazette* would reveal a dozen assorted bankruptcies and County Court Judgements against confectioners every week.
11 Bigger firms were less mercenary, and more willing to take risks. Fry's employed blind soldiers as typists, trained at St Dunstan's.

made their own confectionery. Toffee apples, for instance, were often made from a job lot of windfalls. Once covered, no one had a clue to what they were buying. Bad habits were widespread, like blowing into paper bags before tipping sweets in, or wetting fingers to separate the paper. The increasing use of cellophane was welcome, though it wasn't the hygiene benefits that shopkeepers liked – its crackling acted as an excellent deterrent for would-be shoplifters.

Shopkeepers had few qualms about selling sweets made in Germany, Russia and Hungary, despite protests from British workers who feared for their jobs. 'The public likes a change,' they said, disclaiming responsibility for any lay-offs.

Despite gloomy predictions, the confectionery market was hardly shrinking. Chocolate, rather than tempting people away from boiled sweets, was merely building up its own fan base, an increasing demand for it merely reflecting changing patterns of consumption. Chocolate had brought elegance, of a kind that could never be matched by packets of acid drops or barley sugar, or a bar of toffee. Taste and style were all tied up in it. Chocolates had become an integral part of theatre-going and present-giving. One might give a hostess a box of chocolates. A bag of humbugs, in the same situation, would have been greeted with derision.

For children, decent chocolate was still too formal, too dear, serious stuff for grown-ups. They still preferred sweets with shades of all things childish, described with the comforting language of the nursery – Dolly Dymple, Bunny Bon and Toyplane toffees, Tiny Tots cachous, Curly Murlies, Zoo Mixture, Fairy Crystals, Midget Gems, Sea Shore Pebbles. Horror and fantasy had a part to play, and voodoo was mixed up in it somewhere too. It was as if we could put the bite on our demons, all the things that scared or puzzled us: Black Boys, Black Jacks, Nigger Babies, Jelly Snakes. Even death could be sugared and swallowed – viz.

An early Spangles ad from a more innocent age
(Robert Opie Collection)

FRY'S 1924 EASTER NOVELTIES

FOR PARTICULARS SEE ADVERTISEMENT IN THIS ISSUE

Fry's catalogue for Easter 1924 – an outlandish chocolate bestiary.
Would it not be wonderful to come across a chocolate dromedary
in the 1990s? And maybe, in the Twilight Zone, there is just such
a shop, where a tinkling bell will trigger a scene from some
long-vanished childhood . . . *(British Library)*

(Above) Two Needler's lasses tote one of the firm's giant 1937 Easter eggs. Intended just for display purposes, these over-the-top ova were usually donated to the children's ward of a local hospital *(Below)* If I had a hammer . . . Hard to believe these poor girls spent eight hours a day smashing Brazil nuts. What was their official job description: professional nutcracker, or nutshell removal operative? *(both Brynmor Jones Library, University of Hull)*

The irrepressible Bertie Bassett, cousin of *l'homme* Michelin,
and surely the one with most cause to worry should he ever be
amongst the survivors of an Andean air crash *(British Library)*

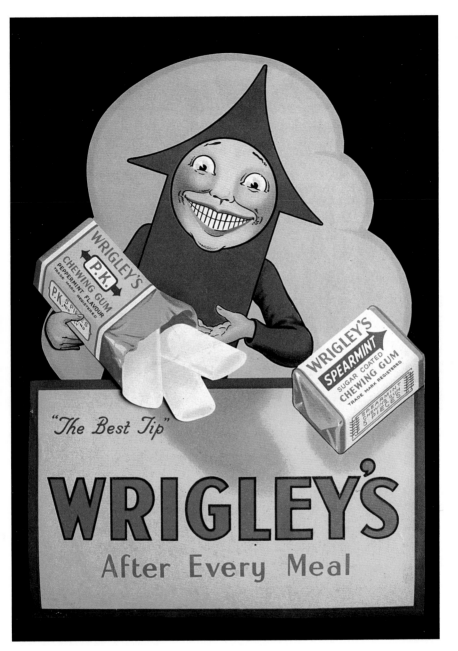

Slightly spooky Wrigley's mascot – grandad to the Gremlins, perhaps?
Not a face you'd like to appear at your window with a chammy leather!
(Robert Opie Collection)

Early advert for the mighty Mars Bar, one which really says
it all in such a simple way *(Robert Opie Collection)*

Fry's 5 Centre, another of those much-loved, much-missed favourites *(Robert Opie Collection)*

Display jars from a 1935 trade show. Not as jam-packed with sweeties as they appear: the sweets are held against the jar sides by a middle crammed full of paper wadding *(Brynmor Jones Library, University of Hull)*

Kelly-In-A-Coffin, a small sugar sarcophagus containing a black or pink candy baby.

Eyes, in various guises, seemed to be a perennial favourite. Bullseyes had been around for ages, just one example of our taste for the ocular. With Cat's Eyes, Hippopotamus Eyes and the wacky Ogo-Pogo Eyes – all from Barratt's – one can't help but wonder if the nation had some kind of spooky eye fetish. As for the charming Laughing Irish Eyes, had distrust of Emerald Isle republicanism reached such heights that the 'bite your enemy' psychology included them, too? Or was it just a kind of sentimental propaganda?

Children did have a taste for chocolate shapes, often moulded into playful guises. Parrots, lobsters, fish and, for some reason labelled separately, bream were popular, though whether backstreet kids used the official sweets-peak – chocolate simulacra – is doubtful. 'Four ounces of aniseed balls and two of them chocolate simulacra please, Mister ...'

Sweets were simply edible toys – and still are. Despite Game Boys, tamagotchis and skateboards, the kids of today still home in on jelly fried eggs, candy bracelets, flying saucers and liquorice watches. They'd easily find their feet in the past, with absurdities like chocolate sardines on toast, candied egg and chips or lamb chops and potatoes, liquorice watches and pipes. Not forgetting sweet cigarettes, of course. The aptly named Jack Tar Smoker's Outfit – 'the famous brands that father smokes, specially blended to suit the juvenile palate' – contained not only cigarettes, but chocolate cigars, matches and a lighter. Frowned on today, such confections gave children a chance to flirt with grown-up eccentricities without being in the slightest danger.

Novelty was the name of the game. Even a hole could raise a smile; witness the success of Lifesavers. The original sweets with a hole, these American imports predated Polos by twenty years and spawned half a dozen imitators.

If you've a hunch, you want some lunch
Try a munch of Lonco Krunch

The Twenties saw a marked increase in liberties taken with the English language. I blame Sir Kreemy Knut, a Douglas Fairbanks Jnr lookalike, who was chief mascot for Sharp's toffee. The letter K, for some reason, was deeply implicated in this kraze. No C was safe from korruption. Customers were confronted by whole racks: Koff-Nips, Stop-Kof, Toffee U-Neek, Kreema, Maskots, Kinema Krunchie, Krispie and Klix. First prize for needless mangling must go to Walter's, who decided that their Swan brand needed a populist make-over: henceforth it must be spelled Swon and sweetshops were flooded with the clumsily named Swon Nuga and Swonkenda. Even the makers of boxed chocolates, a supposedly refined market, couldn't leave well alone – witness Needler's Kiro Assortment. And it would get worse, reaching its nadir in 1935 with the chillingly minimalist K, a harmless nougat bar.

Could we blame children for being so illiterate? Conspiracy theorists (if they existed then) might well have suspected a hidden agenda, a fiendish plot to usurp the mother tongue. Toblerone's latest gimmick was to give away stamps promoting the artificial Ido language, an offshoot of Esperanto. Dentists would surely have preferred would-be linguists to pick up a teach-yourself book. With a staggering 1200 Ido stickers to collect, anyone who completed a set would at least know the Ido for: 'Help, get me to a dentist, my molars are clogged with honeyed Swiss chocolate.'

'Dental destruction' posed such a threat that orthodontic doom-mongers reckoned teeth would disappear within two hundred years. Sheer scare-mongering, retorted confectioners. Of all the places in the world, where did one find the whitest, sturdiest teeth? Why, on sugar plantations of course:

During a railway journey coolies live largely on sugar since there is no time for proper cooking. Its benefits are more than demonstrated by the healthy sets of teeth firmly fixed in the many skulls that litter the wayside. They even use the frayed cane as a toothbrush.

Dead then, but what lovely teeth! 'Sweets are far from a luxury, but a useful part of a modern diet. Sugar is a fuel, producing heat and energy. Soldiers won battles on it.'

But the anti-sugar campaign was gaining ground. Members of the Camp Fire Girls Movement, who aspired to a Healthcraft badge to sow on their sweaters, were required to undergo a two-week withdrawal from sweets and ice-cream. Fortunately for confectioners, who feared the effects of such institutional endorsement, these ideas cut little ice with Baden-Powell's lads. Why, you could even buy chocolate Boy Scouts: Pascall's sold them in boxes of eight, complete with a paper tent.

While adults still liked notional associations with royalty and gentlemen's clubs, confectioners had realized that popular culture – cinema, music halls, big bands – offered the key to sales, especially with children. Roger's Felix Nougat and Sharp's Mickey Mouse Toffee, for instance, were two early examples of sponsorship, tie-ins with cinema's cartoon cat and mouse. Other link-ups with cultural fixations were signalled by Radio Toffee, Ragtime Candy – 'everyone's chewing it' – Jazz Band Suckers and, last but definitely not least, our old friend the letter K was co-opted to work its loopy charms on Keiller's Kinema Krunchies.

One of the decade's noted successes was the Fox's Glacier Mint. Fox and Joyce, two Leicester grocers, had started making sweets in the 1890s. After Joyce quit, Fox recruited his son Eric, previously an Olivetti typewriter salesman in the USA. Originally known as Acme Clear Mint Fingers, the sweets were Eric's invention, the name 'Glacier' suggested by his wife – and quickly registered in 1919. As trade expanded twentyfold during the 1920s, the translucent mints – sixpence a quarter – became universally known as Fox's Glacier Mints – modestly acclaimed as the 'Finest Peppermint in the World'.

In 1924, while digging foundations for a new factory – funded largely by the phenomenal success of Glacier Mints – workmen found traces of a glacier *and* evidence of King Athelstan's Royal Mint. That's the architect's story, anyway. True or not, it earned him a round of applause at the company dinner.

Fox's must have also invested in a battery of Lightning Twisters or something similar. One of 1928's big innovations was – drumroll! – the wrapped Glacier Mint. 'Can be carried in the pocket for days!' boasted the adverts; no small relief to any child who'd ever been forced to say a polite thank-you for a sweet embossed with dust and fibres from someone's jacket pocket.

While die-hards stuck to their fearsome lozenges of cayenne and ginger, modern mint lovers wanted cool – hence the appearance of brands such as Benson's Arctic and Needler's Niagara mints. But following the trend called for caution. One sweetshop owner was forced to publish a grovelling apology for daring to suggest his home-made mints were in any way glacial, that being the word used on his display.

> *I beg to express my sincere regrets and apologies for having recently sold as Fox's Glacier Mints articles which were not of your manufacture. I undertake that I will not again be guilty of this conduct. In consideration of your refraining from taking legal proceedings against me I agree to pay the expenses of publication of this apology.*[12]

---

12 Confectioners hadn't always been so quick off the mark. After all, butterscotch was just as original as glacier. If its inventors had bothered to register it as a trademark they might have cleaned up.

Though snobs doubtless dismissed confectionery as trade, success brought the Foxes some degree of social acceptance. Fox Snr's hobbies were fishing, shooting and, oddly enough, fox-hunting with the Quorn Hunt.

The loathsome conditions under which ice-cream is made will deter anyone from indulging in this questionable luxury...

Well-established by the turn of the century, ice-cream was still largely dominated by Italian immigrants, not cashing in on mythical skills so much as simply opting for a business disdained by British tradesmen. Their stalls first appeared in the 1860s, with some citing the Soho pitch of one Signor Sartorelli, a Venetian, as the very first. Seaside resorts favoured by Londoners – Ramsgate, Brighton and Southend – soon acquired similar stalls and it wasn't long before someone had the idea of adding wheels, enabling them to look for custom – and dodge the officious policemen who nabbed them as common hawkers. Gaudily decorated, the barrows were mobile lessons in Italian culture, featuring Mount Vesuvius, Venetian gondolas, Garibaldi in heroic poses and, with a nod towards topicality, Italians fighting in Tripolitania. After attracting a bad press, mostly centred on the fights around stalls which were often parked outside pubs, half of the traders were forced out of business during the 1900s.

By the end of the World War One they had recovered to be as numerous as ever, a familiar sight on the streets, enticing customers with cries of 'Hokey-pokey, penny a lump'. One lock-up in Clerkenwell had six hundred barrows – just a few of Britain's estimated fifteen thousand.

Moustachioed chaps in straw boaters, crooning an aria or two as they hand out ambrosial ice-cream to rosy-faced children from their pretty barrows ... our cherished view of Italians and their ice-cream. Considering our modern preoccupation with fridges and hygiene, it's curious we should forget that fridges and hygienic wrappings were unknown at the time. Grandma's reminiscences are all very well, but official reports – like this one by the British Institute of Pharmacological Medicine – hint at a much darker picture: 'Manufactured in filthy backyards and dark cellars, exposed to foul emanations both gaseous, liquid and solid, near the sludge from defective drains. The questionable materials used in some of the houses in the Italian quarter include rotten eggs, bad flour, repulsive milk, all excellent media for the ubiquitous microbe.'

Bugs, bugs' legs, fleas, bedstraw, human and animal hair, coaldust, woollen and linen fibres, tobacco, skin scales and muscular tissue – microscopic examination revealed a horrifying catalogue. Even the water used in ices was tainted, teeming with micrococci, bacilli, spirilla and bacterium coli. 'The numbing effect of ice and sweetness of the sugar disguises a hotchpotch of filth. Shop ices are far from perfect, but the street article is seven times worse.'

Nor were the Italians themselves so clean-living, hardly the stripy-blazered and cheerful stereotypes so eagerly mythologized today. On the contrary – newspapers offered dozens of cases that made a complete mockery of such a notion, virtually all involving poverty-stricken immigrants from the boot-shaped homeland.

Three Italians sharing a house in Bradford were fined for keeping wafers, milk and sugar in dirty, fetid conditions. Laughing off Falcarelli's offer to pay his two-pound fine at one shilling a week, magistrates gave him a week to pay the lot. Capuvanio, a recidivist who'd been up for similar offences before, was fined a whopping five pounds, while Antenzio copped his five-pound penalty for keeping custard powder next to the chamber-pot under his bed. Two more Bradford traders were summonsed for storing their wares in a windowless basement alongside old clothes, rabbit skins and dirty bottles. The cellars were also let as a furnished room to a couple with a child.

And if it wasn't blatant disregard for hygiene that landed them in court, it was punch-ups and GBH, like one Signor Gabelli, jailed for stabbing Signor Nocciovelli in a fight over territory in Newport. 'He talked bad to me,' was Gabelli's indignant excuse.

Unfair to Italians? Maybe it was. But even if nine out of ten of them kept their houses in order and scrubbed three times daily with carbolic soap it's hard to see why all these well-publicized cases didn't permanently kill off any romantic notions we may have had about the superiority of Italian ice-cream.

Since most of these Italian were dirt poor and knew very little about vapour compression techniques, they would have stuck with homely methods of refrigeration. Methods of refrigeration were known about for centuries, but developments were slow until the 1920s. The use of salt and ammonia to make ice and frost called for vigilance, the chemical equivalent of plate-spinning, perhaps – OK if you kept your eye on things, disastrous otherwise. The smell and taint of leaked salts quickly turned a batch of ice-cream into cool but smelly stuff disdained even by those who weren't always that fussy. It wasn't until the development of Freon in the late 1920s that refrigeration became the process we rely on so much today.

The origins of the ice-cream cone are disputed. One theory dates it from the St Louis World's Fair in 1903 where Charles Menches, watching girls eating their ice-cream out of holes scooped in cakes, was inspired to produce rolled batters or twists. Another version, also from the fair, tells of a stallholder lobbing scoops of ice-cream to a neighbouring waffle seller – who deftly caught them in a rolled-up waffle and sold them to applauding customers. An unlikely story – but it could well explain the verb 'to waffle'. A wafer factory was already up and running in Manchester in 1895, opened by one Antonio Valvona, who'd learned the art of wafer-making in Brussels. On his heels came a horde of ex-pat Italians: Messrs Fuschillo and

Pompei with a factory in Peckham, and a trio by the names of Coppola, Pompa and Marcantonio who founded the Lambeth Biscuit Co.

Mythology was not confined to ice-cream. Ling's Turkish Delight, for instance, came not from Istanbul but from a garage in South-east London. But who cared? Many people would rather it came from a Forest Hill lock-up than the Middle East. Delight was a rare sentiment where Turks were concerned. 'It is better to buy from our friends than from our unspeakable enemy the Turk!' said one trader, recommending not South London Delight but an American version sold under the curious name Haggis Oriental Rahat. But what had it really got to do with Turks, anyway? Despite the original name – Rahat Lokum, literally 'throat's ease' – anyone could make this simple confection of syrup, honey and lemon juice. Ling's did well enough out of it. Despite being a puzzle to many people, Turkish Delight had a reputation as a sophisticated taste, and even into the 1960s one still came across people who claimed 'this little sweet epitomizes luxury, pleasure and leisure'.

Success broadened Ling's horizons: in 1923 they finally moved eastwards – to the exotic suburbs of Sydenham.

Ice-cream, though, was about to become respectable. Wall's, butchers by trade, first got into it as a sideline to compensate for slack sales of sausages and pies. 'Never eat pork when there's a U in the month,' people said, wisely enough considering the rarity of fridges. Wall's first idea was to sell ice-cream through their usual outlets, butchers and fishmongers. Response was lukewarm – traders couldn't be bothered and shoppers weren't used to asking for ice-cream in the same breath as a pound of tripe.

The idea looked like a loser until a Wall's employee suggested going mobile. Italians had been pushing their trolleys around for years (London alone had two thousand working the streets) but he'd heard tell that, in America, the latest thing was salesmen on trikes. Why didn't Wall's try it in Britain? Reluctantly, his bosses agreed to fork out six pounds for a specially adapted tricycle, first pedalled out on the streets around their West London factory in July 1922. Impact was immediate – despite the two thousand rivals. What chance did a sweaty barrow-pushing Italian have against a smartly jacketed guy with a set of wheels?

Nine more trikes were bought in readiness for the following summer. The 'Stop Me and Buy One' trikes soon became a familiar sight in dozens of towns, and by 1930 Wall's had a fleet of 8500, operating out of 136 depots. As might be expected, shopkeepers hated them. At least Italians walked and so were limited in the degree to which they could cater to the growing market. But the zeal and zippiness of the Wall's salesmen was beginning to make a serious dent in stationary sellers' profits.

The invasion didn't go entirely unchallenged. While no licences were required in London, elsewhere Wall's men – many raw recruits straight from the local labour exchange – were arrested for hawking without a licence. Not such a great problem: with the money they were pulling in, Wall's happily forked out for every licence necessary.

Apart from the ice-cream, one of their best-sellers was SnoFrute, a prism-shaped ice made from real orange juice. Though described as a lolly, the idea of using a stick had yet to be thought of. Wrapped in waxed cardboard, SnoFrute was pushed up into the mouth, rather like today's Calippo. By the 1930s annual sales of SnoFrute (and its milk-based counterpart SnoCreme) reached a peak of 25 million.

While corner shops could make ice-cream in small quantities, since they had no means of long-term storage, they had to sell it quickly or else stand waiting while it melted away. But the wider availability of fridges increasingly meant that anyone could do it: no trikes or Italian ancestry required, just a spoon to stir the mixture with.

PURE DEVONSHIRE
ICE-CREAM
SOLD HERE

'Copies of this full-colour window bill will be supplied to all purchasers of Milkook ice-cream powder' said its maker's advert. Milkook's instructions were simple: just add cold water and freeze. Powder offered one easy method. St Ivel offered bulk ice-cream in liquid form – all the shopkeeper had to do was stick it in his refrigerator and sell it.

No one would ever praise the Pontefract cake as an aesthetic wonder. It looks like, let's face it, a slug that's got on the wrong side of an industrial boot. But, to many, its no-frills appearance – no pretty colours, no sparkle, no scent, no sugariness – was all to the good. It encouraged a non-sissy reputation that advertisers were happy to exploit: 'Men like them. They are the smoker's sweet. They have class appeal and mass appeal.'

Liquorice was a particular favourite with soldiers, a taste picked up during service in the Middle East during World War One: 'When our soldiers captured Johnny Turk he invariably had a supply concealed in his nondescript and voluminous impedimenta.' Shocking turn-out, Yusef, but good taste in sweets!

Noza Lott, writing in *Confectionery Journal*, told a boy's own tale of how a single Pontefract cake once helped him saved six hundred lives. Motoring in the country, he happened on a coal lorry stuck on a level crossing. No way could his little roadster tow it out of danger – and a distant plume of smoke heralded the arrival of a London-bound express. Noza revved up for a dash to the signalbox to sound the alarm but – catastrophe – his engine went. He searched his toolbox for a vital washer. No luck. The seconds ticked away. What about his box of Pontefract cakes? Nibbling a hole in one and – hey presto! – a washer. Fitting it in place, he sped on to the signalbox and managed to save the day![13]

---

13 According to a Sunday newspaper in 1970 one woman sewed

'Liquorice' comes, after some linguistic leapfrogging, from glycyrrhiza, Greek for 'sweet root', its extracted juices being probably nature's sweetest natural substance. Indigenous to Mediterranean lands and renowned for its medicinal powers, liquorice was first brought to England by Dominican monks in the 1560s. The plant's pretty blue flowers did not bloom as vigorously here, but the roots – up to ten feet long, one-and-a-half inches thick and thriving in Pontefract's deep, well-drained soil – were what really mattered. The black juice obtained by boiling them up was used to treat coughs, stomach complaints and bad breath. So jealously guarded was the crop that a by-law of 1701 forbade anyone taking liquorice buds or sets out of the town. The penalty was a half-crown fine, such money to be split between the informant and Pontefract's poor. Yet some smuggling must have gone on – fields of liquorice were known of in Lincolnshire and even as far south as Barnes and Mortlake.

Pontefract cakes were first made in the 1770s by George Dunhill, a local chemist, who added starch to liquorice juice, rolled the black paste into ropes and stamped nipped-off bits into discs. Though the market, at first, was only local, by 1800 Dunhill's Pomfret (the ancient name of Pontefract) cakes were famous. In their heyday the firm turned out 25,000 a day, each one impressed with their coat-of-arms: an owl perched on a gate. Other firms moved in – Ewbank's in 1810, followed by Longstaff's, Robinson & Wordsworth, Weve Monkman, Hillaby's, Voile & Wortley and Wilkinson's.[14] By the mid-nineteenth century a

---

a Liquorice Allsort on her party frock to replace a missing button. On her arrival at the party the host's dog jumped up and gobbled the sweet, thus exposing the poor woman's knickers to the assembled guests. In a similar vein is the story of two kids who, for a joke, replaced their dad's bootlaces with liquorice ones. Very dubious: would any kid want his sweets within a yard of his father's whiffy footwear?

14 Former Labour minister Barbara Castle (continued over)

modest northern town, previously only noteworthy as being the Civil War's last Royalist stronghold, had become Britain's Liquoriceville – its firms, between them, producing around 7 million 'Yorkshire Pennies' every week.

While grown-ups cherished liquorice's medicinal properties,[15] it had a lot of fun potential, too. The 'lite' version, considerably diluted with gelatine and starch, could be extruded, stamped, twisted and looped into a hundred different shapes – an appealing concept to children. Often referred to as Spanish juice[16] – or less commonly Italian juice – liquorice was proud to proclaim its foreign origins. Sticks were stamped with names such as Taranto, Spaniola and Reccio.

Noza Lott's washer story is probably a wind-up, but hardly more far-fetched than the story of how Liquorice Allsorts came about – a story so neat that scepticism is immediately aroused ... One day in 1898, after being spurned by a Leicester wholesaler, a hapless Bassett's rep (probably their one and only) was fumbling to pack away his liquorice samples when he spilled them all over the counter. The hitherto grumpy wholesaler was so delighted by the visual appeal of the mix-up that he changed his mind and placed an order.

If Allsorts were so obviously appealing, surely Bassett would have twigged the idea for himself. Still, what the heck. Let's not drown a nice story with a dollop of cynicism.

---

was a resident of Pontefract's quaintly named Love Lane. Imbued with working-class thrift, Barbara's mother bought their liquorice – Pomfret cakes, twists and Bassetti juice – from Wilkinson's back gate at a tenth of the price others paid in the shops.

15 Pure liquorice juice was regarded as a controlled drug and could only be obtained from pharmacies.

16 'Juice' was a slight misnomer, a term the manufacturers used even when the mix solidified: it looked rather like rubber coal, black and dry, easily broken, attractively shining across its fracture.

Allsorts were officially named in 1898, but the name was not, or could not be, registered. Even though Bassett's are credited with the invention, they were unable to prevent every other liquorice firm copying the idea, as they still do today.

Aero Dynamics

1930–1944

Tired? Hungry? Try this Rowntree's milk chocolate, it'll buck you up in no time. Rowntree's chocolate contains extra cream which specially feeds nerves.

1930s advertisement

It was an age of classics: Mars, Aero, Milky Way, Maltesers, Kit-Kat, Chocolate Orange, Smarties and Rolos – sixty-five years on and they're all still with us. How many other 1930s consumables still satisfy modern tastes, not just as curiosities but as best-sellers? One or two have even attained icon status. Stand a Mars Bar on end and it could easily be a stunt double for the slab in *2001: A Space Odyssey*.

Scene 1: Dawn. Spooky music. A crowd of sweetshop owners dance around a strange brown monolith that has suddenly appeared in their community.

Despite its name, Mars hadn't come from outer space but from Slough, where, in 1932, Forrest Mars set up his one-room factory. Made to his father's recipe, the eponymous bar was a solidified version of malt drinks enjoyed in America's countless drugstores. Mars Snr had already built up a thriving business with it, and it now fell to Forrest to establish a new branch. As soon as the first bars rumbled off the production line, he began an evangelical mission to convert Britain's public: 'It is more than a sweet, it is a food: the eggs, the large amount of milk and butter, the malted milk, all combined form a nutritious tonic.' So ran the long-winded boast on the wrapper. Tagging Mars as 'food chocolate' was an inspired move. Guilt about sweet-eating lingered, especially during the Depression, and it provided the perfect conscience-salving euphemism.

Until Mars arrived, such gutbusters were largely unknown. There were blocks of chocolate, neatly partitioned to encourage self-restraint, and a few cheap choc 'n' caramel bars like Penny Pegs, Penny Puffins and Nora Block, priced to suit kids' pockets and hardly generous enough to put any of them off dinner. Sickliest indulgence was probably provided by chocolate-covered fruit fondants or peppermint creams. But these could at least be eaten with decorum. A lady might partake of a Fry's Chocolate Cream and still look like a lady. The Mars Bar – costing threepence, and triple the size of a Penny Peg – was a fist feed, a gob-blocking, tonsil-painting slab of self-indulgence, which left fangs of caramel drooping from the lips.

Early editions of the Mars Bar were enrobed with Cadbury's chocolate, a fact rarely mentioned now, and one which the company may even find embarrassing. But at the time it was no special secret. Indeed, Mars' adverts emphasized it as a positive bonus. Such 'borrowing' was not unusual. Cadbury's, Rowntree's and other firms had a profitable sideline in selling their chocolate wholesale – couverture as it was known in the trade – and anyone could buy it in 14-pound blocks. All that you had to do was melt it down and pour it over whatever needed covering (or 'enrobing', to use trade terminology). Thus smaller firms were able to produce quality confections without having to invest in expensive plant or pay top wages for a chocolatier. A toffee genius might be lousy at making chocolate, but why spoil a good product when first-class couverture was there for the buying?

In that first year, Forrest managed to shift 2 million of his threepenny Mars Bars. A bigger factory was built and the workforce grew, from twelve to a hundred, every one of them – apart from a small team making Funnyfaces and Dawggies, a range of halfpenny chocolate bars – dedicated to making Mars Bars. And in super-clean conditions, too. A stickler for hygiene, Mars had all production staff line up for fingernail inspection each morning. So efficient was the factory's air-conditioning that no atom of H or O was allowed to loiter in the building for more than twelve minutes.

By 1933, such was the demand for Mars that many shops went short: a peevish situation for the shopkeeper – who wanted to turn customers away? One DIY trader in Glasgow was confident he could make a bar just as good – and cheaper. Displayed in boxes labelled 'Marz Bars, 2d', the Scottish pretender was longer and narrower than the genuine article, but wrapped in identical brown paper and printed with a lookalike red/gold seal. When word of this enterprise got back to Mars they took the cheeky Glaswegian to court for 'passing off'. Under cross-examination by Mars' lawyers (and he'd already made enough money to employ the best) the shopkeeper swore that his assistants had been given strict instructions to say 'our own make' when offering the Marz for sale.

Anxious not to be ripped off again, Mars registered dozens of trade marks. In addition to Mars itself, just to be on the safe side, they also staked a claim on Milky Mars, Mars Mars, Penny Mars and – strategically placed for their next commercial coup – Milky Way, Milky Day and Milky Wave – they hadn't yet decided which one it would be. Also registered in 1933 was Snickers, though there is no record of it being used at the time.

Someone in the company had a sense of mischief – and we might well trace this all the way to the boardroom. A couple of years later, when Rowntree's dreamed up 'Dux' for a new chocolate and roasted-almond bar, someone from Mars went along and registered the name 'Quax'. Hardly a coincidence.

With so much hoo-ha arising from trade marks and name disputes, Mars had been quite lucky himself. It was only a couple of years since the Mars Toffee Company, based at the Planet Works in Castle Bromwich, had gone into liquidation. Had it still been trading – unlikely given debts of £3910 against cash in hand of £5 – confusion would have been inevitable and Forrest Mars certainly wouldn't have found it so easy to win his unique place on the sweetshop shelves.

After the Mars Bar, Britain's chocolate lovers were given, in relatively quick succession, Black Magic (1933), Tiffin and Caramello (1934), Aero, Milky Way and Kit-Kat (1935), Maltesers (1936), Rolos and Smarties (1937).

Forrest – earnestly American and irony-proof – must have thought Energy Balls a brilliant name for his new honeycomb chocolates. But he reckoned without the British love for a good snigger. For some reason people found Energy Balls funny. Renamed Maltesers, Mars' honeycomb spheres, again loosely based on the malt-drink taste, were eagerly promoted as 'the Dri Drink' – an inexpensive alternative to 'food drinks' like Ovaltine and Horlicks, perfect for perky young tennis players and soccer stars: 'I'm not paying 6d for one of those drinks. I get just the same kind of goodness from these Maltesers for only 3d!'

Terry's Chocolate Orange was another of confectionery's glittering prizes, a novel idea still selling well to this day. But it was not totally original. Predating it by some six years came the Chocolate Apple, also by Terry's. For a couple of decades both were sold side by side – until the apple version finally lost its appeal in the 1950s.[1]

'Best Companion to a Cup of Tea' was the polite suggestion for buying a Kit-Kat (or Chocolate Crisp as it was

---

1 A Chocolate Lemon came on to the market in 1979, but the public didn't take to it and it was withdrawn only two years later.

known for the first two years). The change of name came in 1937. Kit-Kat had been registered by Rowntree's in 1911, for no particular reason, other than it was a legendary London club and opinion seemed to be that using establishment names – Albany, Carlton, Burlington, Kit-Kat – as brands offered a kind of social cachet.[2] Following the 'food value' trend, Kit-Kat's slogan later became the slightly bolder, 'A two-course meal for 2d – and butter free!' 'Have a Break' – a catchphrase that's endured for sixty years – was thought up in 1939.

These were good times for Rowntree's. Aero, the one with the bubbles, consolidated their winning streak.[3] Aero had a more racy image than Kit-Kat. But only just. Sparsely clad young couples – only cartoons, of course – were shown lying on a beach … but anyone getting overheated by such scenes would soon be sobered by the message: 'Hot? Tired? Low-spirited? Aero will pick you up. Look at the texture!' Airways had been an alternative name, one of several put forward with the hope of cashing in on the Zeitgeist.[4] Science and modernism were common themes. Bond's Long Wave Assortment, for instance, celebrated the joys of radio; and Wire Chocolates were, one hopes, something to do with speedy communications (though there have been several instances of chocolates with real

---

2 A dubious story reaches me late in the day: the Kit-Kat Club had very low ceilings, and so could accommodate only paintings that were wide but not too high. Such paintings became known in the art world as kit-kats (as verified by the *OED*), possibly another reason for the name of the bar.

3 Over the years Aero has been available in several flavours – lime, orange, peppermint, and most recently cappuccino. Until the 1960s it was also available in 3d and 6d sizes.

4 Airways wasn't wasted: Rowntree's eventually used it for one of their chocolate selections instead. Strangely enough, Aero had been registered by Cadbury's as far back as back in 1910, and while there is no record of them ever selling such a line, a firm called Webster Hill had been selling an Aero chocolate bar during the 1920s.

wire in them, not to mention a veritable scrapyard of heavy-metal shavings).

More significantly, Aero was one of the first British brands to be successfully exported to the USA. 'New English chocolate thrills New Yorkers!' yelled the newspapers.

It wasn't only Aero's own sales that cheered up share-holders. Having patented the formula for their 'cellular chocolate', Rowntree's were able to license production to companies who, despite earnest efforts in the kitchen, hadn't yet worked out how to make a credible version of their own. Nestlé, Cadbury's and Fry's were among the licensees, the latter's Ripple being just one of several imitations.

One brand already well established by this time was Fry's Crunchie, a chocolate-coated version of the broken lumps of honeycomb or 'cinder toffee' often sold loose and especially popular with children. Production was fraught: early versions of the Crunchie proved so fragile that girls in the factory had to use a blowtorch to weld broken bars together. Many also had an unwelcome surprise in store for the purchaser – a total absence of crunchiness. The centres were hollow. Covered only in a single layer of chocolate, any pinhole allowed air to get in and, thus softened, the honeycomb simply collapsed. The solution was simple, if expensive: Crunchies were given a double coating of chocolate, a patch-up job which Fry's craftily turned into a positive sales pitch: 'Crunchie – TWICE covered in chocolate.'

Wrapping was taken for granted by this time. But packaging – a far more sophisticated art altogether – had also made an appearance. One of the zaniest examples (or most ingenious, depending on your viewpoint) was Fuller's Gresham Assortment. After the top layer was polished off, consumers could avoid overexertion by simply pulling a tab on the box side. By dint of an ingenious system of folds built into the box's base, the whole bottom layer and its contents were elevated to the top. How much all this carefully contrived origami added to Gresham's retail price can only be guessed at.

Other boxes relied on more traditional ideas – royal mugshots, for instance, or pseudo-crests which bore a cheeky resemblance to the real thing. With Royal Windsor Chocolates, Prince of Wales and Crown Jewel assortments, patriotism had become marketable again. No copyright existed on the use of 'royal' and it was added with abandon to a rag-tag variety of sweets, chocolates and toffees. Firms thereby enjoyed a hint of royal patronage without risking fraud charges. Royal Buttermints, for instance, had little to do with kings or queens and there was no proof they'd ever been sucked by anyone from the House of Windsor. Then again, who could say otherwise? King George V was unlikely to enter into any unseemly court cases. In any case, it had become a time-honoured custom, a bandwagon that confectioners had ridden ever since Victoria's coronation and the birth of her children. As any mother might be, she was probably flattered to have her daughter's birth celebrated with an inaugural batch of Princess Alice Drops. Confectionery had forged a symbiotic link with events and culture.

But royalty was about to let the nation down big-time. The girls who'd swooned over Edward on his visit to Needler's were no doubt as mad as cats when he took up with 'that woman'. But his abdication wasn't just a blow for royalists – for some confectioners it spelled financial disaster. Millions had been invested. A whole range of Edward VIII toffees, chocolates and assorted sweets stood packed in storerooms, ready for dispatch. Now, all of it had to be dumped. And as soon as that was done they had to start again, working against the clock to cash in on George VI's coronation.

Out came the predictable King Bar and the optimistically named Happy Day chocolate block. Loyalists who intended to brave the crowds in London could buy a cardboard periscope filled with Batger's Princess Toffees. Eat the toffees (or stuff them in your pockets) and find yourself a toehold on the pavement. For kids to wave, there were sticks of rock with red, white and blue streamers attached. But what if they ate the rock first? For those who couldn't make it to London there were plenty of souvenirs. Bubbly would send kids a coronation badge in return for six wrappers, while for grown-ups a tin of Mackintosh's toffees offered a free coronation teaspoon.

Chocolate boxes appeared by the score – but this time there was a catch – a ban on the use of photographs of George and Elizabeth on box lids. Imposed by the Home Office, it was apparently at the request of the king himself. Whether such a ban could be legally enforced is a moot point, but in those days of genuine deference a royal wish was generally enough.

While the new king and queen were unwrapping baubles from well-wishers, a royal cousin of theirs in Romania, Queen Marie, was somewhat taken aback to receive a parcel of fruit gums, a gift from Rockwell Sayer, a Chicago oddball. Reputed to be the 'world champion cat-hater' Sayer had left $400 in his will, with instructions to his executors to buy sweets for famous people who shared his hatred of felines. Among over a hundred others to benefit from this odd will, which included thirty-five handwritten pages of abuse against cats, was Mrs Coolidge, wife of the former US president Calvin, who received a sumptuous box of chocolates. This was her reward for services beyond the call of duty – namely that she'd had the White House cat put down.

British patriotism occasionally surfaced in a more pugilistic form. At a trade show at the Manchester Corn Exchange, a stall promoting Russian sweets was attacked and rifled by angry local tradesmen. 'The Russians are out to create unemployment and unrest in this country,' complained the mob's spokesman by way of justifying the dust-up.

Violence could easily have been avoided. Simply spreading word about the state of Russia's confectionery factories would soon have put off potential customers. Nor would it have been spiteful rumour-mongering – these stories emanated from the highest levels. Among other yucky practices, according to a self-flagellating report in *Pravda*, girls on sugar-boiling duties at the Karl Marx Confectionery Factory in Kiev habitually used their tongues to test temperatures – and always put their samplings back into the mix. Their foreman, stubbornly resisting any pressure to be reconstructed, claimed that tongues were perfect thermometers. And, since they also provided a free supply of phlegmy adhesive, they proved quite useful in the wrapping room, too. A quick lick was all it took to stick the twists of paper. No washing facilities were provided at the factory and, since soap was rationed (4oz a month), girls usually arrived for work already dirty. In an attempt to change all these sloppy habits, bosses were introducing a wide-ranging hygiene programme for the girls, including nit inspection and compulsory manicuring. As in all the best Russian tales, life was lived at freezing point and, bar the sweat of hard work, the factory offered little in the way of heating. One workman was observed untying the dirty rags he used as socks and warming his feet over a vat of boiling fruit.

But Russians weren't the only invaders to give shopkeepers sleepless nights. In their paranoid nightmares, those who made a living selling sweets were permanently under siege. Fifth columnists were everywhere, even in schools ...

Tuck shops, at least in the *Magnet*'s pen-and-ink sketches of Greyfriars and St Jim's, were ivy-licked lodges, their bubbleglass windows full of plum cakes, glittering choc bars and jars of stripy humbugs. A world of beaks, Latin prep and hampers from home, these fantasies for urban kids never mentioned the picket lines set up outside the gates by angry shopkeepers. Tuck shops posed a vile threat to their livelihoods and every week brought fresh complaints, against minor prep schools in Yorkshire and

Derbyshire, right up to the portals of top-notch Harrow. If kids had money to spend, it should be the nearest sweet-shop that profited from it – not some caretaker exploiting his position to lure away their most spendthrift customers. Schools should be ashamed to sponsor such places. Sweets were bad for children's teeth, shopkeepers claimed: a last pathetic bleat against the unfairness of it all. Why not give the blighters breadcrusts or an apple?

Bad for teeth? Were these the same men who protested so loudly whenever one or another health scare hit the headlines? 'It is a fallacy', argued one trade spokesman, 'that sweets are responsible for a superabundance of adiposity' – a bit wordy, admittedly, but an obvious contra-diction to their aforementioned concerns about child welfare. Were sweets bad or not? Why couldn't they make up their minds?

Schools were worry enough – but sweetshops could certainly do without idiots like the Minto Man. Every Saturday, in the village of Huby, near Harrogate, kids eagerly awaited the arrival of this mystery benefactor. Some time during the afternoon – the hour was never the same, as if to keep them on tenterhooks – a large chauffeur-driven car would cruise slowly through the village and, from the rear passenger seat, a well-dressed elderly man would scatter mint humbugs on the pavement. A regular weekend treat, the visits continued for several months – then stopped as suddenly and mysteriously as they had started. Was it a publicity stunt, an act of charity or some private joke the old man eventually tired of? To this day, apart from predictable theories about eccentric million-aires, no one knows exactly who the Minto Man was or what motivated his oddball generosity.[5]

---

5 This tale had an interesting echo sixty years later. Sacked by the *Beano* after fifty-four years, Lord Snooty (alias Lord Marmaduke of Bunkerton) went out in true *noblesse oblige* style by loading a cannon with sweets and showering them over the village for the local kids.

Those who cherish irradiation as a 1990s issue will be surprised to hear of it in the news seventy years ago. 'There are endless possibilities for good in ultra-violet light,' trilled a Viennese doctor in 1929, suggesting that irradiation of chocolate would significantly increase vitality in children and invalids. His experimental Sunshine Chocolate must have sounded irresistible; but, to us with the benefit of hindsight, was rather like labelling the Chernobyl site Sunlight Valley.

But, at that time, irradiation didn't mean enough for anyone to feel scared by it. More concern was expressed over powdered China clay being used to make fondant centres for chocolate creams. Nothing more than a daft rumour, it had all stemmed from an off-the-cuff joke by a lecturer at the Mining School in Camborne. What irresponsible idiocy, thundered confectionery traders. Such ideas all too easily gained credence, especially when voiced by supposedly responsible teachers. And it's true that people were ready to believe the craziest things; like a claim that some jam firms, to feign naturalness where there was only artificial flavouring, were adding tiny wooden pips to their raspberry jam.

Authenticity was a live issue. A cake shop was taken to court by council watchdogs for selling cream buns filled with artificial cream. The judge was not impressed. Cream did not have to imply a dairy product, he pointed out tersely. What about shoe cream, hair cream, face cream? The prosecution refused to give up easily: shoppers would scarcely expect their cakes to contain hair cream, they argued. But the judge dismissed the charge, refusing to accept that any offence had been committed.

Motorists, cyclists, hikers –
all who love the great outdoors –
prefer them for their handiness.

advertisement for Fry's Cartets

Increasing amounts of leisure time were reflected in the style and marketing of confectionery. Theatre, Kinema and Opera assortments catered for the indoors brigade, but it was the great outdoors that called the loudest. Motoring Chocolate, Cruising Toffee – sponsored by Cunard – and Picnic Chocolates were all popular, though there was no suggestion that you had to go on a cruise or own a motor to indulge.

Hikers and cyclists formed the vanguard, their lunch-boxes and knapsacks not properly equipped without at least one of the dozens of picnic-style chocolate bars packed with nuts, raisins and country goodness. Serious dedication to pastoral values was more than apparent in the nomenclature: Rich Pasture, Buttercup and Cowslip toffees; Dairy Milk and Meadowmaid chocolate; Alpine, Orchard and Sylvan assortments. Radiance Toffee, for instance, wasn't just stickjaw for greedy kids: it suggested being full of sunshine and health. Even the odd gleam of wit was allowed, like those caramels with added vitamins – Yeastward Ho!

But some took things too far. Radiance Toffee is one thing – harmless poetry co-opted to the service of marketing – but Radium Schokolade, the latest confection in Germany, quite another. Along with its cocoa and milk, this German wonder bar – surely the only one ever to have a half-life as well as a shelf-life – contained a healthy dose of radium salts. Radioactivity, as already noted, was regarded as a beneficial force and, allegedly, had no adverse effect on the normal chocolate taste. The bar's advertising slogan ran along the lines of 'Eat this and feel great'.

British chemists who heard about it preferred a dose of healthy, self-preserving scepticism instead – leading them to dub the stuff Suicide Chocolate. Still, seeing what British minds had come up with – Bovril Chocolate, Bovril Caramels and Oxo Toffee – many people might have preferred to take their chances with the radium.

Another boon for Britain's stout-thighed weekenders

came in the form of the fizzy drink tablets sold in penny packs. No need to lug all those heavy bottles around. No risk of finding your Woodbines and fishpaste sandwiches soaked with leaked lemonade. Simply find a farmhouse with a tap and – hey presto! – four fizzy drinks for a penny. Just the stuff to fuel an energetic stride to the top of Scafell Pike.[6] There were dozens of brands – Glass Lemon, Toy Squash, Hike-Ade, Coolade, Swizzade, Eiffel Tower, Chef Fizz, Robinade – all of which would make about four glasses. Most popular were lemonade and orangeade, but flavours like raspberryade, limeade, ginger beer and even American cream soda were also available. Slackers who came over faint at the mere thought of hill-walking might prefer to slope off to a cricket match, where a pack of Test Match Fizzers could fulfil much the same function.

Experimenting on the public was nothing new. Nor was using staff as guinea pigs. In one test, mixing Pavlov's theories with fashionable ergonomics, one company divided its typists into three groups. One lot were given sweets every afternoon, the second lot only every other day, and the third lot, poor loves, got none at all. Conclusion – the quickest and neatest typing came from girls who were regularly fed mints and toffees.

Another 1930s fad, psychology, was eagerly adopted as a help in sorting job applicants. Rowntree's, firm champions of the method, claimed that it reduced 'misfits' from 25 per cent to 2 per cent. Tests set for jobseekers included making an arrangement of building blocks, or tapping brass studs in a certain order, speed and accuracy being recorded electronically. In another test, used to ascertain 'willingness to obey', subjects had to squeeze a hand-held dynamometer in response to a pre-programmed series of flashing lights. All in all, a bizarre initiation into what was so often described as a 'sylvan set' works. But since they'd

6 Did they work? My own experiments with Lemfizz cubes in the 1960s are referred to on pages 169–70.

taken on a full-time works shrink in 1922, they had to find something for him to do.

Incentives in Repetitive Work, a sixty-page paper published by the Medical Research Council, purported to be the first 'close-up psychological study of operatives'. Its authors had spent hours observing girls in a sweet factory. Daydreaming, childish behaviour and suspiciously frequent visits to the loo were – surprisingly? – all part of their routine. Even their chatter was noted and classified. Topics, recorded in order of priority, included the opposite sex, grumbles about working practice, film stars, bosses and parents. Bottom of their concerns – most disappointingly, at least according to the observers – came positive comments about their work.

And what was the hardly surprising conclusion of all this? 'Too high a degree of intelligence may be detrimental to success and satisfaction in repetitive work, while a low degree of intelligence affords greater ability to endure monotony.'

Workers in the sweets industry, especially those lucky enough to be with Rowntree's, Fry's, Cadbury's and Mars, were better looked after than many. As well as paying sickness benefit, Fry's even employed a home visitor who doubled up as a chauffeur, taking pale convalescents for a spin in the local countryside to get some fresh air. Some firms undertook to pay for employees' dentures, the cost to be recouped in weekly instalments from their wages. Were dentures so much in demand? If all the tales of tooth-rot from breathing in sugar dust were true perhaps they were.

In one year Mr Nuttall gave £20,000 to various charities, a fortune at the time. Fred Needler, who died in 1932 after suffering from Parkinson's disease, left £147,956 – hardly a grand legacy, considering his phenomenal success, but then most of his riches had been given to good causes.[7]

---

7 'To the memory of Fred Needler, as a token of the enduring affection and esteem of his workforce ...' it said on the memorial

Fry's Christmas treats for Bristol's poor children were a thousand toys for the boys and a thousand dolls for the girls.

But kindness and good intentions could not protect workers from everything. Industry was industry and even the comparatively innocuous world of confectionery involved tasks fraught with hazards. Skin diseases were rife. Grocer's itch, more formally known as sugar dermatitis, was a common ailment. For those who spent all day peeling oranges and lemons, the corrosive effects of citric acid were bad enough, especially in a cut or sore, but there was worse: a mould found in some peels buried itself under fingernails, building up sacs of infected pus that gave sufferers hell. Ice-cream makers on the other hand had no need for a manicurist – constant use of ice and salt stunted nail growth.

In factories with a lax regard for safety laws, absence of efficient extraction led to real risks: a build-up of dusts – from cocoa, starch or sugar – which could easily be ignited by a stray electrical discharge. Daily inhalation of sugar dust was a fast-track way to rotten teeth, while long-term exposure brought the threat of silicosis. Less painful perhaps, but far more startling in its way, was vanillism, an allergic reaction to vanilla which made the eyebrows fall out.

Direct and, by today's standards, disarmingly naïve, much 1930s advertising still ran along the lines of, 'Eat our chocolate, it's rather nice.' For the hard sell they might try, 'It's delicious!' – an exclamation mark the only arm-twisting required. And, with a trusting audience, that worked well enough, especially on those for whom 'delicious' was a new experience.

Budgets were generous. Whole pages in national newspapers were common. Cadbury's, Mackintosh's, and even

---

erected by loyal workers. Hard to imagine anyone having a whip-round for the bosses of Dixons, Burger King or Supasnaps.

smaller firms like Walter's, makers of the famous Palm Toffee, often had the whole front page of the *Daily Sketch* or *Daily Mail* to themselves.

Rubbishing of rivals was frowned on, even if unintentional. When Cadbury's advertised the warming benefits of their Bournvita drink by advising folk to throw away their mufflers, a howl of protest went up from menswear shops and the advert was withdrawn. From then on creativity would be strictly reined in, Cadbury's copywriters with a penchant for the arty-farty limited to harmless drivel like this description of Flake: 'Light as a fairy dancing and as sweet as seventeen.'

But more adventurous firms were thrilled by creativity. Bosses at Needler's gave a nod to the use of maverick humour, zany material that was off-the-wall before Tango and Twix had even finished their NVQ in bricklaying. Their Krispie chocolate (as well as its krazy K, of course) was offered in two varieties: milk, sensibly signified by a churn; and plain, signified by a joiner's tool. Fun indeed. Irony, no doubt symbolized by someone pressing a shirt, had been born.

Eagerness to cash in on current events was not limited to wars and coronations. The discovery of the Loch Ness Monster in 1934 provided a great excuse, with lines such as Coleman's Loch Ness Monster Surprise Bags and Rogall's Monster BB Nougat quickly appearing in shops. Or Payne's Golden Arrow Choc Bar, which, fighting shy of a name change, described itself as 'nearly as big as the Loch Ness Monster'.

Nessie wasn't the only monster on the loose. Down in Leicester they had Peppy the Glacier Bear, the newly recruited mascot for Glacier Mints. Fox's described their six-foot polar as 'a real live personality' – which is pushing it since Peppy was obviously stuffed, a hunting trophy, picked up for a few quid. His head had even been removed at some point, and refitted with a nodding mechanism. Peppy's first enemy was not a cheeky cartoon fox, but a harmless-looking teddy bear. The message – 'accept no imitations' – was meant to imply that a teddy was no substitute for a bloody gigantic polar bear, especially one with a bionic bonce. But the picture of a mean-looking Peppy towering over the quivering teddy looked like a shocking case of bullying.

Those who owned Britain's big brands had an understandable urge to control their marketing, but while sales tactics were increasingly clever and certainly benefited from brainstorming committee sessions, many shopkeepers didn't entirely trust such a centralized approach. 'Go suck a Zube' – a slogan current at the time – was cited by one as an example of sloppy thinking. Wasn't that telling customers to go elsewhere? Surely it should be 'Come suck a Zube'.

Many preferred to go it alone and felt quite capable of attracting their own customers. Trade magazines were full of DIY tips. 'Why not put this card in your window?' suggested one piece:

MONDAY: *Maid rejects youth*
TUESDAY: *Youth contemplates suicide*
WEDNESDAY: *Youth thinks suicide cowardly*
THURSDAY: *Youth sees and buys Slater's chocolates*
FRIDAY: *Maid sees youth and eats Slater's chocolates*
SATURDAY: *Youth promises maid a weekly pound of Slater's chocolates, and maid marries him*

Or why not try a poem, suggested the pundit, a veritable fund of useful ploys:

On tennis courts, in punts, in motors
For Bidwell's sweets we are all voters

Direct mail has a long history. Back then, though, it was handwritten. One sweetshop owner – his letter quoted as an inspiration to others – resorted to tracking down old

95

customers and dropping them a line to ask where they'd got to.

> *Dear Sir,*
> *I have been wondering why I have not lately received your custom as I did previously. I am sorry to notice this as you were such a regular caller. I trust your lack of support is only temporary and that I may soon have the pleasure of seeing you again.*

Women were, as ever, seen as soft targets, especially for emotional blackmail. The DIY tipster, excited by their suggestibility, recommended a carefully contrived placard: 'You have not finished shopping until you've bought the sweets!' Also worth trying, the blatant, 'The children will be good if you take home some sweets.' Or why not place this card alongside a jar of sugar sticks: 'One of these will keep baby quiet for over an hour!' – proof that modern supermarkets can hardly be blamed for originating the practice of ambushing weak-willed customers as they pass through the check-outs.

Confectioners, like lazy husbands, had good reason for keeping women in their place – but both were doomed to Canute-like failure against the tide of progress. Women were smoking more and eating fewer sweets, much to the disgust of many, and not just sweetshop owners. 'It is not natural to refuse sweets. Sugar is heart food as tobacco is heart poison. A pretty woman sucking a sweet is a far more attractive sight than one of her sisters smoking a cigarette', wrote one journalist in the influential *Harpers Bazaar*.

In Germany, some shops displayed prominent notices with the admonition: 'The German woman does not smoke.' Why can't we do the same in Britain? asked one shopkeeper.

But it wasn't all bad news. Sales of cachous, mints and gum had shot up. But since everyone knew such sweets were no more than breath fresheners, women had become self-conscious about asking for them, as if it was a public admission of foul breath and unladylike habits. To prevent lost sales, advised the DIY tipster, sweetshop owners should make up small packets beforehand and display a card with the innocuous message, 'Handy packets for the handbag', thus gallantly saving ladies from having to speak.

Sweets were advertised for the first time on TV – but only as an experiment at a trade show. Sample slogans were simply written out on card and transmitted by camera to a flickering grey screen. Most viewers were distinctly unimpressed. Scepticism was the usual reaction – hardly surprising when there were plenty of traders who still doubted the worth of press advertising. Others, inspired by the scientific buzz, saw TV as a vital key to ever-increasing trade, though they would have another twenty years and another world war to go through before commercial TV came into being.

By the mid-1930s Britain's chocolate firms employed 80,000 of their own cows and used 50 million gallons of milk a year. 'You can't carry a glass and a half of milk in your pocket,' they said, rather obviously, 'but you can carry a block of Cadbury's Dairy Milk.'

Wrapping Britain's annual output of chocolate called for a staggering 2500 tons of aluminium foil. No firm would countenance setting up its own ore-smelting furnace, but if the industry could provide its own milk, why couldn't it become self-sufficient in cocoa? Erratic movements in the world's cocoa markets played havoc with accounting predictions. Why be a slave to it? asked bosses at Rowntree's. Why watch cocoa prices shoot up and down the trading floors when any half-decent gardener with a big enough greenhouse could surely be able to grow a cocoa tree?

A start was made, in the firm's tropical house in York, with seeds specially imported from Dominica. When the first trees, just over one foot high, began to blossom, the flowers were fertilized with the help of a camel-hair brush. Hard to shake off that bizarre image: egg-heads in white coats tickling the reproductive parts of cocoa flowers. A number of pods developed, each about six inches long, but, despite encouragement from two powerful 'daylight' lamps, only nine ripened. And the end result of all this effort? Three bars of chocolate, which Rowntree's proudly presented to Princess Elizabeth.

Vanilla was, until the 1930s, a common ingredient in milk chocolate. Artificial substitutes were available, but some firms insisted on the real thing. Supplies were always problematic. Botanical boffins had successfully grown vanilla orchids in an artificial environment, but despite dedicated fiddling, they couldn't get the damned things to fertilize. Such magic could only be worked by bees, they discovered. A swarm was drafted in to do their duty, but it turned out vanilla was such a choosy plant that only one particular species would do. A hothouse full of temperamental vanilla orchids was hard enough work, but having to fly in bees from the Far East and employ a full-time apiarist to look after them made the whole venture expensively impractical. Faced with the ever-rising costs of vanilla, chocolate-makers chose to phase it out quietly.[8]

Another of the great 1930s brands, Black Magic, was launched in 1933. Development of the assortment involved a survey of over seven thousand people – dealers as well as consumers 'of all classes' – some of these, so it was rumoured, being guests at a 'very superior garden party'. As part of the evaluation (supervised by a team of shrinks from the National Institute of Industrial Psychologists) guinea pigs were given 'units' in numbered wraps of tissue. No clues were given. It may have been a Rowntree's chocolate, or a control sample taken from a rival assortment. All

---

8 Seekers after cheap resources were excited by a mysterious underground sugar spring discovered in Nebraska in 1930. Analysed as Sucaryl Sodium, it had been cited as a possible source of artificial sugar. But no more was ever heard of it.

the tasters had to do was say whether it appealed or not. When the final selection had been decided, a further three thousand people, sampling the chocolates for the first time, voted it a better assortment than any they'd tasted.

Nor was packaging left to chance. The Black Magic box represented, at least according to excited Rowntree's men, 'unparalleled seriousness in its careful planning and calculated scientific knowledge gleaned from research' (and it's only a pity that the box had no room to accommodate such a wonderful claim).

Though a certain fancy style had returned during the 1920s, packaging gurus had a bit of a dilemma. For many people, fancy had become synonymous with expensive and during a recession they were edgy about paying over the odds for anything. Why spend good money on a bit of cardboard and pretty pictures? The Black Magic box, with its plain but elegant lines, set a trend. A further blow for traditional pictorial styles, it also dealt a sharp blow to the career hopes of Judy Shaw and Ruth Skary, students at Willesden Polytechnic who'd just won big prizes – £100 and £50 respectively – for their flowery chocolate box designs.

Between 1933 and 1938 Rowntree's spent £227,000 on advertising Black Magic and sold 3.5 million boxes. Though the name was registered, Rowntree's rights only extended to its use on a chocolate assortment. Black Magic, as a brand name, could be found on all kinds of other products – pencils, lipstick, even vacuum cleaners – but as long as these made no claims to be chocolate assortments no conflict was likely. But Rowntree's bosses were horrified when they heard about the plans of one Edward Hack to market Black Magic laxatives. Court action was swift. The firm's reputation would be irreparably damaged by any such use, they claimed. Confusion was inevitable. People would think that Hack's laxatives were made with Rowntree's chocolate. Or, worse, they might believe that Rowntree's Black Magic chocolates had laxative properties. Since they were frequently a gift from men to their lady friends, such rumours could lead to serious arguments. Hack's lawyers reacted with derision: how could anyone confuse chocolates in a box with Mr Hack's laxatives, sold in glass tubes clearly labelled, 'Black Magic tablets of cascara sagrada.'[9] No right-thinking person would think that a firm well known for its cocoa, chocolate and fruit gums had suddenly diversified into medicinal preparations. Fair arguments. But judges sided with Rowntree's, ordering a ban that scotched Mr Hack's plans and left him to think up a new name. Brown Magic perhaps?

With Kit-Kat, Black Magic and Aero, Rowntree's were on a winning streak. Dirty tricks were unnecessary. When a Fry's employee turned up at Rowntree's York offices and suggested they might like to offer him a fee – £5000, say – in return for the secret recipe of a top-selling Fry's chocolate bar they not only showed him the door – they made sure that police were waiting for him on the other side.

Winning ideas weren't limited to the chocolate industry. Needler's chemists had worked out a new way of making boiled sweets: not rolling them into ropes and cutting them, but depositing the boiled sugar directly into sweet-sized moulds. The old rope method had been automated for some time but, due to trapped air in the mix, fruit drops and suchlike were often cloudy and dull. Now, by using a simple (but closely guarded) formula it became possible to make fruit drops crystal clear – and so the Glacé Fruit Drop was born. Rivals would take another twenty years to work out how it was done, leaving Needler's with a valuable advantage in clear boiled sweets.

> *He did not steal for money, but for a food which his body craved. If his parents had provided for his needs the child would not be troubling this court today...*
>
> American judge, explaining a boy's crime spree

---

9 Translated as 'sacred bark', obtained from the Californian buckthorn tree.

Just as patriots had feared, the gum-chewing habit – foreign, uncouth, corrupting – had caught on with a vengeance. The stuff was even being given away – 'Free packet every fourth turn!' – in machines selling Mackintosh's Chewlets, Wrigley's P.K. or Rowntree's Beech Nut. While the latest brands sounded harmless – O-Pee-Chee, Canadian Indian for robin redbreast being surely the most inoffensive of all – sex, rebellion, even a hint of danger lingered in such names as Gypsy, Black Cat and Mo-Jo. Why, gum companies were even encouraging children to play poker. Nu Chu, which had a pig-tailed Chinaman for a mascot, had a mini playing-card in every pack. Kids had only to collect fifty-two of them and send them off to be swapped for a full-size deck.

With Britain's jaws clicking away like crazy and our moral fibre possibly frayed beyond repair, could it get worse? Well, for the die-hards, it could.

Originally described as 'chewing gum that blows bubbles', bubblegum came into being to cater for the increasing posiness of gum-chewers. They were always trying to show off by tonguing bubbles, pathetically short-lived, thanks to gum's sad lack of elasticity. One early version, Blibber Blabber, made in Germany in 1906, was as sloppy and useless as it sounds. Around the mid-1920s, though, companies were able to make a real go of it. Originally sold as 'bubbly chewing gum', every pack came with 'full directions' for novices. By the 1930s Bubbly, Presto and Rainbow were being bubbled all over Britain, as were jolly-sounding brands like Whiz-Bang and Coo-ee. It goes without saying that this new habit was frowned upon by many, especially grown-ups. Presto and Rainbow, according to gossips, were a prime cause of skin eruptions in young people.[10]

*

10 In the 1950s, rather late in the day, perhaps, to stave off such accusations Rainbow bubblegum came with added vitamin C.

In Trinidad a desperate battle was being waged against witch broom disease, a pestilence that threatened to wipe out the island's cocoa trees – and with them a significant part of the Caribbean economy. Britain, meanwhile, faced an even nastier foe – but that nice Mr Chamberlain would soon smooth things over, wouldn't he? As a thank-you gift for dealing with Adolf so firmly, one well-wisher sent the PM a box of Nestlé's Home Made assortment. Did the lady ask for a refund when war broke out? Sadly, we'll never know.

As hostilities continued, things were sure to get difficult. With Japanese troops overruning many of the Far East's sugar-producing countries, shortages were inevitable. Rationed supplies threatened to displace between thirty and sixty thousand workers. But the Ministry of Food encouraged manufacturers where it could. Sugar wasn't vital, even for the confectionery industry: acceptable toffee and other sweets could be made with pulped apples and treacle. Or what about using plum syrup? Some use had to be found for 1941's surplus crop of 10,000 tons. This gesture brought howls of protest from Britain's jam-makers: why should confectioners get priority?

'Cadbury's Milk Chocolate is a food!' shouted ads – a far from unfamiliar cry during times of war. Even Rolos put in a lame plea for special treatment, describing themselves as a 'perfectly balanced food sweet'. Government ministers were unconvinced, leastways about the Rolos.

Plain chocolate, the Food Ministry suggested, was just as tasty as the milk version. To enforce their point, the Use of Milk (Restriction) Order of 1941 was introduced, banning its use in sweets, ices and biscuits.

From sugar and milk to molasses, a black market opened up for virtually every ingredient. The government issued stern warnings, but manufacturers were desperate enough to pounce on any potential source. But desperation brought risks. One firm who bought black-market starch found it to be Stafford Starch, intended for use in laundries. And there were reports of chewing gum made with that old standby, paraffin wax.

Denial of confectionery had grave effects on Britain's morale. Some crumbs of comfort were vital to avoid unrest. Greengrocers were encouraged to sell children single carrots. If they turned their noses up at the rabbit habit, why not give them toffee carrots – Woolton's Wonders people called them, every bit as tasty as toffee apples, allegedly. Attention was also drawn to the ingenuity of beleaguered Russians, who made tasty treats from carrots, ginger and lemon peel. In the USA one Ohio confectioner tried to whip up interest in spinach ice-cream – and they didn't even have rationing![11]

Sir Winston Churchill still had his jujubes, which he liked to eat during Parliamentary debates. Far from trying to hide the habit, MPs often had to wait while he fiddled in his waistcoat pocket for another. Had Parliament been televised then he would never have got away with such an obvious PR gaffe: publicly eating sweets while Britain's children were driven to carrots and pickled onions ...

Self-sacrifice was all very noble, but hard to encourage when the system could be seen leaking at every seam, as one sweetshop owner observed in a letter to the press:

> *Any shopkeeper in Morecambe who'd shut up shop for want of supplies and taken a walk along the promenade would have met with crowds of WAAFs, many of them carrying 'outers' (boxes of two dozen) of choc bars. They buy them for their landladies and their friends.*

---

11 Another American idea was chocolate dictators – Hitler in milk, Mussolini plain with a pink cream filling. Sales were marginal and they were soon withdrawn. It wasn't until the last two years of the war that things got tight for the Americans. Chewing gum became almost non-existent. Wrigley's resorted to a massive poster campaign depicting an empty packet with the plaintive exhortation to 'Remember this Wrapper!'

A reply from a high-up in the NAAFI appeared the following week.

> *Your correspondent may have been misled. A few empty boxes had been supplied to allow NAAFI customers to take away a few apples that had become available.*

Dreaded by shopkeepers and public alike, rationing was held out as the government's ultimate sanction. In a vain attempt to show they could police themselves, some shops already imposed a system of their own, as a foil to 'professional queueists' and 'shop crawlers' – the kind of people who would buy up anything they could lay their hands on, whether they really needed it or not, just in case they might find a buyer for it. 'Women and children first' was a motto that obviously didn't apply where confectionery was concerned. Clutching their precious pennies, children would often arrive at a shop, only to find that panicked grown-ups had already stripped the shelves. Despicable and selfish, most were agreed. Children should be given priority and this notice from a shop window was typical:

SWEETS AND CHOCOLATE
WILL BE SERVED TO ADULTS
ON SATURDAYS ONLY

It was sadly obvious that the public couldn't be trusted to behave with restraint. Despite his best intentions, Lord Woolton, at least according to one supporter, was 'up against forty million people trying to outwit him'. After months of threats, confectionery rationing finally arrived in July 1942 and coupon books RB11 or RB11a were issued to all adults and children. There was no need to register with a particular shop (as was necessary for meat, fruit and groceries) and these 'personal points' could be taken to any place that sold sweets, as long as it had a licence from the Food Control Committee. No sweets, chocolate or gum could be sold without sight of the purchaser's RB11 and the requisite coupons – issued in four-weekly blocks – snipped out out by the shopkeeper.

The ration, based on weight, was 2oz per person per week (with penny choc and toffee bars counting as 1oz, twopenny bars as 2oz, etc., regardless of exact weight). With one Mars Bar, for instance, equalling two ration points – a whole week's ration gone in a few mouthfuls – it was hardly surprising that many people reverted to boiled sweets which could be made to last.

Many shopkeepers, deliberately or unwittingly, fell foul of the law. 'Sold Sweets Without Coupons' was an almost daily headline in one local newspaper or another. One man, his heart-strings twanged by children staring mournfully at his shelves of empty sweet jars, divided up a block of strawberry jelly and sold the single cubes as sweets. Jelly was unrationed – yet, divided into squares, the law regarded it as confectionery and after someone grassed on him the kind-hearted trader was fined two pounds ten shillings.

Until war broke out, average weekly consumption of confectionery was 6¼oz per person. Multiplied by Britain's population of 45 million, that added up to an awful lot of trade. Now, at a stroke, it had been slashed by two-thirds. Horrified, many shopkeepers felt they were staring ruin in the face. And who would recompense them for the hours spent sorting and collating coupons? Each monthly cycle produced upwards of 8000 million, all of which had to be counted, sent off, counted again, checked against lists to ensure the system was working properly. Besides being a bind, shopkeepers felt slighted: surely they could have been trusted with a much less complex system, whereby coupons were simply cancelled with a rubber stamp?

The public had all kinds of devious ways to get hold of extra sweets. A common fiddle was the tin swap. A man enters a shop and buys a tin of sweets, slipping it into his coat pocket at the same time as reaching for his cash. 'Oops, I've forgotten my money,' he says. 'I'll nip back and get it.' Putting the tin back on the counter, he goes off, supposedly to fetch his money. And here's the trick. It's not the same tin, but a dummy, weighted with a handful of earth and grit. When the man fails to reappear the tin is returned to stock – where it remains until sold to another unwitting customer.

In August 1942 the sweets ration was increased to 3oz. Good news for most people, but shopkeepers were infuriated – not by the increase but by the odd figure. How could they sell 3oz of sweets priced at, say, fivepence or sixpence halfpenny a quarter? Quite apart from taxing an assistant's brain, customers were sure to think they were being diddled somehow. Rationing officials patiently explained: the official ration was 12oz a month, which could be spent any way a customer desired: six purchases of 2oz, or three purchases of 4oz, or whatever. No one had to have 3oz of anything.

With Britain's servicemen exempt from rationing, their NAAFI canteens became the source of fantastic rumours. No wonder men in uniform were so popular with the ladies – it wasn't the brassy buttons or sharply pressed khaki that attracted them, but the pockets full of Mars Bars.

Not all soldiers were so lucky. It wasn't that Dad's Army recruits were too old to swing it with the ladies, but they had no bribes to offer. Home Guard units who applied for extra chocolate to sell to their men were turned down flat. Classed as mere civilians as far as rationing was concerned, they were not entitled to a single extra sweet. ARP wardens, on the other hand, received generous extra supplies – an interesting insight into the long-running feud between Hodges and the lads of Eastgate platoon in the BBC's Dad's Army sitcom.

Once soldiers became prisoners of war they also became civilians, entitled to 3oz of confectionery a week. Relatives who were given charge of the men's RB11s could buy extra sweets on their behalf to send out to the POW camps. Whether the lovingly wrapped parcels arrived intact is another matter. It's a matter of record that guards in the Japanese POW camps took cruel delight in throwing handfuls of sweets on to the ground and watching emaciated prisoners grovel in the dust for them.

Ice-cream makers had been coping with shortages since 1940, but they reacted with disbelieving horror when an all-out ban on production was announced – to begin on 30 September 1942. The government would brook no argument: ice-cream makers used up far too much fat and sugar and their reliance on refrigerated transport was a total waste of resources. And the industry also employed dozens of engineers who would serve their country far better in the forces.

The ices trade felt it had been 'singled out for total extinction'. Would there be any compensation? Not likely. Quite the reverse in fact. Scrap Metal (No.2) Order, which allowed for the confiscation of all non-essential metal, such as iron railings and gates, was now extended to include all the ice-cream equipment – from buckets to wafer holders to freezers – by now lying unused and rusting.

Despite protesting that no such metal was used anywhere in their factory, Terry's of York were ordered to pay a whopping £800 compensation to a customer who found a razor blade in one of his chocolate creams. It was the first complaint against the firm for many years and very unfair, considering how hard bosses were trying to maintain an output despite the privations. But chocolates weren't all they were producing. Like many factories, Terry's had been commandeered by the War Office and their machinery adapted for making all kinds of military gadgets – aircraft propellers in Terry's case. In Glasgow, Cowan's turned out a handy line in anti-submarine devices; while at Cadbury's a company with the faintly sinister name of Bournville Utilities was formed, setting the nimble fingers of its female staff to work making and packaging gas-masks.

Rock Bottom

1945–1960

Two months before VE Day, in March 1945, a goods train rattled out of the sidings at Cadbury's Bournville factory. Its forty brown wagons were packed with chocolate – 35,840,000 2oz bars of it – on their way to Allied Forces in Europe. Intended as hand-outs for starving war-weary civilians, these bars were a mere quarter of a 9000-ton order from the Ministry of Food.

Not everyone welcomed the Choc Express. 'It is undermining the will of the German people to resist occupation,' fumed die-hard newspaper *Koelnische Zeitung*, warning German parents of dire punishments if their children took chocolate from GIs.

Here in Britain, sugar supplies were still desperate. Hardly surprising, since 500,000 precious tons had been requisitioned by the War Office for making synthetic rubber. Despite public impatience to see the back of austerity measures, sweets remained rationed.[1] In America boiled sweets had become valuable currency. Desperate bootleggers were buying as many as they could lay their

---

1 What little sugar Britain had it felt duty-bound to share, lending the USA 10,000 tons to see her through until the next crops. Scientists reckoned they could make sugar from wood – but had yet to prove it.

hands on – any kind of sugary stuff being vital for making hooch.

In Glasgow, even the police who nabbed them had to confess admiration for a gang of ingenious alkies who'd managed to make 85° proof moonshine from a couple of bags of marshmallows. Well, the Government had urged Britain's sweet-starved citizens to improvise ...

There was no shortage of jolly make-do-and-mend ladies to show how. At Morris Motors, for example, the Welfare Department held a talk for workers and their families, advertised on the works noticeboard with the ominous promise: 'Many a good sweet can be made at home over a spirit lamp.' Some people took things to extremes, with all the enthusiasm of DIY winemakers. How else to explain such joys as onion toffee? For those who want to try it, here's the recipe:

> *Boil 1 kilo of onions and 2½ kilos of radishes in 10 litres of water until 1½ litres have evaporated. Boil 10 kilos of sugar and 1½ of syrup, then add four-fifths of the onion liquor. Stir until the required consistency.*

Even children were encouraged to have a go: comics ran recipes for simple sweets and useful tips for making sugar mice or candyfloss (always assuming they could get hold of any sugar). The British, as much as the defeated Germans, had become charity cases.[2] But our transatlantic cousins, under the auspices of CARE (the Co-operative for American Remittances to Europe), would look after us. Untroubled by rationing, they were able to buy $1 million worth of chocolate from Cadbury's. After export to the USA, where it was lovingly repackaged by kind volunteers,

---

2 It wasn't just the sweets that kids missed, but their buying power. Better to buy anything than nothing at all. So desperate were some to cling to their status as junior consumers they willingly traded in their sweet coupons for carrots or pickled onions.

the chocolate was sent back again – to be handed out to the poor kids of Birmingham, in streets not five miles away from Cadbury's factory.

Even Africa felt sorry for us. In an act of charity that mirrored Live Aid – and predated it by forty years – the citizens of Nairobi were asked to give up their sugar coupons: each one donated would provide half a dozen barley sugars or pear drops for one of Britain's orphaned or homeless children. It would be, as one Ugandan newspaper put it, 'a touching demonstration that we children of the mother country do not forget her in times of need'.

But while the public were on rations – blissfully unaware that it would last for years yet – manufacturers had enough ingredients to be getting on with. Production was not yet back to pre-war levels, but it was still far in excess of demand at home and companies relied on exports to keep them afloat until domestic normality returned. Among many temptations tailored especially for foreign markets was the Carol the Redhead fancy tin from Horners.[3] 'This full colour bathing beauty comes with Boy Blue Assortment or Dainty Dinah fruit drops.' Targeted at the overseas male (for some reason presumed to be particularly frustrated) Carol's lid had a cord attached: after the sweets were polished off Carol – bonny, British and buxom – could be hung upon the wall, a tin pin-up for lovelorn toffee-chewers.

Despite overwhelming problems, confectionery bosses believed that 1945 heralded a new age and issued a rallying cry for recruits. There'd be no welcome for 'slavish copiers of old-fashioned recipes'. Those the industry sought now were 'chemists, innovators, men of education, men with practical knowledge and vision'. Young men (or women) who answered the call would not be apprenticed to old

3 British women, apparently, would not buy any sweets whose packaging depicted women, and put pressure on their menfolk not to do so.

geezers with aprons and sugar-rotted fingers – they'd be invested in and educated, enrolled for master classes like Elementary Principles of Confectionery, a two-year course held at Borough Polytechnic.

Great changes were afoot. Like the 'flowpack' – a continuous band of doubled cellophane, sectioned off and heat-sealed to make individual packets. For once, shopkeepers raised a cheer for progress. The 2oz-a-penny trade had bugged them for years: 'ruinous', some called it. What profit was there in weighing out half a dozen sweets for dithering pensioners and snotty-nosed kids? And it all took time. Pre-packs meant less work and guaranteed margins. Advances brought hygiene and presentation benefits, too: toffee packed in the patented 'Flav-o-tainer' bags not only looked good but lasted for longer on display. Palletization had also made an appearance, with nippy little fork-lifts allowing speedier loading of lorries and train wagons; they'd come a long way from Needler's horse and cart.

Yet, in some factories at least, working practices were as old fashioned as ever.

Dipping workers have a permanent chocolate 'glove' – but it never prevents them from scratching their heads, touching their noses or straightening their ties. These same chocolates are then packed into boxes depicting glamorous ladies and lovely pink ribbons. Some chocolates are handled two or three times.

Hard to imagine anyone picking their nose with a chocolate thickened finger, still less a girl tittifying her perm, but there it is, in an official report from Government Hygiene Officers. In Scotland, according to the country's Chief Sanitary Inspector, workers were still making ice-cream with fags dangling from their mouths.

Similar concerns were expressed about the industry's hundreds of outworkers. Employed for pennies to wrap and box sweets the old way, in their kitchens and living rooms, these freelancers had no foremen on their backs and might break off at any time to feed Fido, cut their toenails or pop to the loo.

While World War Two may have been over, Cocoa Wars continued and the battle had crossed from Trinidad to Africa's Gold Coast, where swollen shoot disease had reduced production by a third and threatened economic disaster. In 1891 the country's first shipment of cocoa beans had amounted to a mere 80 tons, but by 1921 annual exports were 305,000 tons – or 40 per cent of the world's production. Now, with 400 million trees and 1.5 million workers involved in one way or another, cocoa production underpinned the entire West African economy.

While botanists blamed swollen shoot on the voracity of the mealy bug, others blamed it on the greed of man. A religious tract – 'for moral and social uplift' – saw a direct link between the disease and the intensity of production imposed by an insatiable desire for chocolate and sugar. Mealy bug be damned – this was the Hand of God at work.

Whatever its causes, swollen shoot had to be tackled. In an uncanny echo of the war, it was the Yanks who flew in to save the day; not paratroopers this time, but a team of boffins headed by Dr Bill Carter from Hawaii's Pineapple Research Unit, a world-renowned expert on mealy bugs.

Back in Britain spivs were everywhere, setting up their folding tables, flogging illicit sweets to jumpy crowds – and disappearing as soon as they heard a rozzer's size 12 footsteps. No dodge was too mean to be exploited. One spiv was observed selling chocolate walnut whips, minus the walnut, for fourpence each – while at the other end of his table, in a separate pile, were the nuts, priced at one shilling and sixpence a quarter. Jumbo sticks of rock also proved a crowd-puller. 'Don't open it now,' buyers were warned, 'there's cops around!' And so they rushed off, delighted with their illicit bargains – until the sticks were unwrapped, and found to be one-third rock, two-thirds thick wooden dowling. No mere opportunism, such cons were organized crime at its meanest. Police had already mounted a nationwide hunt for the man they called 'Mr Rock'.

Not all spivs were men in dodgy suits. One 11-year-old boy who appeared in front of magistrates for selling his homemade lollies to cinema queues told them he'd done it to fund a new pair of football boots. After seeing lollies being made while on holiday, he'd decided anyone could do it. Admirable initiative. But perhaps he'd also read about the Oxford Street toffee-apple seller who made a fifty-pound profit a barrowload – more than enough to cover any fines for illegal trading.

'It is gratifying to see such enterprise,' the young entrepreneur was told, 'but the law is the law.' The bench's fears, they explained, were not about unfair trading or even flouted ration laws, but for hygiene and child labour.

If ambition was one plea, others fell back on older tricks. A Hindu shopkeeper prosecuted for selling chewing gum without points simply answered the charge with, 'No spik English.'

'Did you do it?' persisted the magistrate.

'Yes plizz,' came the reply, and no doubt the magistrate thought something along the lines of 'Chew this then, Gunga Din' as he handed down a fifteen-shilling fine.

Most shopkeepers, mindful of the penalties, stuck to the letter of the law, censoring confectionery even if it was just a gram over the 2oz ration.

> *He took a penknife from his waistcoat pocket and meanly sliced the chocolate in half. It looked like the same knife he used for cleaning his pipe!*
>
> letter in the *Daily Mail*

Yet, for selling a bag with one humbug too few, another shopkeeper found himself in court, charged with underselling. Humbugs were too large to make an exact measure of, he explained in his defence, and too hard to split, so he thought it better to err on the side of rationing rules. Still, the hapless trader was fined five pounds. Whichever way they split it, or didn't, shopkeepers just couldn't win.

As production increased, and shops filled up with sweets that no one had enough coupons to buy, even formerly law-abiding traders began to flout the law. 'A box of chocs for the wife, sir?' When one man to whom this query was directed answered that he did not have his ration book with him he was greeted with a wink. 'That's all right, sir, just drop the coupons round any time.' Such an offer, despite breaking the law, would have been eagerly taken up by most, and kept secret, but this particular miseryguts felt so affronted he wrote to the papers to deplore it.

Acting on a tip-off, police who raided a Doncaster sweet-shop found eight and a half hundred weight of confectionery stacked up in a back room – enough rations for 3,820 people for a week. The boys in blue were convinced they'd nabbed a black marketeer, until they opened up the boxes. Many contained nothing more than papers: mice having long since nibbled any contents. The chocolate had gone into melt-down, forming a solid sticky mass with dead flies and mouse droppings for decoration. Most of the stock (or what was left of it) dated back to before the war. No Mrs Big, as ambitious coppers had fervently hoped, Elsie Williams was an old lady who'd simply stopped caring. 'I ain't never been to school, I'm no scholar,' she said, defending her lack of stock control and telling magistrates she no longer saw any future in the confectionery trade.

So it seems pretty obvious that a shopkeeper's lot, like that of a D'Oyly Carte bobby, was a far from happy one. In addition to the continuing headache of rationing, there appeared to be an increasing obsession with B.O. Not the sort easily eradicated with Lifebuoy soap, but box odour, so strong that it could leave food and confectionery reeking even after being removed from the box, and certainly noticeable enough to frighten off customers. After numerous complaints, the British Carton Association was forced to demand action from their suppliers in Finland and Sweden. Confidence was restored with the announcement of yet another innovation – non-smelly cardboard, or virgin fibre board as it was officially called.

Rappers – impatient customers who knocked loudly on counters to call attention – were another bugbear. But a tinkling shop bell did not always herald trouble (or a delivery of smelly boxes). It might be the rep from Duncan's with his stereoscope. A toy thrown up by the think-tanks of confectionery's brave new world, its purpose was to thrill shopkeepers with 3-D pictures of the latest chocolate boxes. Why this was supposed to be any more effective than seeing a real box is anyone's guess, but science has long tended to have such a bamboozling effect on otherwise sensible people.

In 1949, to celebrate the end of sweet rationing, 7000 Mars Bars were sent out from Slough, one to be given to every Dr Barnardo's child. But it didn't mean that normality had come back overnight. Stampedes followed every rumour of deliveries being made to a shop – but even if true, a batch would sell out in minutes, leaving nothing but empty jars. Euphoria, if any at all, was short-lived. Within months rationing was back in force, albeit increased to 5oz a week. Another half-ounce was granted just the following week – equal to three bullseyes, two and a half humbugs or three acid drops, according to disgruntled pedants. Yet, despite all these strictures, people weren't entirely selfish with their precious sweets: clubbing together in response to appeals, the public was able to send five hundredweight of barley sugar to the homeless victims of a flood in Mablethorpe.

Any suggestion of a link between sweets and tooth decay was still pooh-poohed by those in the industry. 'You can break your tooth on a bullseye. You can pull out a filling with some toffee. But to suggest that sugar is in contact with teeth for long enough to cause decay is pure nonsense,' claimed the Medical Research Council, reporting in the *Lancet* after a two-year research project in which children were fed maximum rations and sent to bed without brushing their teeth. No noticeable decay was reported and in some cases, claimed the MRC, this diet halted decay that had already started. So what was the prime suspect? Lemon – that was the *real* cause of tooth decay, at least according to a group of dentists from Down Under. 'Oh yes,' sneered the *Queensland Dental Journal,* 'it's that darling of dieticians, food faddists, schoolteachers, athletic trainers and every other grandmotherly person for centuries that's to blame.'

But, albeit slowly, the fun was starting to return. A plastic hen that laid bubblegum eggs was just the kind of pet every American kid yearned for, but it was with chocolates that US manufacturers gave their offbeat ingenuity free rein. One box whispered 'Hello Sweetheart' when opened, the voice issuing from a mini-tape-recorder concealed in the base. Another assortment, Spotlight, had a tiny light fitted into its lid: 'Choose your sweets without disturbing your friends! Ideal while watching TV!' A third box had a transparent plastic lid, slotted to allow the bestower to insert their own greetings or, as the makers suggested, a postcard of a favourite holiday resort.

But America did not welcome novelty willy-nilly. In West Virginia cops raided candy stores and impounded fifty 'subversive' chocolate machines. Each chocolate bar came with a miniature hammer & sickle flag, plus a card extolling the joys of life in the USSR. Such actions helped enforce America's tough stance on communism, yet at the same time, during a visit to Moscow, Boyce Powell of the US Embassy in London was singing the praises of Soviet ice-cream: 'I thought the Italians were famous for it but, take it from me, the Russian product can't be beaten.'

Britain preferred a softly-softly approach to exporting its culture. The best way to cash in, would-be exporters were advised, was to put famous landmarks – Big Ben, London buses, Tudor cottages, etc. – on chocolate boxes and toffee tins. Americans had only to see Shakespeare in the red telephone box by Windsor Castle to be overcome by an insatiable desire for toffee.

The British, of course, had their own ideas of fun. Like Toofy – denture-shaped bubblegum that was all the rage in the 1950s. It was so popular that rival gum-makers wanted to cash in, by fair means or foul. Some even resorted to industrial espionage, or so it seemed when Candyco accused rival firm Margo's of illegally copying its moulds. Margo's goofy gum was not only identical in appearance to Candyco's, but also called Toofy – a blatant rip-off that inevitably resulted in a court case. That the original idea was Candyco's, no one disputed, but in the judge's opinion originality did not debar anyone else from copying. To stop any more fuss, however, Margo's agreed to change the name of their gum to Falsies. Satisfied but weary, the judge bemoaned the time and effort wasted on such paltry cases. 'In six months' time the children will not want false teeth, but perhaps false noses.'

Though limited sales of ice-cream had been allowed in 1944, to boost morale, it wasn't until the 1950s that sales returned to anything like pre-war levels, and even then dairy supplies were still squeezed. An ideal time for the ice-lolly to make its mark ...

Walls' SnoFrute and SnoCreme had sold well enough in their day, but it wasn't until just before the war, when someone hit on the idea of putting ice-lollies on a stick, that they really began to take off. For anyone with a bit of wood to spare it looked like a very plump cash cow.

'Hello, that'd be ideal for lolly-sticks,' thought the quaintly named Dorset gardener, Fred Nettlingham, when he found clumps of bamboo growing in a corner of his allotment. After sinking his savings in another twenty-five acres, by 1950 Fred was growing 50 million canes. And he wasn't intending to stop there: with plans for another two hundred acres and a projected annual crop of 450 million sticks, Fred reckoned that Britain could become self-supporting in lolly-sticks, enabling firms to stop expensive imports from China, Italy and the USA.

Nor would Fred's fortunes be upset by any ups and downs in the ice-lolly market: his bamboo could also be sold for use as fishing rods and pea sticks, not to mention switches for whacking naughty schoolkids with.[4] Lolly-stick evangelists saw endless possibilities, like a market for cheap disposable tea stirrers. With candyfloss, lolly and toffee-apple sticks[5] selling at eight shillings a thousand and a minimum order twenty thousand, the rewards attracted all kinds of sharks. There were even reports of lolly-sticks being made from second-hand wood. 'A disgraceful practice,' said magistrates when the culprits landed up in court.

Frupop, Fluky Pops, Koola Fruta, Lucky Koola, Koola Kreem, Sambo, Big Bear and Little Bear, Lik Lap – ice-lollies on sticks were everywhere. In 1952 sales of one favourite, Topsy, totalled 20 million. Flavours were wild, and in addition to the predictable orange, lemon and lime, kids could get dandelion and burdock, liquorice, aniseed, even cough-mixture flavours.

According to the Tin Research Institute, 20 per cent of ice-lollies were contaminated by lead. One theory blamed cheap moulds, their soldered joins being easily dissolved by fruit juice in the lollies. Others suspected that the water was already full of lead before it was used to make lollies. In any case, as sceptics were quick to point out, to

---

4 During the 1950s the market plumped for flat lolly-sticks, since those who researched such things found that they gripped the lolly for longer. So perhaps Fred did eventually become Britain's first corporal-punishment millionaire. Wizelpops, plastic lolly-holders, were patented in 1953, but vanished without trace.

5 Hopefully blunt. Councillors at Broadstairs and other seaside resorts complained that pointed toffee-apple sticks abandoned on the beach were crippling children.

reach danger level a child would have to eat three lollies per day.

The headline 'Ice-lollies Horrify Wearside Wives' was inspired not by lead content, but the unnaturally bright colours of the ice-lollies. Attractive to the childish eye, mums found that stains defied the most vigorous scrubbing.

One problem, from a trade point of view, was a lack of any legal definition of a lolly. Despite calls for standards and regulations, by consumers and from the industry itself, the Ministry of Food was reluctant to act. Ice-lollies were not food, so how could food standards be applied? Most were 95 per cent water, and though officials thought an 85 per cent minimum would be preferable, they did not have any way of enforcing that. Manufacturers might be reined in under the Food and Drugs Act, but that would call for government lawyers to prove ice-lollies were food, and no one had the time. It wasn't until 1955 that any action was taken to impose some standards.

For all that, even if kids cared, they'd rather have taken their chances with poisoned lollies than the fishy ice-cream sold by two Italians in Dundee. Magistrates took a dim view of it, too: citizens might have got used to ersatz butter and powdered egg, but ice-cream made with margarine containing whale oil was one substitute too far.

Americans had ice-lollies, too, though they called them popsicles. Adlai Stevenson, the Democratic Governor of Illinois defeated by Eisenhower in the 1952 presidential race, was seen consoling himself with an ice-lolly. Whether such a common touch did him any good is hard to say: he was defeated by Eisenhower again in 1956.

During the summer of 1952 the bounty hunters were out in force. Not the tanned hedonists of 1980s TV ads, these were short-trousered schoolkids with sticks and nets. Every queen wasp taken to Fry's Somerdale factory earned its captor threepence. For tip-offs on the whereabouts of any nest within a one-mile radius the reward was even better – a whole shilling.[6] Fry's had a dedicated wasp squad on standby to deal with a predicted 7 million of the sugar-hungry stingers. Across the Severn in Wales, Lovell's offered a going rate of sixpence for a queen, and a handsome two shillings for a nest sighting. It made collecting old pop bottles look like pauper's work.

Wasps were a serious problem for retailers too: one fruit stall in Mansfield was besieged by them for six hours. The stallholder thought of spraying them with ammonia, until concerned passing shoppers made him think twice. Eventually the wasps migrated to a cake shop down the street.

It could have been worse: back in 1911 a grocer's shop in Kingston-on-Thames had to be closed for five days until its buzzing plague could be vanquished with a paraffin and water spray.

Coronation year, 1953, began with a complete 'fog out'. But sweetshops had an answer – Smoglets – warm and penetrating, the perfect antidote to those fingers of pollution that reached deep down into the lungs – though, sadly, no insurance against a painful collision with a lamppost.

The public has always been up for a suckable solution to its health problems. In 1859 one shyster made handsome profits from flogging tablets containing sea air. A century later the only change in our endless quest for a wonder cure-all was the replacement of dried ozone with vitamins. Five of Benson's Blackcurrant Vitamin C Health Sweets each day, for instance, and one's body was allegedly fully primed for the fight against illness.

The confectionery industry had a fully staffed health clinic ready to tend Britain's wheezing masses. Stethoscopes, syringes and ear-light things were conspicuous by their absence. Not even a white coat. Waistcoated and

---

6 One can't help wondering how we would today view such potentially injurious ventures being sanctioned by a major confectionery company. Kids would love it, but the potential for litigation would render it impossible.

bewhiskered, peering through half-moon specs, these old-fashioned GPs were hardly pin-ups – but trust and ritual were far more important than the flash of Doctor Kildare's teeth. Dr Smith's Aromatics – 'Medically Approved', the jar said – were one prescription on offer, alongside Dr Thompson's Antiseptic Throat Pastilles, and dozens of others. Loveliest of all in this virtual clinic was Dr Smile, genial champion of Cherry Bronchial Pastilles. But even if Drs Smith and Thompson had really existed, there surely was no such person as Dr Smile (although you rather wish there were, Mary Poppins' GP, perhaps).

While the doctors dealt with no-nonsense coughs and sneezes, airy-fairy complications like lovesickness were left to the female staff, in this case Nurse Grant.

> *Come on Brian, Shirley's waiting*
> *And the picture starts at eight.*
> *With Nurse Grant's you can't go wrong, chum,*
> *They'll just send her sure as fate!*

Think-bubble over young man's Brylcreem-coated head: 'The way to a girl's heart is strewn with Nurse Grant's delicious confectionery ...'

But while the taste may have been sweet, it was hardly likely to stir a girl's latent desires in the same way as a box of some excitingly named chocolate assortment like Glamour, Gala or Broadway. Offering your girl a Nurse Grant's was as likely to turn her on as slipping off your bike clips; and what man would offer his date a Stop Barking pastille? Orolyptus, Victory V, Tics and Zubes were harmless enough, but totally devoid of romance. Medicated Guys had a sexy ring to it, but Men-Lics sounded like dirty talk. As for Grandad's Koffs, the mental picture does not bear thinking of.

With the right mentholly smell to appeal to hypochondriacs, Tunes were really no more than a medicated version of the more glamorous Spangles. All the same, whether meant as romantic offerings or not, being 'twice wrapped' they had to be a great advance on the tatty paper bag with its conglomerated mixture of herbals.

'Chlorophyll is today the biggest best-seller!' While Britons chomped politely on Phyll chewing gum, Americans had gone chlorophyll crazy: as well as gum and lozenges, they'd put the wonder chemical in toothpaste, ointments, insoles, cigarettes and even had chlorophyll-impregnated toilet paper.

Apart from the smog, 1953 looked promising. Batista had released a million tons of sugar from Cuba, and Britain's Ministry of Food had managed to grab itself a bargain – 24,750 tons of Greek raisins – at £5 per ton cheaper than 1952 prices. But the real big news came in February – the end of rationing. For real this time. Even the hardest-hearted government would never have got away with rationing in a year that marked Elizabeth's coronation. To celebrate the occasion – the coronation as well as the end of rationing – Edinburgh firm Duncan's gave away eight thousand pounds of sweets and chocolate to local school-children. A siege at one sweetshop, in Kilburn, London, was filmed by an NBC film crew to show on American network TV.

Union Jack displays made up of sweets would be a great idea, or so someone thought until one Jeremiah pointed out the lack of blue confectionery. Pink, brown and lemony in the main, apart from those dotty Liquorice Allsorts, how many sweets were blue? A bit of a problem, but one soon got round when manufacturers got weaving with a few drums of blue dye.[7]

---

7 A good window display was still worth taking time over. In a precursor to the *Blue Peter* tradition of make-do, can-do shop-keepers were advised on the inventive use of crepe paper, corrugated cardboard, coloured card, silver paint, etc. All a waste of time if the windows were steamed up but not a problem for those who could afford the latest invention – a steamless shop window, made with metal oxide sandwiched between *(continued over)*

Though Scottish folk have traditionally regarded green sweets as unlucky, most of us have no problem there. Blue, though, is a trickier area. While nineties children have taken to blue lemonade and blue Smarties, nature itself provides few blue foods and certainly nothing as bright as turquoise, ultramarine or cyan. Blue Smarties are only a gimmick, after all, an exception that proves the rule. Since confectionery mimics real food in many ways – as chewable, crunchable, suckable fodder – manufacturers have tended to play safe by sticking with natural and socially acceptable colourings.

With the Coronation, Scottish firms had an extra problem. Celebration packs of chocolates and toffees were certainly in order – but how would they be styled? Was the new queen to be Elizabeth I or II? Loyalties were split. They had no wish to offend Scottish customers, many of whom would be fervent nationalists and deemed Elizabeth as the First, but at the end of the day 70 per cent of their sales came from below Hadrian's Wall. In the end the issue was neatly sidestepped by a decision to refer to the new queen as Elizabeth, omitting the number altogether.

The coronation even had an official ice-lolly, Topsy, one of which was to be given to every one of the 32,000 schoolkids lining the Embankment. In addition to royal patronage, as if that wasn't more than enough for any lolly, Topsy displayed certificates from the Royal Institute of Public Health and *Good Housekeeping* magazine. Acclaimed as the biggest kid's party in the world,[8] every child on the Embankment was numbered and ticketed and teachers boasted of being able to locate any child in five minutes. Topsy's makers offered kids a coronation brooch in return for six wrappers. Not all of them knew about the offer and

---

the glass. The only alternative was to keep the doors open all day – a practice frowned on by unions and shopkeepers alike.

8 And the biggest load of free publicity any confectionery firm had ever had – on TV, in the cinema and all over the newspapers.

some became rather upset by being followed, unaware that their pursuers simply wanted to pounce on their discarded wrappers.

Coronation rock, though, was not all it seemed to be (nor was it officially approved) and people were warned to beware of buying any. Spivs had become increasingly sophisticated and the rock was actually made to order for them. Despite its attractive size, it had been pumped up with so much air during the boiling stage that it was virtually hollow.[9]

The young queen would reign over a dwindling empire, but her subjects could rely on always being able to find a few British sweets, even in its furthest-flung corners. Soldiers from the West Africa Frontier Force in hot pursuit of gun-runners entered a village, deserted except for an old woman squatting in dust with a tray of oddments, in which were six packets of Trebor Mints.

1954 SWEETSHOP HIT PARADE
Barratt's Sherbet Fountain (2d)
Devlin's Sports sweet cigarettes (2d for ten)
Dollar Film Star bubblegum (1d strip, plus film-star photo)
Mackintosh's Rolo (6d)
Flying Saucers
Razzle Dazzle chewing gum balls
Blue Star Pure Sherbet Sucker, with liquorice tube (1d)
Big Chief Dream Pipe (liquorice) (1d)
Beat-all Lollies

This isn't the industry's official chart, but a list volunteered from a sweetshop in the provinces. It gives a good idea of what kids were buying.

---

9 Spivs had an even dodgier scam: selling shilling coins for one shilling threepence. Shortage of change was causing anguish in shops, millions of coins having disappeared into electric meters during the cold weather.

Though Yuri Gagarin's space trip was a few years off, junior spacemen had already started to make their appearance in schoolyards. Playground soldiers and junior cowboys had been easy enough to cater for, but what kind of sweets did little astronauts want? Saper's Space Ship Rations, perhaps – candy 'pills' in a variety of colours, each one of which represented a different function – Take-Off Rations, Atmosphere Equalizer, Ultrasonic Stabilizer, Hi-Altitude Fortifier and Inter-Space Rectifier. Kids who saved up the wrappers could qualify for graded ranks in a space-ship crew.

In 1955 Eldorado introduced Milk Frols, milk ice-lollies for which they hoped to win sponsorship from education authorities, as a seasonal substitute for school milk. With fridges rare in homes and schools, keeping dairy products fresh was a major headache during summer months. Crates of school milk were often left outside and by the time the kids came out to play the third-pint bottles were on the turn. Milk tablets had been tried, without much success – but kids would surely welcome a daily delivery of milk lollies.

It wasn't that simple. Milk ice-lollies, far from providing an answer to every kid's soggy-straw nightmares, caused tons of trouble. Legally, an ice-lolly now had to consist of water and fruit juices. Milk Frols were classed not as ice-lollies but as dairy produce and, as such, were subject to dozens of complicated regulations. Several people landed up in court for making or selling them without a licence, including a Paisley café owner who was fined fifty pounds.

Meanwhile, in a Devon quarry, a real milk lake was slowly turning sour in the sun – just a puddle really, a mere fraction of the 2 million gallons dumped by the Milk Marketing Board every week.

Ice-lollies, although packed with, allegedly, vivid colours and heavy metals, had until then escaped the disapproval of dentists and other puritans. Now it turned out they were just as bad for the teeth as sweets – well, at least for the rats and dogs who'd been forced to eat dozens in a university experiment. To combat the threat some local health authorities called for sodium fluoride to be used in chocolate and ice-lollies, an experiment which was tried in Scotland, and quickly abandoned without much explanation.

Though manufacturers felt obliged to give voice to some of the Puritan guilt that still lingered – 'More than a treat, a food!' Wall's said of their ice-cream – these were exciting times in the ice-cream biz. Fresh ideas surfaced all the time, like lollies with ice-cream centres – Lyons Maid's Mivvi and Eldorado's Topper; the latter offered kids their very own boomerang in return for two wrappers. There was even a nationwide Flake famine, brought about by ice-cream firms buying millions to use in their 99s.

With thousands of rival ice-cream vans racing each other for business, turf wars broke out all over Britain. Scotland seemed particularly affected by protection rackets and in cities like Dundee gangs would 'sell' territory for sums up to £850, with promises that interlopers would be seen off. Every rival van would be shadowed by five gang vans and – just to show they meant business – gang members were seen toting axes. Fist fights were frequent, but hostilities often had a touch of farce – like the raspberry-juice fight depicted in Bill Forsyth's film, *Comfort and Joy*. Assumed by most to be a touch of light comedy, at least one such incident was recorded, in Renfrew, between the Izzi and Girasoli families.

Van chimes were the biggest source of aggro, not least with shift workers getting their heads down after a night's labours. One Welshman complained that the sounds carried for three miles down his valley. Others were less disturbed by volume than by style. The 'thin, airy, often sentimental nature of the music presents a travesty of the full-hearted explosive tempo of modern times,' complained one aesthete.

To try to keep the peace with the public, a voluntary code was drawn up.

- Chimes should only be played whilst the van was on the move.
- The volume to be fixed by owner so drivers couldn't turn it up.
- Speakers should point down through the floor to disperse impact.
- Slow tunes were preferred to fast ones.
- Five-second bursts were ample.
- Melodies should not start on odd notes (presumably to avoid upsetting music-lovers who actually enjoyed these mini-extracts).
- Chimes should be kept free of dirt (which distorted the pitch and doubled the annoyance factor).

As if all this wasn't enough, the Performing Rights Society stepped in and demanded a three-guinea fee for every van – this doubtless being the reason why firms were forced to adopt the non-copyright dirges like 'Greensleeves' and 'Blue Danube' that were to mar everyone's peace and quiet for years to come.

Despite their self-imposed code, ice-cream sellers had a narrow escape from inclusion in the Noise Abatement Act and it was only their dubious claim to be involved in the 'conveyancy of perishable commodities for human consumption' that saved them.

In the evenings, though, no one was excused. For sounding his chimes after 8 p.m. a seller in Louth was fined two pounds. Police had lain in wait, eyes peeled, ears cocked. After three bars of 'Greensleeves' had been sounded it was – 'Go, go, go!' – and they moved in to make an arrest.

Even those who kept faith with old ways were not exempt from getting nabbed. 'It is the customer's job to look for you, not the other way around,' Derby magistrates told one

Early advert for Rowntree's Clear Gums (soon to be renamed
Fruit Gums) featuring a freaky fruit figure who must be some
relation to lovable liquorice lad Bertie Bassett *(Nestlé S.A.)*

Two million a day . . . but surely they mean chocolates, not boxes?
(Robert Opie Collection)

Mackintosh's Week-End, a choc and candy assortment with superfluous hyphenation. *(Robert Opie Collection)*

A heartstring tugger that no dutiful son could possibly ignore, even one who looks like an East End villain. 'Yeah, he may have done the Thugg Brothers with a shooter, but he always remembered his old mum . . .' *(Robert Opie Collection)*

Early seventies styles: Cadbury's late lamented Aztec, an austere box of Black Magic, and the neo-psychedelic wrapping of Lyons Maid's Fab ice-lolly *(Robert Opie Collection)*

Three generations of Opal Fruits (oops, sorry, Starburst) *(Robert Opie Collection)*

Free animal picture inside
Fab
Super camera offer See back!
s Maid
Lyons Maid
Lyons

GALLEON FLOWER HOLDER

A wonderfully realistic antique galleon, beautifully made in Staffordshire semi-porcelain. Special holes for flowers. Large hole at the back for emptying and cleaning. 7¼″ high, 9″ across.

Needler's

5/6

Containing ½ lb. (2/- worth) County Chocolates.

"RIPPLE" WATER SET

What could be more natural than this smart Ripple design. Here is a gift for every day use at a truly wonderful price. Containing ¾ lb. (3/- worth) County Chocolates.

6/6

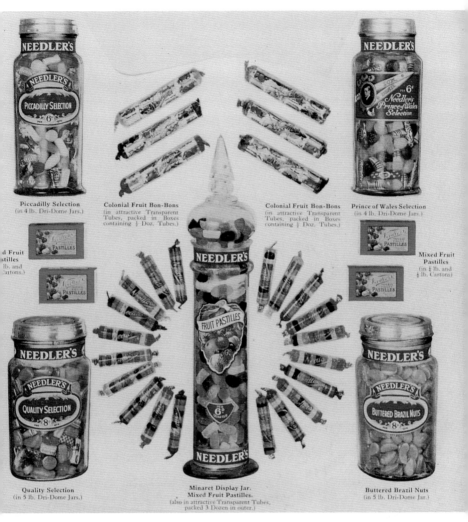

Within the catalogue image:

NEEDLER'S
NEEDLER'S
PICCADILLY SELECTION
PER 6⁰ QTR

Piccadilly Selection
(in 4 lb. Dri-Dome Jars.)

Colonial Fruit Bon-Bons
(in attractive Transparent Tubes, packed in Boxes containing ½ Doz. Tubes.)

Colonial Fruit Bon-Bons
(in attractive Transparent Tubes, packed in Boxes containing ½ Doz. Tubes.)

NEEDLER'S
PER 6⁰ Needler's Prince of Wales Selection

Prince of Wales Selection
(in 4 lb. Dri-Dome Jars.)

d Fruit
stilles
lb. and
artons.)

PASTILLES

NEEDLER'S

FRUIT PASTILLES

6⁰ QUARTER

NEEDLER'S

Mixed Fruit
Pastilles
(in ¼ lb. and ½ lb. Cartons)

PASTILLES

NEEDLER'S
NEEDLER'S
QUALITY SELECTION
8⁰

Quality Selection
(in 5 lb. Dri-Dome Jars.)

Minaret Display Jar.
Mixed Fruit Pastilles.
(also in attractive Transparent Tubes, packed 3 Dozen in outer.)

NEEDLER'S
NEEDLER'S
BUTTERED BRAZIL NUTS
8⁰

Buttered Brazil Nuts
(in 5 lb. Dri-Dome Jar.)

(Above) A page from Needler's 1926 catalogue showing just a few of the company's hundreds of lines (between sixpence and eightpence a quarter), some of which now came packed in the innovative Dri-Dome sweet jars *(Brynmor Jones Library, University of Hull)*

(Left) Needler's novelty choc boxes. Specially designed for the Christmas market, the packaging was often more significant (and more expensive) than the handful of chocolates. But what on earth was 'semi-porcelain', from which the galleon was made? *(Brynmor Jones Library, University of Hull)*

Stop me and buy one – a Wall's ices salesman from the 1920s
(Wall's Ice Cream)

Packing the mint with the hole *(Nestlé S.A.)*

man up in front of the bench for trying to attract kids with a handbell.

In 1960 Mr Softee blew in from Philadelphia to start a new era. According to a survey of Americans, ice-cream was considered effeminate, though that seems hardly surprising when it was brought to them in vans labelled Mr Softee.

The first sweets advertised on TV,[10] during the first-ever commercial break on 22 September 1955, were Murray-mints.[11] Quick to spot the medium's potential, Mars followed with its 'Stars Love Mars' campaign, featuring lovable personalities like Bob Monkhouse, Richard Murdoch, Vera Lynn and Petula Clark.[12] Surprisingly little, if any, of this advertising was aimed at kids; Silmos fruit drops, for instance, were advertised halfway through *Gun Law* at 10.15 p.m.

The public were enraptured by it all. A bag of sweets, simply by appearing on the screen, attained a star status. No longer just a bag, it became an icon, a single branded package simultaneously stared at and recognized by an audience of millions. In a *News Chronicle* poll of favourite ads, Murraymints was voted top.[13] Cadbury-Fry's became confident enough with the new medium to move in on the

---

10 Confectioners' first taste of TV fame came in 1951, when a box of Terry's Spartan chocks was used as a prop in the play *And No Birds Sing*. Not that anyone at Terry's was aware of it, until an excited underling rang the MD at home.

11 When Murray's claimed the record for sucking a single one of their mints was 8 minutes 36 seconds, others were quick to challenge. The record was eventually claimed by a man from Flint: 2 hours, 7 minutes and 12 seconds.

12 A few years later the stars were sacked in favour of the working classes, who used a Mars a day to help them work, rest and play.

13 A competition was run to name the relaxed guardsman seen sucking the eponymous mints – winning entry being the clever Adam Goodmint.

USA where they sponsored a children's programme called *Small Fry Club*.

Confectionery also cropped up many times on TV's *What's My Line*, a panel game in which first-generation media darlings had to guess the occupation of a mystery factory worker. One of their first defeats was by the 'Jelly Baby Vaseliner', a young woman whose job, allegedly, was to shake off the starch from jelly babies after they were turned out of their moulds. A mini-scandal ensued after the boss of Fryer's, pioneer jelly baby-makers and self-appointed guardians of the lore, claimed that no such profession existed.

Further defeats were inflicted on the *WML* panel by a 'dipper' – whose job entailed putting the 'lighted' ends on sweet cigarettes – and an 'essence dispenser', whose function was to measure out the exact amount of mint to go into each batch of Murraymints.[14]

Angry letters about chewing gum stuck on cinema and bus seats were a daily feature of newspapers. While Guernsey's *Evening Press* gave away eleven thousand sticks in an attempt to give the habit a more upmarket image, at London Airport a special squad had to be set up to deal with discarded blobs. Chief culprits, apparently, were Americans, their first instinct on leaving their aeroplanes, like dogs marking territory at a lamppost, being to drop a piece of gum on British soil. One of these recent arrivals was P.K. Wrigley, scion of the gum zillionaire and now president of the company.[15] Fortune stuck

---

14 The public's fascination with the mechanics of the confectionery industry lasted well into the 1980s. Oh, how we chuckled and guffawed as contestants on *The Generation Game* made a dog's breakfast out of folding a simple chocolate box.
15 Wrigley's P.K. chewing gum, first marketed in 1921, stood for 'Packed Tight – Kept Right'. Wrigley's son, born in 1922, was christened Philip K. Since the gum couldn't have been named after him, it seemed pretty obvious that poor Philip had been named after the gum.

to the family like, well, gum to a shoe. As well as now owning no less than eleven yachts and an island off the Californian coast, P.K. also acted as sponsor for eleven baseball clubs.

Rich pickings, but not fairly shared with those at the bottom of the industry. A poor-paying, labour-intensive operation, gathering chicle called for every sapodilla tree to be climbed by a man armed with a machete. On the upward climb a gutter would be hacked from bottom to top, then on the descent diagonal slashes would be cut to connect with the main channel. After collection in canvas bags placed at the bottom of each tree, the sap was slowly boiled, congealing into the loaves that were sent off to America's gum packagers. Workers were away from their families for eight months at a time – fifty pounds being an average payment for their labours – half of which was immediately handed over to middle men in return for food, lodging, machete hire and continuing patronage.

In the Scottish town of Largs, chewing-gum machines, nineteen of them in all, were classed as obstructions under the Burgh Police Act of 1892 and removed. Leeds Council also voted to eradicate bubblegum machines from city streets. According to critics, and there seemed to be plenty, the machines simply attracted crowds of Teddy boys – who were quite likely to smash them up or throw them through a shopkeeper's window if they didn't get a gumball in return for their penny.

In Lincoln a proud police chief informed the city's Watch Committee that the local count of gum machines had been cut from thirty-one to four. Thirteen had been removed for obstruction, but even though another fourteen were on private property and could not be obstructions, officers had managed to impound them as illegal gaming machines – because of the trinkets they contained.

Bubblegum trinkets were also deemed illegal by

magistrates in Bradford,[16] with local shopkeepers hauled up on charges of 'conducting an illegal lottery' – that being defined in official parlance as involving 'a competition not mainly dependent on skill'. But no rivalry was involved, argued defence solicitors, so how could it be described as a competition? As for a lottery, the stakes and prizes were surely far too trivial to be included in such a definition. Magistrates were not swayed and handed out exemplary fines.

Yet the biggest gamble, perhaps, was leaving the gum machines outside. Two youths found guilty of stealing them wholesale asked for ten other offences to be taken into consideration. One youth was assessed for Borstal, his pal fined a whopping £50 with £34 costs, the equivalent of two months' wages. They'd only been after the money – to buy bikes – but what they did with the bubblegum and trinkets is unrecorded.

With the public now making the automatic link between chewing gum, Teddy boys and loutish behaviour, it was no wonder that chewing-gum companies tried to encourage a more wholesome family-orientated image. Wrigley's Ice Hockey, for instance, was a fun game for the whole family, easily set up on the dining-room table after Mum cleared away the tea things: 'With one of you at each end of the table, clench a match between your teeth and push your packet of chewing gum towards your opponent's goal at the far end of the table.' Did kids really have more imagination back then – or merely greater powers to suspend cynicism? Whatever the answer, grown-ups didn't want them imagining too much. Imports of 'pin-up' chewing gum were banned after a Labour MP tabled a Commons question about children buying chewing gum with 'near nude' pictures. Though government solicitors could find

---

16 Bubblegum trinkets cost six shillings a gross, equivalent to a halfpenny each. But with the gum costing only a penny it's no wonder they didn't put too many in.

no grounds for legal action, strangely enough, irregularities had been found in the importer's paperwork, so they were able to assure MPs that no more 'pin-up' gum would be allowed in to corrupt Britain's young folk.

Chewing gum, according to one American professor, made an ideal bait for mousetraps. The gum, pre-chewed to optimum stickiness and substituted for cheese, stuck to the helpless rodent's fangs and, in his panic to shake it off, *sproing!* – the deadly trap was sprung. In a nod towards traditional culling practices, the professor agreed that cheese-flavoured gum, if anyone would care to develop such a thing, would be the real doomsday weapon.

A.J. Pappadakis was a great name for a maker of Turkish delight, even though his label boasted Made in England: West Norwood, in fact. Still, he had lived in Constantinople for a while and boasted that his delight had been certified as authentic by the Turkish ambassador to London. His claims were met with derision by those who considered an address in Asia Minor *de rigueur*. 'This is not Turkish delight but Turkish despair!' moaned one Hajji Bekir of Cairo after sampling a piece of Pappadakis's confection. 'Turkish delight can be made only with water from the Bosphorus, just as Burton beer can only be made with water from the Trent.'[17]

Authenticity is a hazy area when it comes to confectionery. A British couple travelling around America were desperate to find some rock to take home (this being, in the eyes of many, better proof of travel than a smeared ink stamp in a passport). Yet, despite travelling coast to coast from New York to LA, the only sticks they came across were in the gift shop at Niagara Falls. Still, better than nothing, they thought. Back home in Britain, while deciding which friends and relatives would be honoured with a souvenir,

---

17 A yucky misconception: Burton beer was never made from the muddy slush of its local river but with mineralized water from underground strata.

they took a closer look – and discovered they'd gone and bought a dozen sticks of Blackpool rock.

Or was it? British holidaymakers had long had their illusions shattered by the commercial realities involved in rock-making. Somehow it just didn't seem right when small print on labels of Brighton rock revealed origins in Blackpool, while Southport rock was just as likely to be made and wrapped in Margate. So, for all anyone knew, Blackpool rock purchased at Niagara Falls might just as easily have been made in Weston-Super-Mare or Bridlington.

A garbled gazetteer wasn't the only thing that caused concern. According to health watchdogs, some manufacturers were still using a chemical called rhodamine B to create rock's familiar pink colouring. Suspected of being carcinogenic, it had been banned by law as long ago as 1957[18] – yet it seemed millions of such poisonously tinted sticks were still being sold from Britain's countless seaside stalls. One guilty company was ordered to destroy the three tons it held in stock, and recall sticks from as far afield as Lowestoft, Southport and Torquay.

Rock, like many other items of confectionery, had a hazy history, cluttered with myths and tall tales. Some seaside resorts made it a matter of pride to claim credit as its birthplace, one such being the port of Lancaster, once an unloading point for West Indian cane sugar. While the quality stuff went off to various factories, locals were able to buy up any water-damaged cargo at knock-down prices. Being tainted with salt water it wasn't that much of a bargain and its main use was to be combined with soap and brick dust to make holystones, used for scrubbing ships' decks. In 1820 a cheapskate by the name of Fishwick decided to use up some of this dodgy sugar to make sticks

18 The clampdown on dodgy ingredients continued apace. Needler's Bronchial Pastilles, popular since the 1900s, finally ceased production in the 1960s when chloroform was banned from use in food.

of toffee. Despite a distinctive tang, it was eagerly snapped up by kids and anyone else who couldn't afford first-class sweets. When nearby Morecambe became a resort, Fishwick opened a stall on the promenade and began selling his 'lollipops'[19] to holidaymakers. Others soon followed, in Morecambe, Fleetwood and elsewhere. Later, a copycat trader, who coloured his version bright pink to attract buyers, was nicknamed Dynamite Dick because of his product's resemblance to sticks of explosive.

Rock was soon sold everywhere and by the mid-nineteenth century had become as much a part of the seaside experience as cockles and mussels. All-the-way-through names didn't appear for another twenty years. Originally just a gimmick, the idea probably originated with a group of apprentices messing about. Playfully adding star and flower shapes to lumps of still-molten rock they noticed that, when extruded, the shapes diminished in size but still went all the way through. Words were an obvious next step. In the beginning the word was 'MINT', but it didn't take long for someone to spot the potential for self-promotion.[20]

Claims for originating lettered rock have also been made by the Isle of Man, where a local confectioner, Bill Quiggen, made a special batch for Prince Albert's 1847 visit, with the words 'Welcome, Prince Albert, to Mona' running all the way through. But its potential has never been limited to advertising seaside resorts. In Welling-borough, in the 1950s, letters were replaced by the final

---

19 The first official record of 'lollipop' dates back to 1754, in the *Dictionary of Vulgar Tongue*, defining it as 'sweet lozenges purchased by children'. No mention of a stick, and no reason to suppose a lollipop had to have one. The word itself probably came from 'lolly', northern dialect for tongue.

20 I doubt if there's ever been rock with Llanfairpwllgwyngyllgogerychwyrndrobwll-llantysiliogogogoch all the way through, but one firm did win an order from Oslo for 122 sticks with the legend 'Anre Bendikson A/S Lyd Studio'.

score of a victorious away game. After the result was relayed by telephone, the rock was niftily made and was ready for sale at Wellingborough station as the football special full of ecstatic fans steamed to a halt. And in York, after Athens police made an exchange visit, a special batch of rock was made with Athens Police all the way through – though I don't know if it was in English or Greek.

Besides being lettered, rock could be moulded into virtually any shape. This was holiday stuff, so the more fun the better. Carrots, Bass bottles, celery, fish fry-ups, oysters, sardines on toast, shellfish and pairs of kippers are just a few of the countless forms in which it has been sold to an adoring public. How many teeth have been lost or broken by rock's clamp-like grip is unknown, but it must be thousands.

One man at least was safe from such risks – comedian Ken Dodd. His trade-mark teeth had famously been insured for £10,000, but the policy had strict conditions. As well as insisting he brush his gnashers three times a day, it specified a total ban on seaside rock.

Sweets were an integral part of life at Christ Church Junior Mixed and Infants School. Bartering went on constantly: in the corners, alongside the walls of the toilet, in the changing rooms. There were whisperings and mutterings as thick as a Popish plot – and all over whether so-and-so deserved to get a Black Jack.

Sweets were, still are, tokens and currency. Friends, lifelong or temporary, could be bought for a single Spangle (Old English variety excepted, since few liked them and in currency terms they were as negotiable as a Mongolian tugrik). Kids who grew up in the days of Roy Rogers and the Lone Ranger were sure to be Spangles fans. Introduced by Mars in 1948 at threepence a packet – 'Double wrapped to keep all the flavour in and all the dirt out!' – Spangles were probably the first sweets to be widely known as a packaged brand rather than just a bag of generic miscellania. As well as the standard fruit flavours, Spangles came in varieties. Acid drops, barley sugar, peppermint and blackcurrant all had their fans, as did golden mint, lime and liquorice. Old English had few fans because its flavours were so odd: with some vaguely medicinal and others reminiscent of your gran's linen cupboard, no one could be quite sure what these flavours were supposed to be. One thing was sure, we didn't like them. Nevertheless, Spangles were number one.[21]

With the right sweet, the services of a slave could be yours, at least till the end of playtime, time enough to be piggy-backed around the yard a dozen times. Some kids' servitude seemed to extend beyond playtime, beyond the school gates even, but what deals were involved there are unknown.

Many children, me included, naïvely believed that Love Hearts were an essential part of courtship, a romantic King's Shilling: once a girl accepted one she had to be your girlfriend. This was how our mums and dads met, surely? Some boys (old before their years?) would even plan a sting, carefully removing the wrapper and fixing the order of sweets so that one's chosen belle picked out a particular message. Originally designed as 'conversation lozenges' for shy Victorians, our post-war version came with such messages as: *It's OK, Run For It, OK Baby, Hi Dad* and obscure greetings such as *Hairzy Doats*[22] and *Ali Baba*, presumably only understandable to clued-up kids.

Despite their cloying perfume, Parma Violets were another favourite, and were oddly addictive, though it was this same scent that made others disdain them as girls' stuff. It wasn't until recently that I ever thought of asking

---

21 When a mystery flavour was included in packs in 1964, 78,000 amateur sleuths set out to identify it.
22 Doats, according to the OED, means to talk foolishly or ramble, but, as yet, the cultural meaning of Ali Baba has proved beyond this researcher.

questions, like what connection did they have with violets? Or Parma come to that?

Though sweets were confected fakes anyway – sweet tobacco, liquorice shoelaces, rock peas and potatoes, even sheets of Eating Paper – there were all kinds of double-bluffs: copies of copies, as it were. Those cornets and wafers, for instance, that had foamy marshmallow in place of the ice-cream.

Liquorice remained a perennial favourite, exerting the same charms on us as it must have done on our grandads fifty years previously. One advantage, for those who made it, was that its multitudinous formations could be quickly renamed to keep abreast of crazes and cultural shifts. David's Sling (liquorice primed with a small gobstopper) was timeless enough to be inoffensive, even biblically educational. Bullets – comfits in joined-together tubes – were still popular, though some makers now opted for the less belligerent name Pencil Cases. Twisty Telegraph Wires were renamed Electric Drills to reflect the post-war craze for DIY, while the nascent Space Age was celebrated with Rockets, a comfit jammed in one end of a liquorice tube.

Across the road from our school was a launderette. No obvious temptations for schoolkids there, one might think, except they had a bubblegum machine affixed to the wall. Why? Certainly not to cater for the old biddies who sat watching their smalls whirling in sudsy orbit. No, it can only have been a cynical attempt to exploit us kids. Not just to take our pennies either, but to tempt us to cross a busy street at dinnertimes when no lollipop man was on duty. At the time I joined the bubblegum gang (renegades who went out despite the headmaster's warning) packs came with cards depicting kings and queens of England. The first additions to my collection were Lady Jane Grey, monarchy's nine-day wonder, and a rather stern portrait of Henry VII.

Gum packets have never carried a Government Health Warning, but perhaps they've never needed one when parents and class goody-goodies always had a plentiful store of gruesome fables. Swallow gum and you died. It stuck halfway down your windpipe, starving you of air. Right at the end, a bubble burst out of your mouth. But that was your last gasp – undignified and sticky – and by then it was too late. Or, if it got through, it ended up wrapped around your insides like so many rubber bands, cutting off blood supplies, causing deadly atrophy of various organs. Doctors couldn't save you: by the time an ambulance got you to Casualty the evil gum was so entangled that nothing could be done. Even the autopsy had to be abandoned halfway through as the pathologist's instruments got impossibly bogged down in ivory-coloured goo. Scare stories, of course, but all in a good cause. People were only passing on the lore, what other people had told them. Most kids dismissed such tales. Even if they were true, death was surely preferable to being called a sissy. You could always tell kids who weren't quite sure: they chewed with great care, as refined as old duchesses – and when the gum lost its taste they spat it as far away as possible.

After school came the long walk home. Long? For this adult, it's a ten-minute walk. Back then, though, it was an untroubled dawdle, with at least half a dozen sweetshops en route. With their brass doorlatches smoothed wafer-thin by millions of sweaty thumb actions, those shops were part of our little lives. Window displays were functional, never clever – packets of PG Tips, boxes of Daz, combs on a card – there not to seduce, merely inform. And, alongside such household necessities, the sweets, boxes with flaps of waxed paper peeled back to show off their contents – the translucent greens and oranges of Sports Mixture, candy shrimps, pink and foamy, aniseed balls the colour of dried blood. Cup-Tie Chews, Fairy Milk Drops, Martian Space Gum and Granny's Teeth, Chimps, Calypso Joes and Cocojax. Eagle Lollies and Dan Dare liquorice bars. On hot days wasps buzzed lazily around the boxes of liquorice laces and pipes but, far from putting us off, the insects were a good omen, proof of succulence and sweetness.

Marketed with kids in mind, Cadbury's Dairy Milk came in half a dozen sizes – 1d, 2d, 3d and 6d bars being the ones in our price range, the last also offering a variety of flavours like strawberry, marzipan, peppermint and Turkish delight.

These shops were all run by little old ladies, or so it seemed. As patiently as gold-panners, they garnered their income from farthings, pennies and threepenny bits. It's hard to believe anyone made a living. What profit can there have been in a single chew, four pink candy shrimps or a penny Arrow bar? Economically, ergonomically, could it possibly have been worth the carpet-slippered trudge from the back room to sell half a dozen chews to a kid in a grubby shirt? Any profit – a farthing, if that – would be more than offset by the cost of replacing the energy expended. Maybe they didn't care. Not so much a business as a branch of the social services; these kindly souls who ran our sweetshops were only in it for a chance to pat kiddies on the head.

Sentimental tosh! They were more mercenary than we imagined, waiting like patient websters for kids to spill out of school with a hot threepenny bit stamped into a sticky palm. 'This is Barratt Country!' yelled their wholesalers. 'Where you strike gold every schoolday and holiday of the year.' Barker and Dobson were no less straightforward with their line 'B & D = LSD' – a slogan dropped for obvious reasons in the 1960s.[23] Yet, for all their kind enquiries about our mums and our schoolwork, at the end of the day, that's all we were, little consumers, easily pleased, short-trousered magpies attracted by the sparkle of sugar and the fragrance of synthetic raspberry, eager to be part of each and every craze that swept Britain's schoolyards on a regular basis.

One shop, on a corner by the nearby secondary modern, had a marvellous machine that dispensed penny bottles of

23 To older confectioners, LSD had a more cynical meaning than pounds, shillings and pence – Live, slave and die.

pop. Solid and functional at counter level, it was surmounted by a huge sphere of glass full of soda water. Kids picked a flavour, the shopkeeper added a slug of brightly coloured syrup to one of the thin-necked bottles and topped it up with water, which bubbled, gurgled and belched its way through tin pipework and into the narrow bottle. A serious junior with a sherbet dab, who'd had it drummed into him that drinking in the street was common, I watched with a mix of disapproval and envy as these kids strutted and swigged simultaneously, oblivious to society's edicts. How cool and rebellious they looked, and how I longed to copy them.

Unlike many kids, I was conscientious about dropping sweet papers and lolly wrappers. Litterbugs did get nabbed by bobbies and hauled off to face justice. Excuses were treated with magisterial derision. They were only small bits, protested one youth, in court for dropping paper in Hyde Park. All very well, but as the JP pointed out, fining him seven and six,'If everyone threw away a small piece the place would look like a snow storm!'[24]

At school, then, using sweets as our currency, we learned many of the guiding principles of adult life – purchasing power, trade-offs, bribery, blackmail, even a kind of prostitution. But many sweets still came to us for free – or nearly free – from old folk who'd reward you for running an errand. If you were lucky you'd get a penny to spend as you liked, but cheapskates would try to palm you off with a sweet of unknown origins: nothing that any normal kid would want, but some hard-boiled, rhubarb-flavoured creation, a chocolate lime filled with gritty Grade Z chocolate, or a herbal horror that had been kicking around the bottom of their shopping bag for weeks, or kept in a trouser

---

24 Why not throw sweets at weddings, suggested the Archdeacon of Chesterfield, having seen this admirable custom on holiday in Italy: 'Confetti is hideous and hard to clear up, but sweets can be picked up by the children afterwards.'

pocket in close proximity to … we could only shudder to think. These sweets were far too personal, well beyond any best-by date, so that even the hardest boilings had softened and acquired a kind of animal coat, wrinkled like a new-born rat and suspiciously fluffy. It made you feel sick but you had to smile and say thank you very much, slip it in – then spit it into a drain at the first opportunity. One I remember getting rid of in just that way, a distinctive green sweet with a red stripe – which lay there for days, as bright as a traffic light. I was scared stiff that the lady who gave it to me would see it lying there and know I'd spat it out, ungrateful and unfeeling.

Did the owners of that launderette realize their bubblegum machine helped end a way of life? Despite moves against free-standing machines, local authorities confessed themselves powerless to act against a vending machine affixed to the wall of a private house.[25] The trade was up in arms. That would mean any Tom, Dick or Harry could cash in on a passing public. Look at what was happening. To compensate for a slump of sales due to the derationing of sweets, even fish and chip shops had started to sell them. 'Fish and confectionery are like night and day,' spluttered nearby sweetshop owners. 'It's fantastic for a fish and chip shop to sell sweets. Just as fantastic as if we sold bicycling accessories.'

With competition on every front – launderettes, garages and now chip shops – the traditional sweetshop didn't stand a chance. After all, while few traders had the will or the necessary expertise to diversify into meat or vegetables, anyone could sell sweets. They needed no special know-ledge, no special conditions, no licences. The sweetshop, at

---

25 But how much money was there in it, anyway? With a chew dispensing machine costing thirteen pounds eight shillings, you'd have to sell over three thousand penny chews just to cover the cost, and even then the margins must have been pretty minimal.

the end of the day, was entirely devoid of any protection.

Debts and bankruptcies had long been a fact of life, but by 1960 county court judgements against sweetshops were averaging twelve a week. Britain's social tapestry was coming apart. Loose threads became laddered rips, worn patches turned into holes. The streets were emptying. The old ladies were sitting in their armchairs, listening to ticking clocks, fading away. It was a social disaster. And, under any other circumstances, an economic one, too. But Britain's big manufacturers weren't that bothered. Any bad debts were easily absorbed. For every old lady who went to the wall, a new outlet was opened in a petrol station, bingo hall or self-service mart. Even chemists were selling sweets alongside the toothbrushes.

Yet the same economic Darwinism also began to touch many manufacturers. Just as dinosaurs scarcely noticed the eerie light cast by the meteor that was to end their reign, so these firms did not notice any portents in the sodium-grey glow now bathing the nation's parlours. The arrival of TV shifted the whole balance of the industry … permanently. Only firms with enough spare cash could take full advantage of the new medium. And as soon as they started they began to take an increasing market share, leaving poorer competitors to wither away or be weakened enough for a takeover.

Candy, Man!

The Swinging Sixties

*How long you will be in retirement I do not
know. You must be fully prepared. If you are
smokers bring your cigarettes, if you are
sweet-eaters bring your sweets.*

Judge in the Great Train Robbery trial

With his blond pudding bowl, NHS specs and cowboy gear,
the Milky Bar Kid epitomized post-war childhood. It was
1961 when he first rode into town, and we've loved him
ever since. As geeky as he looked, there wasn't one boy who
didn't harbour secret dreams of having his popularity.
Such divine status couldn't be bought at any price, but for
four and ninepence and two Milky Bar wrappers you could
get a hat like his, while the whole caboodle – suit, hat, rifle –
could be yours for just twelve shillings plus four wrappers
from the bigger sixpenny bar.[1]

---

1 We loved Indians, too. Two days before the Popemobile
appeared to ferry celebs around in full view of adoring fans,
Chief Big Arrow toured Britain on the back of a Mini pick-up,
complete with wigwam and campfire. As kids gathered, Big
Chief handed out free samples of penny Arrow bars, now with
tribal customs and words on the wrappers. Also on offer, for
half a dozen wrappers, were a bow and arrow.

Child stars had a long history in sweet advertising. Fry's Five Boys chocolate, first sold in 1902, was still around in the 1960s; and so was the boy himself – now a pensioner and living in Providence, Rhode Island. Lindsey Poulton was only 4 years old when photographed for the famous wrapper, which featured him in five guises, morphing through the personifications of Desperation, Pacification, Expectation, Acclamation and, lastly, Realization – it's Fry's. Good acting? Not exactly. Desperation's tears, which must have moved a hundred million mums to guilty appeasement, were actually brought on by an ammonia-soaked cloth draped around his neck – cruel exploitation that would never be allowed today. Little Lindsey's smile in the last of the five cameos was, supposedly, brought on by a loving parent placating him with Fry's chocolate – but maybe it was just that someone took the choking rags away.[2] Five Boys is one of the most cherished brands. By the time it last appeared in sweetshops in 1971 the wrapper showed five very individual boys, but it had enjoyed a run of almost seventy years and been loved by children of four generations.

'Don't forget the fruit gums, Mum' – a 1960s TV classic – was another example of emotional blackmail, refined by masters and so full of pathos that it's never been forgotten by those of us who grew up with it. The pivotal staring-out-of-the-window role starred a youthful Dennis Waterman, years before he achieved pin-up status as shaggy-haired Carter in *The Sweeney* and Terry in *Minder*, with direction by Lindsay Anderson, later famous for seminal 1960s films *If...* and *This Sporting Life*. As for the kindly mother, as an icon she has to rank a close third behind mothers Mary and Teresa. It's probable that the actress never played such a serious role again.

---

2 A modern agent would have had Lindsey on a royalty deal, setting him up for life, but Fry's had bought copyright in the images for a one-off two hundred pounds.

But these were idealized kids. In the real world they were rather less angelic.

On Whit Monday 1962 a holiday coach speeding up the M1 had its windscreen shattered by a gobstopper dropped from a bridge. Disaster was prevented only by the quick wits of the driver, who screeched to a halt on the hard shoulder. His three-dozen daytrippers, who'd been looking forward to a cockle-fuelled knees-up at Blackpool and now had three hours to wait for a replacement coach, no doubt felt that God had singled them out for punishment.[3]

A thoughtless way to dispose of an old sweet, certainly, but part of me likes to think that the attack was more than naked yobbism. Since Chancellor Selwyn Lloyd had just introduced his 'Lollipop Tax' – a whacking 15 per cent purchase tax on sweets, chocolate, gum and ice-cream – a snotty-nosed David, his sling primed with a gobstopper, would have been the perfect symbolical protest. But no, realism triumphs. Idle hooliganism is all it was: just a kid bored with a bullseye that lasted too long.

The confectionery biz has suffered many a seismic upset, but the arrival of Galaxy[4] milk chocolate in the early Sixties was Krakatoa and Vesuvius combined. It wasn't so much the shock, perhaps, as the gobsmacking cheek. There'd been dozens of chocolate bars before – Rowntree's Elect, Needler's Kreema, Fry's Five Boys – but none had ever dared consider themselves a serious challenge to Cadbury's Dairy Milk. Galaxy did. And, made by Mars, it was American too.

Secretly made and marketed in Scandinavia by a Mars

---

3 Or had it fallen from the sky? The 'slipping gobstopper' was a derisive name given to Telstar after reports that the pioneering satellite was dropping from its orbit.
4 Why Galaxy? Well, an obvious connection with Mars and Milky Way, but also a clever link from Galactic to lactic, pertaining to milk.

subsidiary, Galaxy got a ready thumbs-up there, quickly capturing a half share of the Norwegian market. The next guinea pig to be given a nibble – Northern Ireland – fluffed up its fur, rolled over and squeaked its satisfaction. In 1960 Galaxy went on sale in mainland UK. It never achieved its ambition of seizing Dairy Milk's crown, but has been snapping at its tail for nearly forty years. Not bad for a firm who'd started out 'borrowing' Cadbury's reputation to sell their products.

Childhood was undergoing great changes. Its chants, its games, its rituals, all were constantly evolving, tugged hither and thither between folk traditions and the new ways, aping what was seen on telly. Despite these changes, the old ways would take a long time to finally die out. Sugarolly water or Popololly – a DIY liquorice drink much cherished by ragmuffins too poor to afford bottles of fizzy pop – survived into the 1960s.[5] Diced liquorice was added to a bottle of warm sugared water and after being given a vigorous shake it was laid down until the liquor acquired a lovely black colour, the deeper the better. In Scotland and the north they even had a special day for it, Spanish Juice Sunday or Spo Sunday, when children sold their inky nectar door to door, a drink for one pin being the recommended price.

> *Spanish Liquorice Water*
> *Fit for a lady's daughter*
> *Two spoonsful a pin*
> *And a little drop in*
> *Spanish Liquorice Water*

---

5 In France, in the eighteenth and nineteenth centuries, coco (liquorice water) sellers were a common sight in the streets and parks, selling the milky-coloured drinks from a flask carried on the back. In Arabia, they still drink *suhss* – a potent liquorice drink made from the steeped roots.

As the bottle's water level dropped, so the juice became increasingly potent, and therefore more desirable.[6] Sugarolly was the most common of these home-made drinks, but they could be made with other ingredients, too. Palm Sunday was celebrated, in some parts of Yorkshire, with Palm Juice, made with cachous steeped in water.

> *In the liquorice fields of Pontefract*
> *My love and I did meet*
> *And many a burdened liquorice bush*
> *Was blooming around our feet.*
>
> John Betjeman

Sounds idyllic, doesn't it? But by the 1960s Sir John's blue-remembered flowers were almost extinct, at least in Britain. Since homegrown plants took anything from three to five years to reach maturity, factories had relied on cheaper (and better) foreign supplies for decades. In the 1920s Britain's liquorice growing had provided a modest living for about ten small-time growers, but by 1964 Pontefract had only one liquorice farmer left, Ernest Carter, who still cultivated five acres. Even for him, though, it was more of a hobby than a viable business.

Liquorice, or the industry attached to it, had been considerably rationalized. Bassett's had taken over Pontefract liquorice-makers Voile & Wortley in 1955 and, more recently, had snapped up Wilkinson's for £1 million. Not that the old firm had ever been run by a Wilkinson. It belonged to a family named Marshall, Wilkinson being an accountant who had put up some of the capital and whose name had been used for obscure tax reasons. Nor, oddly enough, was there a Bassett in charge of Bassett's, and hadn't been since George, its founder, had died in 1886.

---

6 It wasn't just child's play. Black Sugar, a similar liquor, was often prescribed by doctors as a medicinal tonic.

Many sweets, in one way or another, occupied a unique place in our culture, each having its own rituals or oddball stories attached. Liquorice Allsorts were no exception. One fan always fed the black ones to his prize greyhound, swearing by them for giving the dog's coat a glossy shine. Cows were quite partial to them, too. Flossie, a personal milk machine owned by a Clitheroe smallholder, chewed and ruminated her way through ten tons a year. Quality Allsorts, at £237 a ton, would have made an annual bill of £2370 – but factory rejects could be picked up for a mere £10 a ton, half the price of the farmer's usual cattle feed. For cost-cutting nous his idea beats using dead sheep. Risks seem minimal: turning Bertie is infinitely preferable to a dose of mad cow disease.

At Bassett's in Sheffield two thousand factory girls eagerly awaiting a visit by *Goldfinger* star Honor Blackman were disappointed when 'indisposition' made her three hours late and the visit had to be cancelled. Ms Blackman's diplomatic excuse would these days be treated far more sceptically, but Bassett's personnel manager, the hunkily named Ralph Mountain, arranged for the delivery of a box of Liquorice Allsorts to cheer up the actress.

Endorsement from stars of the day had always been craved by confectioners,[7] but the sporting heroes and music-hall turns of old were now being elbowed aside by the stars of pop, TV and film. The chance to earn extra cash by lending their monicker to various products was something few stars turned their noses up at and their agents even touted for business in confectionery's trade press. Pin-up rock 'n' rollers like Marty Wilde and Tommy Steele were, it seemed, only too willing to have their mugshots attached to lollies and toffee bars. Chubby

---

7 'Voice' confectionery – lozenges and gums popular at the turn of the century – was endorsed by a variety of actors and singers, including diva Adelina Patti who gave her name to Hollway's Pattines.

Checker's Peppermint Twisters, for instance, came with a photo of Chubby himself, along with instructions for doing the twist.[8]

To promote his new single *Candy Man*,[9] Brian Poole gave a stick of rock to each panel member of TV's *Juke Box Jury*. Maybe he hoped that a watching rock-factory owner would offer a fabulous fee to make sticks with Tremoloes all the way through ...

'We're getting about two tons thrown at us every night,' moaned Beatle George Harrison a few days after he'd let slip that jelly babies were his favourite sweets.

Originally known as unclaimed babies – sold forty to a bag – these squidgy homunculi had been invented a whole century previously by an Austrian named Steinboch, one of Europe's many itinerant confectioners who wandered from town to town offering their expertise. He arrived in Lancashire in 1864 and took a job at Fryer's, makers of the Victory V lozenge, for whom his first offering was the jelly baby. Though Steinboch's idea was never trademarked – and many copycats cashed in on the craze: Bassett's, Lion and Wilkinson's to name but three – Fryer's always insisted on their credentials as inventors.[10]

---

8 Such contracts didn't always work out amicably: Pinky and Perky had to take out an injunction against one man who paid for a year's rights to use their name on his sweets, but then just carried on regardless.

9 The pop world is notorious for adding all kinds of hip meanings to straight words. Donovan's *Candy Man*, far from being some lovable old guy from the sweet shop, made regular trips to North Africa – and the Morocco's finest he brought back was not a brand of Turkish Delight. In the clubs of London, Sweeties was a slang term for Preludin, sold at a going rate of twenty-four for a pound.

10 Black jelly babies were undeniably popular – Bassett's cashed in by launching All Blacks – but was it an encouraging sign of multiracial harmony? PM's wife Mary Wilson, on a visit to Fryer's, made a point of quizzing bosses about the number of 'coloured' people they employed in the factory.

Yes, all will wonder, there's no doubt
How we are made, till they find out
But as a fact, head, feet and belly
Are all made from the purest jelly
And nicely flavoured too.

For Victorians, unclaimed babies had unpleasant suggestions of loose morals, hints of housemaids being undone and cruelly cast out. A name-change was called for. Bright babies was pleasing and far more refined, and no one then saw anything amiss in nigger babies to describe the liquorice-flavoured ones. After World War One, in a touching display of new world optimism, they were rechristened peace babies.

Originally a northern eccentricity – cotton-mill workers swore by them for keeping down lint in their throats while weaving – jelly babies won many more fans after one of the characters in radio's weekly *ITMA* comedy kept up a running joke about them.

But back to the Beatles … When the boss of Fryer's heard that Ringo was having his tonsils out he sent a 4lb box of jelly babies to the hospital.[11] 'I'm not a Beatles fan myself,' he told reporters, 'but all the girls here are crazy about them. I'm sure they've had an impact on sales. Not that I approve of them being thrown around,' he added snootily. 'They are far too nice to be used like that.'

Jellified figures had become astoundingly popular. To cash in on *Dr Who*, jelly Daleks made an appearance and proved an instant hit, while jelly cowboys and Indians also sold well. Not so jelly guardsmen; perhaps there was something slightly too treacherous about biting such a symbol of state.

---

11 Firms were falling over themselves to share the pop limelight. *My Boy Lollipop* singer Millie received a 42lb lollipop from Tyler's lollies, along with 216 normal-sized ones. They were presented by fellow pop star Chris Sandford, alias *Coronation Street*'s Walter Potts.

Three years later, thanks to 'improved technology', Payne's (one of several southern firms now cashing in) played midwife to a jelly baby with a navel. This ever-so-slightly-rude gimmick, a probable side-effect of the Permissive Society, hit headlines for a day, but was quickly dismissed by others. Fryer's, speaking in their official role as Creator, responded sniffily to any suggestion that they'd been upstaged. 'Jelly babies are bought to eat. Fryer's were the first to make them and we'll be producing our usual 2500 a minute for a long time yet.'

The perennial appeal of jelly babies is worth considering. Is it sublimated cannibalism? Or something sexual, an urge to nibble at bodily parts? In a survey, eight out of ten addicts confessed to biting the heads off first. Most also confessed an especial fancy for the black ones – though none would buy a pack containing all black babies.

Bassett's claimed that their new babies – also with belly buttons – were more human and baby-like than ever before. They even had a name. And what might that be? Why, Reg, of course. For, as Bassett's pointed out, their JBs were conceived from registered design No.885406. So, it's worth asking, if only to annoy, why not Des?

When it came to relieving kids of their pocket money, Beatlemania offered undreamed-of potential. Spilling through the school gates and straight into the nearest sweetshop, kids couldn't get enough Beatle-backed items: Beatles gum, for instance, which came complete with wallet-sized snaps. Not just any old repackaged publicity shots, mind, but exclusive pics by a photographer who shadowed the group for four weeks, just to snatch a few minutes' snapping each day. For their co-operation the Fab Four were paid a four-figure sum: no specific numerals were mentioned, but it was described by one of A & BC's bosses as 'a breathtaking amount'.

Understandably enough, everyone wanted a slice of pop's profitable pie. Official endorsement didn't come cheap, but the need for a sizeable bung could be easily sidestepped with some clever thinking. For instance, if reps said Beat-All lollies in the right way when talking to shopkeepers it might easily be mistaken for Beatle lollies. Bosses at the firm which made Beat-All hotly denied that their reps had been given any such instructions. And it was true that Beat-All lollies had been around since Bill Haley's day, years before the Beatles appeared – but then why had the wrapper been redesigned to include a guitar and the slogan 'It's Fab!'?

The Beatles may have been literally flavour of the month, but prudent companies had to hedge their bets. Beatlemania had great potential and could not be ignored, but the business world had seen nothing like it before. Who knew how long such merchandising mania might last? Hence the expeditious appearance of Dave Clark Five lollies and rock as soon as the DC5's *Glad All Over* ousted the Beatles from number one.

Quick as they were to spot profit in the youth market, without inside advice confectionery firms could find themselves hopelessly adrift. In a promotion aimed at every teenager who owned a Dansette record player, Rowntree's were offering a Smarties LP – virtually half the price of a normal album at fifteen shillings and threepence – featuring tracks by such pop progressives as Ray Conniff, Burl Ives and Mike and Bernie Winters, not to mention the memorably forgettable André Kustelanetz.

TV and confectionery were made for each other, a perfect example of financial symbiosis. Tie-ins were nothing new – we had Mickey Mouse Family Assortment and Felix Toffee back in the 1930s – but, with the spread of TV, such product association really came into its own. Sweets brought revenue to commercial TV, and in return TV lent its glamour and fun to hundreds of lines. *Danger Man, Dr Who, The Man From UNCLE, The Monkees* – all brought added charisma to a raft of confections, from bubblegum and sweet cigarettes to ice-lollies. Even the wooden performances of Lady Penelope and Parker, her

154

faithful chauffeur, could be used to sell Fab, the first ice-lolly made specially for girls. Influences bounced back and forth, until it became impossible to tell who was influencing whom. Ads became cameo performances for the characters, and the full-length programmes they came from became a *de facto* endorsement of the ad.

One of the first TV tie-ins was the *Take Your Pick*/ Cadbury's Lucky Numbers promotion. Each chocolate in the Cadbury's assortment had a numbered wrapper, and punters who correctly guessed the public's five favourites in the right order were invited to a special edition of the *Take Your Pick* gameshow, to be held at the London Palladium and hosted by genial 'quiz inquisitor' Michael Miles. Prizes ranged from a Ford Zodiac to a rusty wheel nut.

Norman Vaughn, host of TV's *Sunday Night At The London Palladium,* also made a very profitable pact with Cadbury's. At one time, in 1964, he was everywhere with his 'Roses grown on you' slogan (a catchphrase still remembered over thirty years later) and his trademark thumbs-up sign, gleefully copied by every junior.

An early casualty of the new cut-throat commercialism was the Trebor lion, one of TV's early stars, a real-live big cat being walked in the park by a 1960s dolly bird. All done by mirrors, claimed sceptics, refusing to believe that anyone would be so reckless. But it hardly mattered what the truth was: lions and bulldogs, those dangerous pets of patriotism, had had their day. Flags and heroes were out. TV stars, both live and hand-operated, were the new champions of confectionery and could name their price. Lenny the Lion, hardly a heavyweight in leonine stakes, signed a lucrative contract with Trebor Mints and the real flesh-and-blood beast was sent to a home for old lions.

Over at the BBC, the *What's My Line* panel was still being stumped by a procession of sweets workers who turned up to test their wits. But vigilance was necessary. Mere plebs, these factory hands couldn't be expected to understand the protocols of TV. Bubblegum-worker Jessie Patching barely escaped being hustled off for a tongue amputation when she nearly gave the name of her employers – an excommunicable offence in TV-dom. Guest panellist Eartha Kitt meanwhile was allowed four plugs for her show at London's Talk of the Town nightspot.

As marketing got ever slicker, there were inevitable complaints about rip-offs. Kids snapped up anything to do with football, but one Crawley dad went bananas when a local newsagent took his son's threepence pocket money in return for a pack containing five pieces of popcorn and a 1962 Romford v. West Ham programme. He got his son a refund, but only after he'd made complaints to the local consumer council.

Still, it's nice to know that, despite such hardline marketing, the confectionery industry's philanthropic traditions remained undimmed. When bosses at Parkinson's heard about an old Glasgow lady who'd been buying 4oz of their barley sugar twists every day for twenty years, they generously arranged a free supply for life. Mrs Couper was over the moon. No one had ever been so nice to her before – not in her 106 years.

Despite a 1968 survey in which a staggering 72 out of 250 people alleged that chocolate gave them a headache (leading doctors to suspect it as a major cause of migraine), the chocolate box had become, over the years, the standard measure of affection. The bigger the expectations, the bigger the box. When London's notorious Windmill Theatre finally closed its doors in 1964, local sweetshops reported a boom in sales, with numbers of furtive men buying the largest and prettiest boxes of chocolates as farewell gifts for the theatre's dancing girls. 'I don't know what I'll do now,' said one sad gent, handing over a box of Black Magic to his favourite barmaid.

While some of Britain's oldest pensioners had only just got used to the Gregorian calendar, now it had been annexed by marketing men, turned into an almanac of company-sponsored dates, all kinds of new-fangled red letter days for men worry about. No excuse was too shameless. 'Don't forget this is "Be Sweet To Your Secretary Week"', announced Terry's in October 1968. 'How about giving her a box of Contrast?'

With every Sunday paper full of envious stories about the goings-on of the Permissive Society, the best place for this kind of bribery – if local JP Lady Osborn was to be believed – was Welwyn Garden City, a veritable Sodom served by InterCity services from King's Cross. 'Girls give themselves for a box of chocolates,' she said, referring to a steep rise in local rates of illegitimacy. A bag of barley sugars or a stick of gum may have bought delights for men in bombed-out Berlin or war-torn Hamburg, but in Welwyn Garden City in 1965 – surely not?

If sweets and chocolates – as overtures, offerings or naked bribes – had long been part of every suitor's game plan, women themselves were not above using confectionery to get their way. Like a girl employed to pack tins of humbugs at Parkinson's Doncaster factory, who hit on the idea of enclosing notes with details of her name, address and age and the plaintive plea: 'If single, drop a line. If married never mind.' One recipient (sadly married) was so impressed with this novel precaution against being left on the shelf that he reported it to his local paper. An interesting sociological note: the enterprising lass obviously felt safe to assume that humbugs were a masculine purchase. Certainly, one didn't expect to see a woman with her cheeks distended by a humbug, but what if there'd been some tweedy, fag-smoking, humbug-sucking Sister George type out there who'd offered to take the girl up?

At the opening of an exhibition of chocolate boxes, Dame Gladys Cooper, a choc box pin-up from the 1900s, expressed a wish for the return of pretty girls on box lids. Not likely, one company rep admitted privately. Foreign buyers weren't too fussed, but British women apparently disdaineded such pictures.[12]

But while chocolate's fashions came and went, some of the stuff itself had a spookily long shelf-life. Clearing out his drawers one day in 1963, a Kettering man found a tin box of chocolate. The box, one of 100,000 sent to Boer War troops by Queen Victoria, had been there since 1900, saved after his return from Africa and forgotten. After trying a piece, Percy Tressler pronounced it fine, but said he'd rather keep the rest as a souvenir because of its happy memories.[13] By weird coincidence, in the same year in the same town, a man who bought an Easter egg for his nephew found it crawling with grubs. On investigation, council officials found the eggs to be part of a four-hundredweight batch – but compared with Victoria's, this was fresh stock, dating back a mere twelve years.

If chocolate was Cupid's food and manna God's food, Satan's response to it must have been gum. Once again, moral danger seemed to come with the wrapper. In 1966 A & BC was taken to court after Hove residents, led by a local headmistress, made official complaints about obscenity in the firm's bubblegum cards. The series in question, *Martian Attack on Earth*, included such graphic horrors as a pilot struggling to escape a burning aircraft and a dog being killed by a ray-gun. 'We appeal to all those who care about

---

12 The same rep boasted about his firm's Royal Household Chocolates, of which the Queen Mother apparently got through 50lb every year.

13 War chocolate has turned up at regular intervals. The bar which hit the news in 1991 belonged to the same batch as Percy's. Whether its original owner, Lance-Corporal Willie Fryer, had intended to eat it will never be known, but after his death in 1901 the tin became a family heirloom. Not quite sacrosanct: 'experts' who were invited to taste a small section swore that it was definitely a milk chocolate, not plain. After this verdict only three of the six pieces remained, probably the first time that a family heirloom has been eaten by people rather than woodworm.

children and their upbringing to tackle any trader who sells them,' said protesters. 'Children buy these horrific cards without hindrance. Some are even starting a collection.'

After a quiet word, one shopkeeper removed offending packs from his shelves, explaining his actions with the parroted phrase, 'blood-curdling'. But the cards sold well in shops near schools and those traders, reluctant to surrender such a moneyspinner, refused to have anything to do with such censorship. Until, that is, police arrived and carted away their stocks, citing the Obscene Publications Act as authority.

The case against A & BC, brought under the Obscene Publications Act, cited 43 of the 73-card set as examples of corrupting horror. But while even the defending QC admitted the pictures were distasteful, they were not obscene. Magistrates agreed: 'We deplore all of these cards – but cannot say that they amount to any offence.'

While hard-line teetotallers expressed concern even about ice-lollies flavoured with cider or shandy, the moral dangers posed by liqueur chocolates were taken seriously by a wider cross-section of society. Introduced originally to save lazy music-hall audiences from having to queue for the bar, liqueur chocs were now available in all kinds of shops and might easily fall into the hands of children. One brand, imported from Italy, even bore the unashamedly honest name Happy Tipsy. To illustrate the ever-present dangers such chocolates posed to impressionable youngsters and the weak-willed, one Tory MP, Sir Cyril Black, produced a fifteen-inch liqueur chocolate during a speech in the House of Commons. Unmoved, customers cheerfully carried on buying them by the ton (or should that be the pint?). Hardliners in Scotland and Ulster did score one small victory, managing to have the sale of Babycham chocolates restricted to licensed premises.

Another example of confectionery's malign influence was the widespread fiddling of chewing-gum machines. In 1964 nearly three hundred two-pfennig pieces were recovered from machines at Margate railway station. Local traders were doubly outraged – fiddled ... and by foreigners! Some returning tourist must have told everyone about the German coin's similarity to our sixpence – but it's hard to believe that Hansel, Gretel *et al.* were making an eight-hour train and ferry trip just for the thrill of getting a few cut-price sweets. A German student was eventually caught red-handed by a vigilant shopkeeper. Hauled off to court, she was duly made an example of and fined five pounds.

Free sweets had always been hard to resist and kids would take all kinds of risks to get hold of some. With soap coupons now a common give-away, the latest dare was to nick any left sticking out of people's letterboxes. There was apparently no shortage of bent grocers happy to swap them for lollies, chews and sherbet.

Fräulein X was lucky she lived in the 1960s. Stealing sweets had always been a common crime, but penalties were once much heavier. At the turn of the century, for nicking sweets worth two and sixpence, four teenagers each got fourteen days in prison – followed by four years in reformatory. Another boy, aged only 8, who visited a sweetshop and claimed to be on an errand from his school, took away 3lb of chocolate, 2lb of acid drops and 5lb of cough drops after asking for the bill to be sent to his headmaster. When rumbled, he received a week in the workhouse. Sugar, if not the original fatal attraction, must have come a close second. A Liverpool lad who jumped on the back of a lorryload of sugar to grab a handful was crippled for life when he slipped and his legs were crushed under the back wheels.

But latter-day confectionery crimes – especially pre-planned ones – could still pull in an occasional spell of porridge. In 1965 a Kirkby housewife who complained to Barker & Dobson that her son had cut his mouth on a pin in one of their sweets (producing a partly chewed toffee with the pin still embedded as proof) was given £10 by way of apology. At Edmondson's she received £5 for the same story; and again at Tavener's, though here, for variety, the pin was changed for a nail. 'Yes, I found it so easy,' she told Liverpool City Magistrates, admitting to 27 similar offences. Her reign of trickery had netted her a grand total of £116 – and now, a six-month prison sentence.

1966 TOP TWENTY

1. Mars Bar	11. Smarties
2. Cadbury's Dairy Milk	12. Fruit Spangles
3. Wrigley's Spearmint	13. Rolo
4. Milky Way	14. Bounty
5. Polo	15. Fruit Gums
6. Kit-Kat	16. Fry's Chocolate Creme
7. Crunchie	17. Trebor Mints
8. Wrigley's Arrowmint	18. Opal Fruits
9. Fruit Pastilles	19. Flake
10. Maltesers	20. Bar Six

In the 1960s 'the charts' ruled our lives: pop charts for teenagers and even, as here, a confectionery chart to help the new breed of marketing men and sales analysts. A 60/40 per cent split in favour of chocolate is fairly easy to discern, but to draw great sociological conclusions from this would be risky. A forensic psychologist could, no doubt, read all kind of things into individual preferences, but any opinions – the reader's included – would seem equally valid. I prefer to think that people like what they like and leave the paperwork to the eggheads. There's always one who believes our idiosyncrasies can be made into a science.

Sweets – and the way people ate them – offered vital clues to the consumers' characters, at least according to the guide devised by an American shrink. Suckers, according to Professor Bill Schlackman, were calm, contemplative types, though they could also be 'smug, self-satisfied, lacking in drive and ambition.' Chewers were extroverts. But the ones to be wary of were the crunchers. Not necessarily people who buy Crunchies, these are the folk who gnash and grind like a stone-crushing machine sorting a truckful of granite. Impulsive and volatile, such people were liable to fly off at all kinds of tangents. If they were cannibals, these would be the ones who gnawed the bones.

For some people, sweets, chocolates and ice-cream still carried all kinds of serious social meanings. Not merely observations about psychology and etiquette, but even bringing up all those old chestnuts about gender and what was suitable for who.

'Confectionery eating isn't a masculine occupation,' said a Dutch company as an excuse (and they'd need a damned good one) to introduce tobacco-flavoured sweets. It was the first of several proposals for confectionery with 'masculine flavours' – an idea which, luckily, has never been mentioned again.

If the Dutch hadn't quite grasped the sweets plot, other foreigners were still full of enthusiasm. The Russians, undeterred by their rough treatment back in the 1930s, were giving it another go. 'Your customers will go for Soviet sweets in a big way,' shouted their adverts. 'They're new and deliciously different.' And they might well have been, but who could pronounce such goodies as Griliaj V. Shokolade, Mischa Kosopaly, Mischka na Savere and Raboya Sheika – simple sweets maybe, but as tongue-twisting as a troika full of Russian poets. Anyway, those Commies had some neck, considering they'd just banned the import of American gum and were even searching incoming parcels to make sure. Several consignments had been found already and their contents dumped. Besides, anyone with libertarian sympathies would surely make it a point of principle to boycott Soviet sweets and, instead, make a point of showing their faces at London's well-publicized Czechoslovakian Taste-In …

WIN THE COLD WAR –
DISPLAY VICTORY V ON YOUR COUNTER!

This was nothing more than a clever quip, of course. But a few years previously, especially for citizens worried by the East-West stand-off turning into a nuclear pillow fight, confectioners Harlow's had perfected a timely cash-in – Anti Fall-Out Sweets. Their recipe involved sugar-coating a magical concentrate – ashodine – claimed by its inventor, one Professor Cripps, to protect anyone who swallowed it from lethal fall-out. Packed with essential minerals, ashodine promised to meet the human body's require-ments in full – thereby 'physically preventing' any more being absorbed. Tests were conducted by eating the sweets and washing them down with a manly swig of radioactive iodine. Despite Harlow's earnest faith in the idea, Defence Ministry officials remained apathetic, so squashing any prospects of a fortune-making government order. Britain and its allies eventually won a reprieve from phosphores-cent death, but no record exists of what happened to Professor Cripps and his acolytes.[14]

Cold War would have been a good epithet for continuing rivalries over ice-cream sales. In the early 1960s, when the Tonibell van first cruised on to my estate, I sensed trouble. It looked like an invasion from a future that could not be avoided. Gleaming, aerodynamic, slicked-back, Cadillac pink, the van's Space Age image was marred only by a joy-riding cow on the roof.

Until Tonibell and Mr Softee muscled in, door-to-door ice-cream had been a weekend treat, for Saturday teatimes and Sunday lunchtimes, a monopoly enjoyed by Dytham's Ices. Square and solid, Mr D's van was as unflashy as you could get. Eschewing tinkly versions of 'Greensleeves', Mr Dytham used a handbell, solid and commanding: a dependable technique in an age when children still jumped to the sound of gong and whistle. On Saturdays, as

---

14 There is no truth to the rumour that Mars purchased the professor's formula with a view to using it in a new choc bar named Iso-Topic.

a treat, kids would be given a pudding basin and sent out to get ice-cream to have with their tinned strawberries or peach slices. It looked like the auditions for *Oliver!* – a queue of kids with bowls held up in supplication to the sliding glass hatchway. Mr D, bespectacled and chubby, a cheerful doppelgänger for Billy Cotton, the 'Wakey-Wake Hi!' bandleader, filled each bowl with pats of ice-cream, as thick and yellow as frozen butter.

Since few families had fridges, the whole procedure seemed like devilishly clever timing. Did Mr Dytham plan his itinerary with military precision? Or was it us, all having our tea at the same time, but ever so slightly staggered to take into account his van's progress from Shakespeare Road to Masefield Crescent to Wordsworth Close?

Tonibell made no effort to mesh with our mealtimes. A chancer, he could appear at any old time, weekday teatimes for instance, so that harassed mums were pestered into providing unbudgeted sixpences for cornets and ice-lollies. Then, when we sat down to our beans on toast, half of it ended up scraped into the bin.

Tonibell … the cutesy name bugged me for a start, and his tunic, with its Tonibell logo woven across the pocket, was far too smart. We ragged Tonibell in a way we'd never have dreamed of with amiable Mr Dytham, flagging him down just for the fun of it and then running off. Or we'd cheekily demand his broken cones and stand there nibbling them, acting silly. 'Know how to make a brilliant bomb, Toni?' I asked him one time. His real name was Roy, but the nickname was inevitable. When he shook his head I smacked a box of Bluebell matches down on to the pavement, so hard that it exploded into flames and sent a jet of grey sulphurous smoke into the air. 'I'm sure Mr Bluebell wouldn't like to see you doing that with his matches,' Toni grumbled. He slammed shut his glass hatchway to cut off the choking smoke and drove off to find some nicer children. After that, in the hope we'd leave him alone, he began to miss out the stop nearest our house. But we just jumped on our bikes and gave chase.

Mr Softee was a more welcome interloper, with me at least.[15] I was charmed by the van's figurehead, a goofy guy with a cornet for a head. But what we didn't know was that Tonibell and Mr Softee were both playing the same game, blowing air into their ice-cream, bulking it up so it was, in effect, not much more than frozen froth. We'd simply assumed their ice-cream owed its softness and whirliness to some amazing new recipe. Then one day, after seeing Roy loading up his machine with what looked suspiciously like dried milk powder, I started to ask myself questions – like why did his van pump out so much foul-looking smoke from its back end? Simple: it came from the machine that produced the air. Ice-cream? We were paying out good pocket money for something that was little more than cold water and milk powder.

Tonibell and Mr Softee knew their spells, though. Mr Dytham could do you a lovely wafer, with a square of grease-proof to hold it by, but who cared about good manners now that the Oyster had arrived – a pair of shell-shaped wafers containing a squidgy dollop of ice-cream. And, knocking Mr Dytham's solitary bottle of red raspberry gunk for six, these guys (an Americanism that's entirely apt) had whole battalions of squeezy plastic bottles containing exciting new sauces – butterscotch, chocolate, maple syrup – to perk up the ice-cream. It had become a visual delight as well as a tasty experience. And, to this day, I still remember that Mr Softee jingle. Question: if I heard it today, would I be powerless to resist, walking out, zombie-like, into the street to buy a cone?

---

15 While Mr Softee visited Britain to set up his ice-cream franchises, elsewhere the sell was harder. The US destroyer *Forrest Sherman* visited African ports, its mission to give away sweets. Uncle Sam's latest brainwave was to 'defeat communism without firing a single shot'. A couple of years later, in Indo-China, they decided to try bombs instead.

Cute-sounding, by design, Tonibell was actually a division of BAT, the notorious tobacco multinational, and Roy, for all his smartly tunic'd authority, was just an eager but humble franchisee. '£2000 a year profit' boasted Tonibell's recruitment ads, and Roy must have been so convinced he'd seen the future of ice-cream that he'd happily put up five hundred pounds of his own money to buy his place on ice-cream's front line, facing council estate kids and the doleful stare of doomed Mr Dytham. As righteous anti-Americans, had we known all this background dirt at the time we could have made Roy's Disneyfied van a scapegoat for every Yankee sin from the Sand Creek Massacre to Vietnam.

But honourable mentions are in order, too. During World War Two, Wall's had loaned their redundant vans to the National Blood Transfusion Service, and, more recently, Mr Softee saved a Brighton woman's life. Well, sort of. All Mr Softee vans had a generator, and during the bad winter of 1962–3, anticipating power cuts, the franchisee in Brighton offered them to the local hospital. When one did occur, a van duly set off on a mercy mission. A power line for the hospital's oxygen tent was thrown from an upstairs window and connected up. In this way, thanks to Mr Softee, an elderly woman was kept alive for two hours before mains electricity was restored. Whether she had to listen to 'Greensleeves' at the same time is unknown.

Ironically enough, in the end, it was Mr Dytham who nearly killed me. So olde worlde, so eager to serve, so determined not to let one kid's sixpence slip from his hands, when he saw me in his rear-view mirror pedalling furiously in pursuit to buy a cone, he braked immediately. Excellent reflexes for a pensioner. Mine weren't half as quick and I smashed into the back of the van.

'All right son?' asked Mr Dytham cheerily, as if he couldn't see my split lip and the gash on my shin. 'Sixpenny cone, is it?'

*

In some ways confectionery turned out to be more of a currency at my grammar school than it had been in the juniors. Some kids, easily kidded, took it all too literally. When A & BC gave away Confederate dollars with their Civil War bubblegum, these simple souls actually took fistfuls into the foreign counters of high street banks in the hope of receiving spendable British cash in exchange.

From the basic four-bit packs of Beech Nut, to varieties like Bag o' Gold, Fruit Sandwich, Sambo and Blackcat, the choice of gum was staggering. Beatmint – 'specially aimed at teenagers' it said; though wasn't it all? – was heavily pushed on Radio Luxembourg and young groovers also had Fab, which came with minuscule pictures of pop stars. There was gum to cater for all idiosyncrasies. Chiclets and Snips, for instance, pieces the size of a matchhead, could only be chewed between two teeth in a kind of nervy tut-tut-tutting way. Others preferred the bulk approach, cramming four or five sticks in their mouths at once so they had a jaw-aching plum-sized lump that, in the wrong circumstances, could certainly prove fatal.

If gum-chewing made teachers despair, blowing a bubble as they talked to you was enough to freak them out. At Falmouth Grammar School a sullen fifth former (with the apt name of Douglas Kain) ruined the annual school photograph by blowing an enormous pink dirigible just as the camera panned across his part of the line-up. Bubbling in class was an offence punishable by DT, though with our ineffectual RE teacher retribution came in the form of a weary lecture including verses from Corinthians II. Other masters preferred a pro-active approach, seizing kids by the neck and doing some neat fingerwork to extract the gum from the culprit's mouth, leaving him gagging on the taste of chalk and waxy fingernails – punishment enough.

Sweets were banned in class, of course, but what child had ever taken notice of that rule? The ones who got copped were those who, despite well-meant advice, just couldn't control their baser instincts to slurp or crunch. To a teacher the sound of a boiled sweet moving from one cheek to another was as loud as someone overturning a desk. Trouble could be avoided by attention to technique: I could dispose of a whole bag of crisps during Double Physics without making a single crackle, holding each one against my tongue until it turned to mush and then letting it slip quietly down the hatch: all the flavours, none of the grief. None of the crispness, admittedly, but the taste of victory was enough.

If our headmaster had nightmares, they were probably littered by the plastic strips torn from the end of Tip Tops and spat out. Our yard was full of them. At only twopence, kids could afford to buy Tip Tops by the handful and often walked around the yard with four or five poking out of their blazer pockets, like gigantic trainspotting pens – absurdly surreal when, like Dali's watches, they began to melt and droop. Some townspeople actually believed that raspberry-coloured stains on our shirts were part of the school colours: white with scarlet polka dots.

A tuck shop! My new school had a real tuck shop. How excited I'd been when I first found out. But it was nothing like the places I'd pictured when, after reading Jennings and Bunter stories, I'd mentally bodyguarded the Fat Owl as he headed for the Greyfriars tuck shop to stock up on iced buns, ginger beer and humbugs. Our tuck shop was the caretaker's broom cupboard, scarcely bigger than a telephone box and reeking of wet mops and Jeyes Fluid – none of which discouraged long queues from forming every lunchtime and squabbles breaking out among the brushes and buckets. It was run by the caretaker, as an unofficial sinecure to supplement his meagre salary. A cheery enough fellow, though he could have scrubbed up before changing from one function to the other. Or even put on gloves. Modern-day hygiene freaks would faint at the cracks, cuts and bleach sores on hands that counted out golf ball chewing gums and Sports Mixtures. But we kids hardly cared. Sterility was easily restored by a quick wipe on a blazer sleeve.

School mythology told of one occasion when the door had accidentally been left unlocked and the whole stock disappeared. Now it was *de rigueur* to check the handle at every passing, just as some people cannot pass a payphone without feeling compelled to finger the Returned Coins tray.

Elsewhere, tuck shops were still sources of aggro. I can't recall any such trouble at ours – maybe its trade was too modest – but the tuck shop at Doncaster Grammar School was boycotted by local wholesalers after protests from shopkeepers. It was a display of solidarity with the couple who'd recently taken over a sweetshop near the school. They'd been hoping for plentiful profits from the kids and were enraged to find that most of them were broke by hometime, when they were passing the shop.

For my schoolmates and I there were half a dozen shops on our two-mile hike between home and school and we must have played a modest part in helping some of these shopkeepers – for sure a dying breed by then – stave off bankruptcy for a little while longer. Our tastes were eclectic and fickle. We'd try all the oral techniques – sucking, crunching, slurping, chewing – on a rota basis, so heaven knows what Professor Bill Schlackmann would have made of us. Our choices depended on a host of variables: the weather, pocket money, our moods, loyalty to schoolboy tradition, or whatever the latest craze happened to be.

Despite a steadfast refusal to honour the spirit of the Trades Descriptions Act, Lemfizz cubes were still a favourite. Supposedly perfect for making one's own effervescent drinks, experiments seemed forever doomed. They'd make a cup of orange-ified brew, drinkable, but effervescent only in the loosest sense and given an offputting gravelly texture by swirling grains of sugar that refused to dissolve. Far better to eat them as fizzy sweets in their own right. Best nibbled at or licked; eating a whole tablet at once was quite reckless. They frothed wildly, causing you to slobber and froth like a dog crazed by hydrophobia – green hydrophobia – a sight which in the eyes of many only confirmed our mental instability.

Fab lollies, as advertised by the charming Lady Penelope, were a colourful cooling treat in those lovely post-exam days before summer holidays started, but, for sheer icy value, nothing could match the Jubbly. These huge tetrahedrons of orange ice were prized for their long-lasting quality, but once thirst was satisfied they could get boring. Apart from the ever-present risk of frostbite, since they had to be held in the hand for so long, sucking too hard could drain out every bit of orange flavouring, so that you were left holding a messy and tasteless iceberg.

One curiosity that disappeared from sweetshops around this time was the liquorice stick, six-inch lengths cut from the plant. I can't recall anything except an aching tongue and splinters stuck between the teeth, but others swear they were delicious and claim to remember them with fondness. A bit of a poor excuse for confectionery – or so I've always assumed – but maybe it was nothing to do with lack of money and making do. People still chew matchsticks, so it's quite possible that liquorice sticks answered some deep-seated gnawing urge, a Western version of chewing betel leaves. With the extinction of Britain's domestic growers, liquorice sticks died a natural death, but even if they'd survived they would certainly have been banned, for fear of any poor mite getting a splinter in his tongue.

By the time we reached 13, sweet cigarettes had been replaced by real ones – but we'd had plenty of years to practise the techniques. Some packs of sweet cigarettes were designed with an uncanny – some would say cynical – resemblance to the real thing: Westerfield, Old Mall, Marlborough. Other manufacturers pulled no punches at all with their Camel, Kent, Chesterfield and Lucky Strike – exact facsimile packets which surely indicates some kind of arrangement with tobacco companies. To whose benefit? The recipe – icing sugar, gum arabic and gelatine rolled into a thin rope and chopped into lengths – was so easy anyone could cash in. Prize for the most blatant attempt at association must go to Junior Service, a cynicism pointed up all the more by the advert's lovely period sketch – an idyllic childhood setting, Swallows and Amazons kids – all with fake smokes a-dangling from their lips.

One can see a certain logic behind sweet cigs endorsed by James Bond or Napoleon Solo, since these spy types were rarely seen without an elegant king-size in their hands. Gun Law ones fitted in with hard-smoking cowboys and Wyatt Earp, who had a pack named in his honour, no doubt clenched his teeth on a tip or two, but, *pace* the Lone Ranger brand, does anyone recall the masked one ever crashing the ash to Tonto?

It's true that Popeye was a smoker, though of a pipe, but there's something dodgy about linking smokes with the likes of Noddy, Sooty, Andy Pandy, Yogi Bear and the wholesome family in *Chitty Chitty Bang Bang*. As for the Dalek brand – ridiculous! A cartoon character did at least possess the necessary limbs (I recall Tom the cat smoking a cigar on more than one occasion) but how on earth could a Dalek manage it?

Packets of Dixon of Dock Green brand, showing PC Dixon sternly wagging his Met-issue pencil, were the first to be cellophane wrapped (for authenticity rather than freshness). But the genial wiseacre was never seen lighting up a Woodbine prior to his end-of-story homily.[16] Then again, why was he so often standing outside the police station? Could it be that what we thought was frosty breath was really shameful evidence of a secret habit?

Yet, while most adults still saw no harm in this childish mimicry of their vices, others were quick to decry anything that encouraged grown-up sins – gambling, for instance, which, at least according to one member of radio's *Any Questions* panel, was encouraged by the sale of children's lucky bags.

---

16 The same applies to 007 chewing gum: did you ever see Bond slipping out a wad and sticking it under the table before sipping his cocktails?

One oddity from childhood's make-believe tobacconists' was Surname. Each packet came with a surname and crest. When you'd managed to get your name, you could cut it out and send off for a transparent badge into which your 'family crest' could be proudly inserted.[17] Fine for Britain's Smiths, Browns and Johnsons, but the Patels and Zimmermans must have felt really left out. A cute idea, killed stone dead by our burgeoning multicultural society.

But just because my schoolmates and I had moved on to cigarettes – regulation No.6 or the laughable Diplomat (great name, shame about the size) – we still had the sweet-buying habit. Even as we smoked, we carried on chewing gum, licking lollies and sucking sweets.

Apart from penny pop machines, a sad rarity by then, buying pop usually called for sharing. Cans were rare and expensive, as were individual bottles. For kids it was more economical to chip in for a big bottle and take turns, wiping the previous kid's spit off the rim. Or not, as the case might be. While some considered it essential hygiene, to others sharing spit was akin to being blood brothers. Only nancy boys bothered to wipe it off. And what was the point? Did they believe their shirt sleeves had antiseptic properties?

One of the first pop firms to introduce cans, under the Suncharm label, were Shaw's of Huddersfield, just one of the thousand or so firms still making a living from pop in 1960. Apart from a few national brands like Corona, pop was a business of fiefdoms, local fizz factories with local markets. Rotherham's thirsty were catered for by Hague's pop factory, where the future Tory leader once had a summer job. The works were eventually sold to Boddington's when the family decided to consolidate its wealth to help fund young William's political career.

---

17 Strangely enough, the College of Arms has no knowledge of this. Surely it can't have been a cynical hoax on the nation's kiddies?

The large bottles were heavy and, understandably, mums were reluctant to add more weight to their shopping bags. Many fizz fans relied on deliveries. The Corona lorry came to us on Friday evenings. We weren't regular customers, but every other week I'd manage to pester my mum into sending me out for a bottle of limeade or ginger beer. Then one day, in the same ominous manner as Tonibell, the Alpine lorry rumbled into view, stacked with rattling bottles, like giant test-tubes glowing with crystal-clear colours: red, green and orange. Now and then, in a moment of silence, you could hear the bottles jingling in their crates, a tintinnabulation that excited kids as much as a belly dancer's finger cymbals heightened the expectations of a stripshow audience. A man knocked at our door and made us an unrefusable offer – three bottles for two and six (Corona was one shilling and twopence a bottle). Alpine's bottles were bigger, fatter and temptingly contoured. My mum fell for it. Three whole bottles! Fizzy heaven.

Cherryade, limeade, dandelion and burdock,[18] American ice-cream soda, lemonade, orangeade – whichever flavour we chose, they all had one thing in common: tepidness. Pop was rarely cold when bought from the shop and few people had a fridge in which to chill it. Bottles fetched from the chip shop across the road were even worse – kept on a shelf above the chip fryers, just to keep them at a steady 60°. But no one complained. Kids were

---

18 Could pop actually be made from such wasteground weeds? It's not a question any of us asked at the time, but I've always wondered. Each plant was already known separately for its medicinal properties – as cure for a variety of ills such as gallstones, scurvy and rashes. But their marriage as a catch-all cure is undated. Nor do we know who first had the idea of adding some fizz, but the decision helped this odd combo through into the twentieth century. The taste is an enduring one, mixed up as it is in a classless childhood nostalgia, as well known by snotty-nosed tenement kids as by crinolined young ladies.

only too grateful for the fizz. Some talk of claret with beef, others of Chablis with *fruits de mer*, but when it comes to blissful matches, could anything really beat that childhood classic of tepid lemonade with egg and chips?

> *By the end of 1964 we'll be chomping our way through £48m worth of crisps.*
>
> Trade press headline

Schoolkids' habits were changing. By the mid-1960s our dosh (mostly embezzled dinner money) was just as likely to be spent on crisps as sweets.

For almost half a century, from the 1920s until well into the 1960s, crisps had been synonymous with Smith's, an unfussy English name that was a perfect foil to the potato's gimmicky pretensions. After all, the idea had come from France. Frank Smith, ex-manager of a wholesale grocer's in London, invested ten thousand pounds and set up Smith's Potato Crisps in a converted store behind Cricklewood's famous Crown Hotel. Despite some initial wariness from the British public, Smith's twopenny bags of crisps eventually caught on and within a few years he'd opened six more factories to cope with demand. 'Six times the food value of boiled potatoes!' boasted ads. 'All vitamins retained.' And, lest anyone thought this mere puffery, the words MEDICAL OPINION were appended to chivvy along any ditherers. Crisps were not flippant but sensible, an integral part of a well-planned diet.

Salt in a twist of blue paper was added in 1922 and, for Frank, fortune smiled. After World War Two Smith's could count nearly six hundred competitors, many of them demobbed soldiers looking for a profitable business to go into – but few lasted long enough to offer any serious challenge to Smiths' supremacy.

In the 1960s, to get across just how swinging their 'scene' was, Smith's recruited chat-show host Simon Dee to endorse their brand. But while vast sums were being spent on promotion, employees at several Smith's factories were collecting their P45s. Smith's pre-eminence had been badly shaken by the arrival of Golden Wonder. Although the potato variety from which the company took its name was useless for making crisps, 'Golden Wonder' had the perfect ring about it. Their bags featured Poppa Crispin, a cheeky chappie in a tam-o'-shanter, and the new Rayophone version, launched in 1965, guaranteed to keep crisps 'crackle fresh' – an irresistible promise to those who'd previously resigned themselves to a fifty-fifty chance of staleness. Previously regarded as pub snacks or al fresco nibbles for trainspotters, crisps now began to look more like *fun*. Promoted on TV by the likes of Freddy Trueman, Diana Dors and Mr Pastry, Golden Wonder crisps soon had their own show on Fab 208, Radio Luxembourg.

The biggest advance came with the ready-salted. Nostalgists claim to miss those little blue twists of salt, but in truth they were pretty grim. Sprinkling was the theory, but the salt, damp and clogged, fell out in lumps which just dropped through gaps between the crisps.[19]

With its share of the market now expanding by 10 per cent a year, Golden Wonder opened its third factory and the real battle began. Just as the 1960s bequeathed us the creative wonders of the Beatles, Hendrix and the Moody Blues, so it also ushered in cheese and onion, roast chicken and salt 'n' vinegar – the last tested on Geordies first, just to make sure. Not only those, but Bovril, Oxo and smoky bacon, while the glam 1970s would bring us exotica such as prawn cocktail, tomato sauce and curry. For creativity and innovation, the world of crisps has never again matched these two decades.

Technology was as important as taste: Golden Wonder's

---

19 In a clumsy attempt to cash in on nostalgia, separate salt was reintroduced in the 1970s, now packaged in hygienic, damp-proof sachets. But consumers were too used to ready-salted to be swayed by this gimmick.

peanuts were not just thrown in any old bag but came 'packed in a cushion of pure clean air'. Meanwhile British children were busily collecting their old crisp packets – over nine million of them – and since Golden Wonder had pledged twopence for every five, it raised nearly £16,000 for British athletes training for the Mexico Olympics in 1968.

The Planets Sweet

1970s

The best decades always deserve an epithet – Naughty Nineties, Roaring Twenties, Swinging Sixties. Such titles are usually awarded in retrospect, but why wait? This next one, suggested Cadbury's, might be remembered as the 'diggin' groovin' earth-moving motor-cycling' Seventies. An interesting viewpoint, and a catchy tune too – but with a little ® attached. Tagged as commercial property, this was not a free contribution to Britain's rich store of colloquialisms.

No, they weren't giving too much away. Aztec's[1] spot-the-ball competition offered a first prize of an all-expenses-paid trip to Mexico City for the World Cup. But Scrooge must have had a descendant working in the promotions department: who else could have suggested the second prize: a stingy five pounds? It was barely enough to buy a football and a Mexican hat.

More enticing, perhaps, was the Fry's Turkish Delight competition, in which punters were given the chance to win 'five beautiful slaves'. As a come-on, adverts featured five young nubiles in belly-dancing gear – delightful enough to tempt punters without a need for subliminal

---

1 Aztec wasn't entirely off-the-wall: Cadbury's sold bars of Mexican plain chocolate back in the 1920s.

prompts. Yet, parked in the background, cryptic *Abbey Road* style, was a Ford with the registration NOB 284F.[2]

Conspiracy theories about the 1969–70 moon landings are ten a penny. Here's another: the space race may well have been sponsored by the world's confectionery industry, judging by the mileage they managed to squeeze from it.[3] Everything went space-shaped: Dobson's Moon Pebbles, for instance, were boiled sweets specifically minted to 'capture the imagination of Space Age youngsters'. Zoom ice-lollies had been around since the mid-1960s, as had Sky Ray, but next off the launch pad came Orbit, Saturn and Sky Rocket ice-lollies – our spacecraft on a stick. Askey's baked a rocket-shaped ice-cream cone (great idea, but the pointy bit went downwards) and Beecham's gave us Splashdown powdered drinks – smart repackaging for an idea that dated back forty years. (A galactic bureau de change would been handy, too, somewhere to cash in all that Moon Money and Space Coins bubblegum.)

As for Terry's Moonlight – just a simple coincidence, the name more likely inspired by the drippy imagery of romance than anything to do with Neil Armstrong and the Bacofoiled ironmongery of NASA's Apollo programme.[4] Yet, could moonlight ever exert the same magic, now that we'd all seen a workman going up to change the bulb?

Space-agers or not, Britain's kids still found time for more traditional games. In back gardens and on waste ground, cowboys and Indians lived on, playing out age-old

---

2 Is it so far-fetched? Adverts for a famous bubble bath around that time certainly featured the word 'sex' subtly woven into a formation of background foliage.

3 Flying Saucers, rice-paper pods still popular today, were merely a clever remarketing of what was once a common method of taking medicinal powders.

4 Now, any girl who demanded moonlight and roses from her fella could have both, so long as neither forgot it was now Moonlight™ and Roses™.

rivalries against a soundtrack of cracking gun caps and slobbery war cries. Tommy Atkinson took over as Milky Bar Kid Mk II and immediately launched an appeal for deputies. Volunteers would get their stars as soon as they sent in six Milky Bar wrappers and a four-penny stamp.[5]

Rocket lollies? Milky Bars? Sherbet dabs? For some kids such names were already an embarrassment. Facing pressure to act grown up, these kids would be found holed up in a den of corrugated tin sheets and railway sleepers, puzzling over the picture in *Tit Bits* and debating with themselves which looked coolest, Beatmint chewing gum or Yellow Submarine sweet cigarettes. They were, perhaps, the last of the ragamuffins, the last generation of kids to be allowed to wander Britain's dumps and woods and railway sidings. Not wishing to be associated with little kids, but too young to visit pubs, they chose to define themselves by a sulky rejection of chocolate buttons and dolly mixtures. Yet it was still important to have those kids to feel superior to. Though they still defined themselves in relation to older kids and younger kids, it wouldn't be long before they could free themselves of that altogether, take their cue from TV and commercially led ideas of what childhood should be and how much could be milked from it ... And in a twisted kind of way, TV would give them the OK to be kids again, once it had defined ice-lollies as fashion statements ...

For grown-up do-gooders, these sugar ciggies were no better than full-strength lung-clogging Woodbines. Wasn't it high time such 'dangerous confectionery' was banned, as it had been in some states of the USA? Minnesota led the way as far back as 1957 with a proposal to ban sales to anyone under 18 (as if anyone over that age would want to

---

5 The Kid was an icon and Nestlé were prepared to go to great lengths to defend their best brand. A posse of QCs and business lawyers could be rounded up in hours. In 1972, Clark's were hunted down and forced to rename their Big Milky white chocolate to White Delight.

be seen dead buying a pack). Sceptics choked at the idea: if candy fakes were such a great way to make youngsters into fag-addicts, the world's tobacco giants would have cottoned on long ago and set up their own subsidiaries to make them. But who was to say they hadn't? It would have been the perfect American conspiracy.

Could sweet cigarettes really be any more dangerous than all the other candied simulacra children loved so much? Jokes aside, no one would seriously suggest that jelly babies encouraged cannibalism, or that those chewy fried eggs brainwashed lads into expecting fry-ups from dutiful wives.[6] Adults read far too much into childish play. At the end of the day, kids knew they weren't Sioux braves or members of the *Fireball XL5* crew. Moving on to grown-up vices was probably inevitable, whether you practised on dummy versions or not.

Sir Keith Joseph, Tory Health Minister, promised to address MPs' concerns. But changes were slow.[7] For the rest of the decade sweet cigarettes stuck it out, endorsed by an unholy alliance of cartoon favourites and pop stars: Tom and Jerry and Yogi Bear joined by the likes of Gary Glitter, David Bowie, Slade and Gilbert O'Sullivan. Not until the 1980s were any changes made, voluntary ones which were little more than cosmetic. Red tips disappeared and 'candy sticks' was adopted as the official nomenclature – as if mere semantics would discourage children from playing grown-ups.[8] Changes were harder to make elsewhere. Chocolate

---

6 Though it wouldn't be too long before it was suggested that Black Jacks turned kids into racists.
7 The Dutch took a tougher line. Not only were sweet ciggies banned, but TV adverts for other sweets had to conform to strict rules: they could only be shown after 8 p.m., use no children, and have a toothbrush icon superimposed throughout.
8 By the 1990s it was more or less back to square one, with lookalike sweet cigs imported from less high-minded places in Europe, although many shopkeepers, depending on their own views, refused to stock them.

cigars might have been restyled as choc sticks or choc tubes or something, but a pipe was so manifestly pipe-shaped, how else could you describe it? Stick a 'this way up' sticker on it and call it a liquorice candle-snuffer? Still, pipes hardly contained the same dangers: sweet cigs may or may not have helped children imagine themselves as Napoleon Solo or Jason King – but how much cool could a kid acquire by toting a limp liquorice pipe?

Decimalization was always bound to cause rows. New coinage wasn't the problem so much as shoppers' suspicions that it provided a perfect smokescreen for price hikes – mistrust which the media was all too happy to stoke up. The only thing new about Rowntree's 'New Size' five-pence Kit-Kat, according to the BBC's *Nationwide*, was how much shorter it was than the pre-decimal version. A court case quickly followed in which Rowntree's alleged serious harm to their reputation and Auntie had to dip into her purse to pay hefty damages.

But such backdoor price rises – and, Kit-Kat apart, there were plenty of real ones to come – were small change compared to the introduction of VAT on confectionery. Had it been classed as food, it would have been exempt, but despite fierce lobbying from the industry, Treasury officials stoutly refused to recognize its claims – a concession willingly granted to the makers of crisps and savoury snacks, now arch-rivals for schoolchildren's pocket money.

By 1972 crisps and snacks had an annual market worth £100 million, already double its 1964 figure. Half of these profits belonged to Golden Wonder, now undisputed kings of the crisp scene. Left with a sad 25 per cent, Smith's could at least still lay claim to good pub sales. Theirs were the crisps that parents bought for their kids, along with a lukewarm lemonade, before abandoning them in what the pub jokingly called a garden. But modern consumers, people who ate crisps out of choice, wanted to buy into a better image. Golden Wonder happily obliged, plying them with exotic flavours – prawn cocktail, roast chicken,

Oxo, tomato ketchup and even crisps which boasted of 'added protein'.

Tudor, small nationally but a significant player up North, adopted Henry VIII as their logo. 'Henry was renowned for his liking for good food,' they explained. To emphasize their affinity with this regal epicure, Tudor bosses introduced brown sauce flavour corn snacks, adding to a range which already included kipper and baked bean crisps.[9]

Smith's were not taking this rivalry lying down. One might even say they were hopping mad ... In 1975, to mark the return of blue bags of salt, a sack race was held in Covent Garden, with Michael Aspel as referee and various suits from Smith's press-ganged into showing their fun side by sack-racing in giant Salt 'n' Shake bags. Afterwards one of them made a less-than-startling confession about the old blue twists: only 95 per cent of Smith's packets had ever contained one. Many had none, while others had two or even three. But such slapdash presentation was now a thing of the past: their state-of-the-art sachet slinging machine (it probably had a more official name) was accurate to 0.001 per cent. Though describing blue bags as an innovation would be stretching it somewhat, Smith's board was convinced they'd seen the future. 'People don't like odd shapes,' they said, introducing Square Crisps, which were 'the most dramatic addition to the UK market since our founder thought of blue twists of salt' (note that 'our founder' with its give-away trace of adoration).

Their faith was touching. Surveys, questionnaires, market reports, all were pored over as if they were holy texts. Any true crisp fan could have put them straight, and saved them a massive consultancy fee to boot. Odd shapes were half the appeal. People had a lot of time for the potato. They loved its off-the-wall knobbliness. Crisps were enjoyed as a lucky dip: big 'uns you could brandish as trophies, a cornerful of titchy fragments saved till last and

9 I believe these to be two separate varieties, but who can be sure?

tipped down the throat like a fountain of cheesiness. Yes, a square crisp might catch their attention, but only for its freak value. Who, apart from anal retentives, wanted such an orderly bagful? Perhaps Smiths had forgotten that 'square' was still a pejorative term.

It's hard to believe that a quarter of a century has passed since R. White's Secret Lemonade Drinker first tiptoed down to the fridge. Pop had got trendy at last, literally and culturally cool. Tizer introduced their Fizzyologist and the Cresta bear donned his shades and uttered the immortal sign-off, 'It's frothy, man!'

The biggest innovation of all was probably the ring-pull, a relief to all those who'd croaked with thirst while hunting for a bottle opener – but not so welcome to Britain's growing league of greenies. Inevitable, unavoidable, cans were the only response to our dismal failure to honour the bottle-deposit system. Once regarded as something akin to a civic duty, as people got wealthier and lazier taking back empty pop bottles became extremely uncool, left to kids who were trying to scrape together extra pocket money. But did they realize how close they were to a fortune? If they'd put their minds to it, many could have eschewed CSEs and taken early retirement. Barr's, makers of Irn-Bru, were losing 10 million bottles a year, while Coca-Cola estimated annual losses of £20 million due to the cost of replacing unreturned empties.

'There's one million pounds out there in lost deposits,' said a disappointed Coca-Cola spokesman. 'There's sixpence on a family-size bottle, you know. If you take four back, you've got enough for a loaf of bread!'

Since these appeals fell on deaf ears, no-deposit bottles seemed like a logical step. When they met with resistance (ten thousand empties being dumped outside the Cadbury-Schweppes HQ in full view of Britain's TV cameras), cans were the only alternative.

Further clashes with greens were inevitable when Trebor and other firms changed their sweet jars from glass to PVC.

Seen as a brilliant idea by pioneers in the late 1960s – no breakages, no deposits, no need for washing, just dump 'em – few dreamed that, a decade later, those who advocated wider use of plastic would be as popular as double-glazing salesmen.

Not all firms were so wasteful. A few small trees were undoubtedly saved by Pascall's decision to introduce sweet jars with only half a label, though their real intention was merely for customers to get a better view of the contents. A good idea, yet the narrowness of the labels made for some cranky hyphenation: Golden Butter-mints; Black-currant Eclairs; Murray-mints.

Despite powerful TV backing for branded products, loose sweets – 'weigh-outs' – still accounted for a third of Britain's confectionery sales. In 1961, 307,000 tons clattered out on to the scales and ten years later the figure was virtually unchanged at 305,000 tons. Down slightly as a percentage of total sales, such tonnage was remarkably healthy and the manufacture of boiled sweets still provided a good living for a dozen or so firms: Parke's, Hall's, Dobson's, Needler's and Parkinson's, for instance. Trebor alone still had thirty different weigh-outs. While no one could prevent the extinction of Britain's sweetshops, its newsagents and off-licences could put on a good show, some noted for arrays of up to a hundred different jars.

Phul-Nana and Shem-el-Nessim cachous were, according to their ads, 'still around' – hardly bad going for sweets from the 1890s – but new lines came out all the time. California Fruit Chews, Toffy Froot Splits, Froot Drops, Glitter Fruits: rejigged names for old favourites, maybe, but if a bit of repackaging could keep the market fresh, all well and good. Even old favourites could be new again, like the unexciting barley sugars and acid drops now cunningly styled as 'Old-Fashioned Sweets'.[10]

---

10 Nostalgia was everywhere. Sharp's resurrected Sir Kreemy Knut, pressing him into service as a mascot for their toffee.

If there was one thing people liked about weigh-outs it was the honesty. They told you exactly what they were, no ambivalence, no wisecracks, no doubt. Pear drops may not have been exactly fruity (what *was* that nail-varnish smell?) and Tyne-Tees Mixture could have included anything really, but with names like chocolate limes, pineapple chunks, strawberry pips and sherbet lemons even a fool would know what they were buying. The named brands, by comparison, were marvels of ambiguity. Even familiarity with the TV ads wasn't always a help. Sure, everyone knew that Bounty contained coconut and that Mars was bursting with 'milk, sugar and thick, thick chocolate'. Yet, without prior knowledge, what clues could anyone glean from names like Cabana, Ticket or Loot?

But boiled sweets had another advantage. It wasn't just the sweets themselves: for many people etiquette and ritual were just as important as the sugar fix. Buying a quarter of barley sugars, Everton mints or Tom Thumb drops took time and it was well-nigh impossible to conduct any such transaction without engaging in chat or pleasantries. The sweet jars and the weighing-out ceremony were parts of a street communion. Even the names rang out like a litany: 'I'll have four ounces of three noughts, red coughs, clearmints, strawberry sherberts ...'

Revealing one's tastes to a shopkeeper was almost intimate, a kind of confession. It called for the same trust you'd place in a doctor or solicitor. A relationship was necessary. People would – still do – go out of their way to visit the same shop, a place where one's habits were known and indulged without question or comment – much as they are in a local pub.

Now just a cheap cartoon, Sir K had originally been a live person. Not, alas, some dotty aristo, but a rep named Nobby Clarke, co-opted from Sharp's sales team. Arriving by Rolls, Sir Kreemy, a pocket hero at only five foot tall, was a regular visitor at shows and seaside resorts during the 1950s and a great favourite with children.

But the retail world was gathering speed. With customers no more than inconvenient appendages to their cash, there were many businessmen who would condemn these relaxed transactions to history. Slowness and profit were mutually exclusive concepts. Maximum throughput equalled optimum return. They were already trying to condition us with their vending machines, supermarket stands and filling-station displays. By the 1970s a body could walk into some places, buy a Picnic, Mars or a pre-packed bag of Murraymints and depart without uttering a single syllable. But how many wanted such a life? As long as sweets maintained a psychological connection with affection, most people would still crave the human touch with their sweets.

Our continued devotion to sugar goods did not go unnoticed by the big players. Although by the end of the decade chocolate would account for a staggering 70 per cent of all confectionery sales, the remaining 30 per cent was too juicy to ignore. The smartest marketing brains in the industry would never sway pensioners and kids from their loyalty to weigh-outs and other sugary miscellania. If they wanted a cut of the profits, they'd have to buy the firms that made them ...

'Cider is the fastest-growing product in the teenage refreshment market,' crowed a Wall's man. 'Bulmer's have transformed cider from a local yokel drink into a nationally known youth refresher.' A good fight was always fun, like this Wall's v. Lyons Maid spat over cider-flavoured ice-lollies. Lyons had been first, with Apple Jack, but Wall's claimed their Cider Gold contained the genuine stuff, from Bulmer's. The West Country seemed to have become the marketeer's Arcadia. Holidaying suits couldn't wait to get back to their desks and start selling it to us. Close behind cider-lollies came 'Cornish' dairy ice-cream – 'thick and rich, honey-coloured ice-cream from the heart of the country.' Everyone knew about Devon cream teas, even people who'd lived on sterilized milk all their lives – but was Cornwall really the birthplace of ice-cream's *ne plus ultra?* Despite browsing a century's worth of confectionery trade journals, I never once came across it.[11] Cornwall's claim was as mythical as the Italian connection. Dig below those meadows and it was all tin and arsenic, with the highest levels of radon gas in the UK. No matter: all they had to do was make up a dreamy pick 'n' mix – the 1930s, the West Country, the seaside, art deco lettering, stir in words like dairy, butter and cream – and wishful thinking would do the rest. Even Cornish Treasure Choc-ice, it seems, ran no risk of over-egging the pudding.[12] One can't help wondering if ice-cream would have been so attractive with a Bedfordshire or Essex tag.

But the Nostalgia Express (or should that be a slow train on a country branch?) had only just left. Wall's then went on to try to reinvent the cornet. By adding a gay canopy and painting a wagon wheel on its side panels, a dumpy freezer could be transformed into an 'Old Fashioned Cornets' barrow – 'as trundled by Italians in nineteenth and early twentieth centuries. A magnet for thousands who remember the hokey-pokey man.'[13] And, presumably, a must-avoid for anyone who recalled an attack of the squitters brought on by ice-cream made with contaminated water.

Lyons were, on the face of it, serious rivals – but not nearly serious enough for some people. With the two

---

11 To be fair, perhaps it dated back to 1959, with the arrival of Lyons Maid's Cornish Mivvi. Mivvi? Now what kind of word is that? Some old Cornish language? No, actually it's a dialect word meaning marvel, which seems to make sense, though it's also old slang for a downmarket boarding house landlady.
12 To celebrate their successes, the entire Lyons Maid sales team of 550 reps was invited to a performance of the *Lyons Maid Story*, a 'spectacular' at London's Talk of the Town.
13 'Hokey-pokey, penny a lump' is a cry our grans remember. It comes from the Italian '*O che poco*', meaning 'Oh, how little' – the bargain price, not the size of the ice-cream.

companies accounting for four-fifths of all sales (not just lollies and choc-ices for the corner shop, but juicy wholesale accounts with supermarkets, restaurants and catering companies), the monopolies watchdog decided to take a closer look, especially at their 'parallel pricing policy' – an arrangement which showed many of the features of a collaboration. Bricks, the ice-cream industry's equivalent to the Gold Standard,[14] had been sold by both companies at identical prices since 1964, every increase by one firm exactly matched by the other. They were also joint owners of the Total Refrigeration Company, a firm that leased cabinets to shopkeepers. Wall's and Lyons Maid reacted angrily to any implications of shady dealings. Hadn't they already been investigated and vindicated by the Prices and Incomes Board in 1970?

Orbit chewing gum – introduced by Wrigley's in 1977 – wasn't another attempt to cash in on the space race, merely a play on the word Sorbitol, an artificial sweetener used in its 'sugar-free' recipe. In the hope of official endorsement, samples were dispatched to every one of Britain's dentists. Another newcomer, Freedent, was especially formulated for denture wearers. 'Does not stick!' boasted its adverts.

What worried many, though, was not the gum sticking to false teeth, but the way it adhered to virtually every other surface in the country. Every single paving slab in Britain must have been decorated with at least one white blob. Tourist attractions were particularly vulnerable: the deacon of Canterbury Cathedral even lamented his discovery of a glob stuck between the pages of a prayer book.

Mindful of their public duty (and the vast profits they made from gum), Wrigley's donated £25,000 to the 'Wrap it and bin it' campaign. Hardly worth a sneeze. At five

---

14 The year 1977 saw the launch of the Jubilee Brick. Not literally launched; it wasn't a missile for angry republicans, but merely a block of ice-cream from Midland Counties.

pence per blob, the total cost of removing an estimated 1400 million pieces of gum (no, I don't know who made this estimate and how it was arrived at) from Britain's streets would be around £70 million. Wrigley's contribution would have paid for the removal of a mere half a million pieces.

Jubilee year also saw the death of Peter Knight Wrigley. His name lives on – or his initials, at least. Do gum-chewers realize they are holding a thumb-sized memorial in their hands? P.K.'s is a damned curious legacy, when you think of it: no mere tombstone, nor even a towering cenotaph, just a trillion greyish blobs firmly glued to the planet, from cathedrals to shanty towns – like the kid who leaves his Juicy Fruit under the school desk, but replicated countless times. When Chernobyl and Sellafield are sweet pastureland once again, that gum will still be there. Rubbery, water-resistant, self-protectingly evasive as they flatten themselves to the pavement, these blobs will probably outlast mankind itself. Who knows, in the mutant genetic soup of a post-nuclear world, DNA lying dormant in all that long-dried saliva may well emerge to take some role in evolution's reboot.

Victorian gum had paraffin wax, modern versions have polyvinyl acetates. All perfectly safe, of course. Who cares, anyway? Tell a kid his gum contains polyvinyl acetates and he'll shrug. There are more scary ingredients. In 1977 a rumour swept through schoolyards in the USA that Bubble Yum contained spiders' eggs. Swallow the stuff and, boy, major trouble. A week later dozens of tiny websters hatched out and – mad as hell – they chewed their way out to freedom through your belly button. Life Savers Inc, the company who made Bubble Yum, were so fearful for their profits they were forced to place page-sized ads in American newspapers, reading simply: 'IT IS NOT TRUE THAT BUBBLE YUM CONTAINS SPIDERS' EGGS!'

By the mid-1970s Cadbury's marketing department seemed to have gone into creative overdrive. Kicking off with Oranges & Lemons, Almond Islands and Old Jamaica, they'd gone on in footstomping form to bring us Hazel In Sweet Disguises, a choc bar that must have owed its zany name to 1968's John Fred and the Playboy Band's hit 'Judy in Disguise with Glasses', itself a parody of 'Lucy in the Sky with Diamonds'. The gingham-wrapped Country Style, Rumba, with rum, and Gold Mine, with little honeycomb bits, all arrived in 1975 and are all gone now. The following year brought us a classic, admittedly, in Cadbury's Caramel (though it was only a repackaged version of their earlier Caramello).

The bigger the build-up, it seemed, the floppier the flop. Whistler was, according to company hype, 'One of the most thoroughly researched brands ever introduced by the company. Its extra crunchy formula is expected to capture a sizeable part of a £92 million market.' Yet it signally failed to capture even an honourable fraction.

Coffee and Walnut sounded like a good enough concept, but if a bar ever begged for oblivion it had to be Cadbury's Nunch. 'The nunchiest bar ever,' they said. Confectioners had added enough oddball nouns and random Ks to the English language – all very colourful and relatively harmless – but messing with adjectives was surely a step too far.

Even long-established brands – our beloved Aztec, for instance – would no longer be tolerated if they didn't perform well enough. Launched as a rival to Mars and undoubtedly popular, in the long term Aztec just couldn't dent its rival's sales and had to go.

Curly Wurly proved to be an enduring success, but things looked slightly dodgy in the early days after a deluge of mail from angry mothers complaining that Curly Wurly's chocolate coating flaked off at the slightest touch, ruining clothes, carpets and cushion covers. The recoil from an especially tough bar could trigger a positive fusillade of chocolate bits. To be fair, sticking chocolate to toffee had always been a problem for confectioners, but a rapid revamp was essential if Cadbury's were to avoid the risk of having to withdraw Curly Wurly from sale.

Although Galaxy had certainly taken a share of a market once virtually monopolized by Dairy Milk, any danger of it taking over as Britain's favourite seemed to have receded. Cadbury's could relax a little – until Yorkie arrived. Until now, despite a dozen successful and much-loved brands, Rowntree's had never really been in the frame with a straightforward bar of chocolate. They'd had a few – Elect in the 1920s, Motoring Chocolate in the 1930s – but nothing with any long-term mileage. Yorkie might do it, though. Thick, chunky and muscular, Yorkie, named after their home town, was a bar with attitude. It had abandoned all pretence of elegance. Ounce for ounce it offered little more than a standard bar of Dairy Milk – but purchasers who removed its wrapper felt they had discovered chocolate's answer to Dr Who's telephone box.

Within a year of its launch in 1977 Yorkie was tail-gating Dairy Milk in confectionery's top five.

1978 TOP TWENTY-FIVE

1. *Mars (Mars)*
2. *Kit-Kat (Rown)*
3. *Dairy Milk (Cad)*
4. *Twix (Mars)*
5. *Yorkie (Rown)*
6. *Milky Way (Mars)*
7. *Bounty (Mars)*
8. *Maltesers (Mars)*
9. *Aero (Rown)*
10. *Smarties (Rown)*
11. *Galaxy (Mars)*
12. *Banjo (Rown)*
13. *Whole Nut (Cad)*
14. *Fruit & Nut (Cad)*
15. *Flake (Cad)*
16. *Crunchie (Cad)*
17. *Double Decker (Cad)*
18. *Wrigley's Spearmint*
19. *Callard & Bowser's Toffee*
20. *Polos (Rown)*
21. *Rolo (Rown)*
22. *Fruit Pastilles (Rown)*
23. *Opal Fruits (Mars)*
24. *Marathon (Mars)*
25. *Topic (Mars)*

(And, slipping to a sad 42, Nutty)

Was the Mars Bar unassailable? This was its third decade at number one. Not only that, the company didn't make a product that wasn't in confectionery's Top Thirty. Every single one of its dozen brands was a winner. Unlike Rowntree's and Cadbury's, Mars spent no time on speculating on the possible tastes of the British public.

For all the hype about new brands, three-quarters of 1978's 'hit parade' dated back to the 1930s. It was a chart dominated by golden oldies. Constantly beguiled by ephemera, every conceivable combination of taste and form, we stuck to our guns. We knew what we liked. Firms wanted instant hits, but getting a nation to change its tastes took more skill than turning around an oil tanker. It would never turn any of these new bars into standards without years of testing.

Straitjacketed in post-modern irony, it seems hard to believe that TV cop Kojak could ever have been flavour of the month, but in 1975 sweetshops were eagerly awaiting deliveries of Kojak lollies, confident they'd be snapped up by the four o'clock stampede of schoolkids. What 10-year-old didn't want to look like a slaphead Big Apple cop?

Children's tastes had become inextricably tied up with fashions in TV, cinema and pop. It was a costly game. Buying the rights to use brands like *Happy Days*, *Star Wars*, *Superman* and *Mr Men* on their ice-lollies would cost Lyons Maid millions.

But some tie-ins were utterly crass, laughable attempts to add glamour to old-fashioned lines that were better left alone. Did anyone seriously expect New Avengers Marshmallows to catch on? TV's hard-kicking special agents endorsing the fluffiest, squidgiest, most spineless sweets ever invented? Whose wet idea was that? To compound the clumsiness, each pack came with 'Purdey's special marshmallow recipes'. Special assignments, yes, but special recipes? It hardly fitted in with the private life we'd imagined for Britain's favourite dolly bird. Was that really all she got up to in her Mayfair mews flat – changed out of thigh-boots, put on a frilly apron and reached for the mixing bowl?

Smaller companies, like Blue Bird, had to look further downmarket for their tie-in opportunities, but still, it would have cost them a fat fee to get Eddie Waring's cheery fizzog on their It's A Knockout Lollies.

Even when official endorsement wasn't available, some judicious tweaking of pack designs could work wonders. Trebor, past master with Beat-all Lollies, tried it again. Kids crowding into shops in search of some hero-endorsed sweets would make straight for the box illustrated with an Incredible Hulk lookalike and the legend Hunk Chew, without ever realizing it was a less-than-subtle *trompe l'oeil* and the label narrowly avoided charges of passing off by actually reading Hunk of Chew. Thank heavens for poor grammar.

Children may have been easy prey for the craze-mongers, but at the same time they were incredibly eclectic, able to encompass ancient and modern, switching from ice-lolly spaceships to chocolate choo-choos in the same walk home from school. They loved Stan Laurel as much as they did Marc Bolan. Firms looking for hooks on which to hang their products could never take anything for granted. Just as Cadbury's brought out a Bay City Rollers Curly Wurly (offering a tartan rosette and scarf for just 85p) who should pop up on *Top of the Pops* but Stan and Ollie, singing 'On The Trail of the Lonesome Pine'. To cash in on this reincarnation groove, Ollie's Lollies were rushed out. No need for a new product either: all they had to do was design a new packet. At the end of the day, Pop Star sweet cigs were no different to Dixon of Dock Green's.

Crazes, by definition, come and go. Few merit a footnote in confectionery's history, but some are worth remembering ... Space Dust, introduced in 1978, was the first genuinely new idea for some time. Its sugary granules encapsulated harmless CO_2 gas under pressure – a reckless trick that had taken General Foods, makers of Maxwell House, years to get right. Combined with juvenile saliva, Space Dust let loose a cannonade of mouth-based explosions – a far cry from the mild-mannered fizz of sherbet and kali. Big kids loved it, but smaller children were often distressed by the firecracker effect, especially those who shoved in a whole grubby handful. Trusting pensioners who took some from their grandchildren risked having their dental plates blown away, while those with genuine teeth were in for wild agonies if a particle landed in a cavity. The Space Dust sachet even had a rather mocking tone, somewhat reminiscent of that tipsy-looking moon on the cover of seminal 1970s album *In the Court of the Crimson King*.

As an update on traditional Love Hearts, Swizzel's Hippy Bits were a great idea, but rather clumsily executed, a pop-up thesaurus of youth slang that didn't quite know where it was coming from. *Groovy* belonged to the Beatles years, while *Swing It* and *Age Gap* dated back to Beatnik days. *Pop Art, Love Power, Faith* and *Action* were perhaps more in tune with the hippy ethos – but even hippies were out of date by the time these sweets arrived in the shops.

'Our baby will rank as the biggest, most successful new product in UK sweets trading for many years' – so reckoned the makers of Ipsos, sinking £500,000 into a sales campaign. The gimmick here was the packaging rather than the tiny fruit drops themselves: Lego-style inter-locking plastic boxes, which the company suggested could be collected and used to make interesting constructions – castles, dogs and ducks. A castle? Their example looked more like the Bureau of State Security in some Mittel European communist state. In any case, it would have needed around eighty boxes to make any decent attempt at such a construction. Even the angular-looking mutt would have called for thirty-odd packs.

Marketed by Nicholas, the company who made Aspros, Ipsos were yet another attempt by them to break into confectionery. Their Merijel sounded too much like a burns ointment to find favour, but with Ipsos they were more successful, despite complaints about the sweets' similarity to pills. This wasn't idle nannying, but genuine folk wisdom. In one year, 1952, eight children died as a result of scoffing pills that looked too much like sweeties.[15]

Increasingly, packaging was becoming as important as the contents. Kids didn't care that much about what they stuffed in their mouths but seemed increasingly self-conscious about what they were seen to choose.

Not that children had any monopoly on crazes. Grown-ups could be just as easily swayed. With muesli and yogurt hailed as the great panaceas, it wasn't long before some cross-fertilization with confectionery occurred. As well as Yoggets, sweets from Pascalls, and a Yogurt Maid ice-lolly, muesli bars were everywhere. Meltis Harvest was among the first of these puritanically dry sticks, not forgetting the oddly named Swisskit. Intended as a play on 'biscuit', this latter sounded, to me at least, more like a penknife. From Granary Foods, a company based in Burton-on-Trent, came Kalibu, a bar packed with healthy negatives: no refined sugar, no oxalic acid, no caffeine, no theobromine. Eschewing the drawbacks of cocoa, its pseudo chocolate coating was made from carob. 'Minimizes the threat of acne to teenagers,' they proudly claimed.

The 1970s was a golden age for peripherals, but how many have survived the intervening years? Do people still take their kids to the park for a game with their Polo frisbee? Would anyone dare go out in public wearing their Curly Wurly Flasher Badge? I doubt it. Yet I'd like to believe that somewhere, today, bent beneath a car bonnet, is a man wearing his Yorkie anorak. Once smart, with smooth-running zipper and jauntily swinging toggles, it is now hopelessly ripped and greased-up. Yet its owner still dreams

---

15 As late as 1994, eight Oldham children ended up in hospital after mistaking LSD tabs for sweets, while in a more tragic case a toddler died after mistaking her mother's iron tablets for sweets. Doctors struggled for twenty-four hours to save her, but she had taken three times the lethal overdose.

of life as a trucker: the caffs, the open road, steamy lay-by sessions with willing hitchhikers ...

'PROFIT DIPS!' No, it wasn't a new line to sell alongside Fun Dips, Double Dips and Sherbet Dips, but a business-pages headline, a gloomy warning about the future. Bassett's profits had dropped from £2.8 million to £1.3 million – peanuts compared to Cadbury's £21 million profits. With capital and marketing costs thrashing smaller companies, a firm of stockbrokers, Sheppard and Chase, predicted that Britain's sweets industry would be increasingly dominated by the big boys – Rowntree-Mackintosh, Mars and Cadbury's.

The new Star Bar – 'a substantial eat product' – had £500,000 allocated to it, as did Rowntree's Cabana. They could even sink £600,000 into the launch of Splicer, a ten-pence chew bar – though 10 million would have to be sold before they reached break-even point. Global brands were the business, each one a long-term strategic investment.

Years after I left junior school, when I no longer had much to do with that part of town, I often had nostalgia flash-backs, misty collages of steam trains, kids in grey jumpers, the *Watch with Mother* flower unfolding on a black-and-white TV. And the penny pop machine. Yet sometimes I couldn't help wondering if it wasn't down to false-memory syndrome. Those I mentioned it to looked puzzled, sceptical, shaking their heads in a kindly way, smiling behind my back. Surely someone must have known what I was talking about? It couldn't have been the only one in the country, surely? Then one day in the late 1970s, walking around that area and thinking how small it all looked, as if I'd freakishly grown and might topple to the ground at any moment, I happened to pass by the shop. The door handle seemed tiny in my hand, the headroom restricted. What did I want? Just a packet of Polos, no more than an excuse to go in, really. As I waited in the dusty silence, from the back came the sounds of a TV. Eventually an old man in a brown knitted waistcoast came out and, just as he rattled aside the curtain that separated his living quarters, I glimpsed the pop machine in the back passageway, disused and dusty, half dismantled. The fantasy response is obvious: one takes out one's wallet and offers the bemused troglodyte a wad of notes in return for his old scrap. I probably never thought of it. I probably had no money, anyway. For years afterwards I regretted not seizing the moment. And still do. If only I'd bought it, I could have restored it, polished it, loved it with Brasso and yellow dusters, and dispensed penny bottles to myself and my children.

Careless Wispas

1980s

*These Fisherman's Friend super strong mints
really make you blow!*

1980s press ad

For the half-dozen firms in confectionery's Premier League, winnings could be colossal. But just to join their game cost £500,000. And these were hard-nosed players, quite happy to double or treble the stakes. Rowntree's Drifter, for instance, was a bet with a staggering £1.75 million riding on it.[1]

To invest so much in a mere chocolate bar looks like lunacy – until one takes into account the way its nominal value can be inflated by hype. Being delicious was no longer enough. In fact, as a *raison d'être*, it looked pretty pathetic. To hack it, a new chocolate bar had to be much more than the sum of its parts. A chocolate bar is a chocolate bar is a chocolate bar. But as a brand it might be shaped as many things: a lifestyle statement, a fashion accessory, a daily bite. Choc bars, some smart Alec decided, might even take the place of prayer books, chocolate rosary beads for folk who lived in the fast lane.

---

1 Cautious spending, though, compared with the money thrown at established brands – Smarties meriting upwards of £3 million spent on its annual advertising budget.

'The experience of Drifter contrasts with the hectic pace of modern life.' Sold as meditation while-U-chew, your Drifter offered a 'relaxed casual lifestyle' – all two minutes' worth. Those last crumbs of wafer falling to your feet were as ominous as those old public phone-box pips.

There were other fantasies for rent. Sex, for instance, always a winner. Not that innuendo was so new: Walnut Whip had been under suspicion for years, the object of many a titter, without ever needing a push from ad agency whizz kids. Now, though – with the Flake advert, for instance – the nudge-nudging was insistent enough to knock an elephant sideways. Kids had their sweet cigarettes, they reasoned – why shouldn't adults have some fun, too? But did they seriously believe that anyone was picturing a Flake as anything other than a Flake? Why, if it had a similarity to anything it was a rotted twiglet, not a part of any male from this planet. Such innuendo, though it got Flake talked about, wasn't really what most people wanted. Old-fashioned values still held, albeit in updated form. Rowntree's did it with Yorkie – thick, square and chunky – and a hunk in an unbuttoned shirt to bait the honey trap. So popular was this ex-*Poldark* actor with female viewers of the TV advert that Rowntree's had to set up a special office to cope with the demand for signed pin-ups.

But nudge-nudge stuff was really for the hoi polloi. To some people chocolate was far too serious to be used as some kind of *Carry On* prop. These *soi-disant* connoisseurs, well-placed enough to have contacts on all the broadsheets, had their own society, and a house mag, *Chocolate News*, printed with chocolate-scented ink. Chocophiles delighted in trivia: they only had to nibble a square and they could tell you what country the cocoa beans had come from and the name of a little shop in Brussels where it had been purchased, and pronounce the centres in perfect French. These people would no more buy a Yorkie than have their hair cut at a place called Marilyn's Modes. Their agenda was to elevate chocolate from its humble past, give it gravitas, reinvent it as a topic they could weave around with the same kind of bullshit oenophiles attached to simple plonk. They were convinced that sex was in the chocolate already, coded into its molecules. God had laced cocoa with chemicals that made a bee-line for the libido. But they were talking about sex as something, well, spiritual almost, not sticky moments with randy truck drivers.

But once the media got a whiff of sex the message was bound to be sensationalized. It was the excuse thousands of addicts had been waiting for. Now they could load their supermarket trolleys with Dairy Milk, Yorkies and Mars Bars and excuse their weakness with a stream of psycho-babble. They weren't guzzlers after all – how unfair their detractors had been! – but turbo-charged lovers.[2]

For connoisseurs, chocolate's heritage – Aztecs and all that jazz – was just as important as any supposed aphro-disiac qualities. High priests apparently drank chocolate prior to sacrificing a teenage girl or two; and afterwards, too, as a celebration tipple while drudges mopped up virgins' blood from the terraces. Magic, myth, sex and paganism – here was a fantasy that blended all the right ingredients – and made chocolate lovers feel better about their addiction.

With Cadbury's Aztec sadly retired in 1978, one might think other firms would have twigged the limited appeal of history. But no, now that chocolate had acquired a fan base with more money than sense, here came Inca, from Rowntree's. No mere bar, mind you (Aztec had always been a bit down-market) but a *collection* in three flavours: roast hazelnut, walnut and orange and apricot truffle.

---

2 This ploy to crank up sales has been tried by everyone from prawn fishers to cheese-makers. Yet the shelves of Soho's sex shops and love boutiques seem oddly bereft of Dairy Milk and Yorkies (as well as prawns and Cheddar). Isn't that enough to disprove such wacky claims? If establishments that specialize in fleecing dissatisfied lovers don't buy the idea, there can't be much in it.

Collection? It reeks of hobbyism at its worst: who but a bad-breathed tanktop would collect bars of chocolate? Others obviously attached more attractive values to the word. Alongside Inca in the shops, those who cared would be thrilled to come across the Henri Nestlé Collection – 'for discerning choc lovers'. And to prove that foreign names still had allure, Payne's were pushing their Anton Berg milk chocolates.

1988 TOP TWENTY BOXES

1. Quality Street	11. Matchmakers
2. Roses	12. Toffifee
3. Milk Tray	13. Contrast
4. After Eight	14. Neapolitans
5. Ferrero Rocher	15. Harlequin
6. Black Magic	16. Weekend
7. All Gold	17. Eclipse
8. Dairy Box	18. Mint Leaves
9. Chocolate Orange	19. Twilight
10. Biarritz	20. Terry's A/D Mints

Chocolates had always been packaged with added snob value, yet the way we'd done it in the old days seemed more excusable – that is, far too clumsily to cause offence to even the staunchest socialist.

Introduced in 1962, After Eights are still, thirty-five years later, at number four in Britain's choc-box charts. Originally part of a range (or even a collection!) which included a chocolate bar and a boxed assortment (both dropped after a couple of years), After Eights hail from a vanished era, a time when the hostess trolley, Blue Nun and wafer-thin mints were all part of British efforts at upward mobility.

We chose, quite arbitrarily, but by common consent, to invest after-dinner mints with all kinds of elitist values and 'high society', however tongue-in-cheek, remains an integral part of the brand image. After Eights are the communion wafers of social acceptance, the ritual end to a black-tie dinner party. Yet the one shown on TV is as unreal and laughable as the Ferrero ambassador's reception: a fantasy social occasion, complete with moustachioed colonels and white-gloved ladies, in a mythical house in a non-existent England.

Reality is so much different. After Eights[3] are not purchased from Fortnum and Mason, but from security-grilled off-licences on inner-city estates. Instead of being politely shared with fellow guests, they are bought (or shoplifted) by the lonesome, the greedy and the bulimic, people who scoff a whole box in one go, in private, at any time of day, while watching *Noel's House Party* and waiting for a lottery ticket to change their lives.

If After Eights are to be found at dinner tables, it'll be in one of Britain's innumerable curry houses, one to each saucer when the coffee arrives, a heavy hint that time's up and the waiters want to go home.

With Yorkie proving such a hit, rivals issued an edict to the gnomes in their kitchens: 'Make it chunky!' And to counter what was perceived as a 'conservative image', Dairy Milk, Whole Nut and Fruit & Nut bars were redesigned with a chunkier outline, redefining them (in trade parlance) as 'self-eats, with increased pick-up appeal'. Nestlé did much the same with Dairy Crunch.

The enduring success of Aero – now coming up to its half-centenary – had long been a cause of angst at Cadbury's Bournville HQ. In the 1930s Fry's had launched a bar named Ripple – but it never caused many. A decent enough rival in the bubbly chocolate stakes (understandably so since it was one of several rivals made under licence to Rowntree's patented recipe), it would never knock Aero

---

3 Cadbury's tried to cash in with their neatly named Royal Mints. At the time, the mid-1960s, Britons were chomping through a staggering 150 tons every week, which makes it look less like a dinner party than feeding time at the elephant house.

from its pedestal, and by 1940 it had been consigned to the industry's capacious dustbin.

But people liked bubbly chocolate. That it was, after all, half air seemed to matter not one jot. We looked on it not as a con trick, but as a playful novelty. There had to be an element of the practical joke in confectionery, even masochism, one might say. Like the powdered sherbet that had us coughing our little lungs up, the gobstoppers that nearly asphyxiated us, the Murraymints with a grip so strong they could pull out teeth, liquorice that left us looking like clowns. What fun they all were. If firms wanted to sell us chocolate riddled with holes, well, we were only too glad to have a chance to buy it.

The idea was too good a moneyspinner to let slip. Cadbury's were determined to have another go … Known originally as P.46, Wispa was one of several new products dreamed up by Cadbury's in the mid-1970s, made in answer to a brief calling for a bar to 'build on Cadbury's Dairy Milk heritage in a pure chocolate countline format, exploring all possible textures, configurations and resultant eats'. Quite a mouthful, then, even before it left the drawing board. And if that wasn't ambitious enough, the new bar should also be 'young, active, trendy, convenient'.

First trialled in 1976 and, for some reason, shelved, Cadbury's aerated chocolate wasn't given another test-run until the 1980s. P.46 might have ended up as Rondo, K.O. or Vista. Rollers was another suggestion that was scratched. Maybe it sounded too much like Rolos (the mangled vowels of yokels and oily rags, remember, can so easily end in lost sales). Or maybe the name held unfortunate hints of heaviness, reminded people of steamrollers.[4] Something lighter, airier, frothier was called for. Wispier even. And, by remarkable coincidence, Wisp was already in Cadbury's piggy-bank

---

4 Waste not, want not. They could always add a 'St' and create a brand called Strollers, as they did in the mid-1990s.

of registered trade marks. Yes, Wisp was nearly there – but not quite. Light and fairy-like, certainly, but maybe a shade too much like 'lisp'. No one must be offended. Adding an 'a' provided a quick fix for that dilemma.

So intense was the secrecy surrounding Wispa that it made Trappist monks look like chatterboxes. All waste paper – draft designs for wrappers, tasting reports, marketing predictions – was shredded, incinerated and – who knows? – buried in concrete. As launch date approached, the first Wispas were packed in plain boxes and transported to selected wholesalers in unmarked vans.

'It's as significant to us at Cadbury's as the Metro was to Austin Rover,' said a spokesman.

Yet this first launch, in 1981, actually proved *too* successful. Even with a new £12 million production line turning out 500,000 Wispas a week, Cadbury's couldn't meet demand. TV ads, featuring the stars of *Hi-De-Hi* and *It Ain't Half Hot, Mum* were postponed. Modern PR folk, though, are expert at extracting valuable publicity even from failure: newspapers happily printed their hyped-up and judiciously planted stories of shopkeepers scrapping over the limited supplies. Wow! Get this – here was a chocolate bar so good that normally docile citizens were prepared to resort to fisticuffs to get hold of some.

A relaunch in 1983 went rather more smoothly, and within a few weeks of going on sale Wispa reached the number four slot in Britain's chocolate hit parade. A welcome success in its own right, Wispa might also be seen as the cavalry coming over the hill – rescuing Cadbury's from twenty years of decline, during which the company had been steadily losing market share to Mars and Rowntree's. By 1984, thanks in no small part to Wispa, Cadbury's profits had shot up 40 per cent to £130 million.

The Wispa Department has a great ring to it, doesn't it? Surreal, romantic, sinister even, a euphemistically named ministry in a Big Brother state ... But no, to Cadbury's, it is all deadly serious. Staffed by a hundred dedicated

205

employees (this being personnel-speak rather than a declaration of faith), machines run 'non-stop' (though actually only for twenty-three hours a day). Vats of chocolate are kept at a steady 30° (by computer-controlled thermostat rather than a foreman's finger) and Wispa's bubbles are so uniform that each one can be exactly calibrated to between 0.2mm and 0.3mm. At any one time the stores have stocks of paper for 275 million wraps. Such details are dutifully copied down by children who send off for material for school projects (and authors too, of course).

Real pedants will have spotted a serious mistake in my copy. It may even be a legal blunder of some kind. Am I the only spoilsport who keeps writing Wispa with a capital 'W' when it should, strictly speaking, be wispa?

'The lower-case letters say, "Pick me up and eat me,"' burbled the marketing department, but the question has to be asked: if that's true, why isn't all chocolate sold using the same lower-case psychology? Conversely, if it turned out to be true, what message is given by upper-case letters? If wispa says, 'Pick me up and eat me', what would WISPA say? Would it be perceived as a shouted order rather than a polite suggestion?

Just to make sure everyone noticed this brilliant lower-case wheeze, a Wispa ad was projected – amidst predictable protests – on to the dome of St Paul's Cathedral, a sacrilege sanctioned only in return for a sizeable bung to the fund for restoration of the Whispering Gallery. (Geddit?)

Wispa's success persuaded Rowntree's to reissue Aero in a chunkier format. And high time too. Didn't the old-style Aero smack too much of self-discipline, its half-dozen sections marked with little lines to promote restraint and discourage gluttony? Hell, these were the 1980s, a decade with the motto, 'Be greedy, take as much as you want, throw away the old restraints' – and even chocolate had to fit in.

The success of Yorkie and Wispa didn't mean that Cadbury's or Rowntree's had finally discovered a magic formula. Both companies still had a dedicated turkey department, where white-shirted acolytes could waste the odd £500,000 without getting into too much trouble. Was there ever a P.29 or a P.41? Probably, but we'll never know. For every success there were always half a dozen failures, trumpeted loudly and then hushed up and never talked about. Cadbury's Silk and Ticket, this latter a 'substantial self-consumption' line, both took a dive, as did their Tribute, a chocolate assortment aimed specifically at men. Tribute's emphasis was on nuts (the presumption being that orange creams were soft and distinctly un-macho, whereas hard nuts speak for themselves). But men weren't interested. Nor was anyone strongly minded to dip into Cadbury's Heritage assortment. The word heritage was surely ill-starred, but it was somewhat more homely than Rowntree's bizarrely named Kassidic Assortment!

After years of being out-Smartied by Rowntree's, Cadbury's had fought back. Now it was Mars' turn to put the boot in. The Slough mob had been plotting revenge ever since Kit-Kat – now with a whopping 16 per cent share of the brand-name market – knocked the Mars Bar (albeit temporarily) from its top spot.

M&Ms, first issued to GIs in World War Two as part of rations, were America's Smarties and the British were notorious copycats. And hadn't M&Ms recently featured in that blockbusting film, *ET*? If kids thought they could befriend their own alien with the help of a few colourful sweeties they'd be sure to switch brands ... Yet others doubted the wisdom of Mars' attempt to tackle Smarties – not just a giant brand in itself, but one so very close to the hearts of British people. Even if commercial victory proved possible, what if the natives despised the victors? Humiliating Smarties would be as acceptable as kicking a cat.

Launched in 1987, after a successful two-year test period in the Tyne-Tees region, the M&M assault was backed by a serious £7 million campaign, plotted with the help of kingmakers Saatchi and Saatchi. In response, Rowntree's increased the Smarties advertising budget by 25 per cent. 'Smarties are not just sweets,' said a loyal spokesman from J. Walter Thompson, their ad agency since 1938.

In a suspiciously timed incident at New York's Kennedy Airport, US customs men arrested a Rowntree's rep bringing in some Smarties with his commercial samples. The red ones, said the officers, looked just like a certain hard drug. A special squad from the US Food and Drug Administration was summoned. The sweets were cleared of being deadly narcotics but, just as seriously, it turned out that the gaily coloured buttons were packed with E numbers.

'Green ones are OK,' the FAD men decreed. 'Yellow and pink – OK. Not red. Say, you know these guys have got cochineal pigment? That's barred here in the States.'

After sorting through seven thousand Smarties, helped by his children, the Rowntree's rep was left with eight hundred red ones. After being ritually dissolved in hot water, the resulting sludge was flushed down the Kennedy Airport toilets.

'Trade and food regulations are so complex we need a computer programe to keep track,' moaned a Rowntree's spokesman.

To comply with all the laws and social customs of its eighty markets, the company had to produce Smarties in no less than six different colour sets.[5] They'd been playing with Smarties for years – but most people had probably never even noticed. The dark brown, for instance, originally had a plain chocolate centre, while the light brown one, positively exotic, had a coffee-flavoured filling.[6] This latter

---

5 They'd also been producing a three-finger Kit-Kat for Middle East markets, while in Japan they preferred a single extra-long stick, known, predictably enough, as Kit-Kat Stick.
6 And after the war they were all plain, due to the shortage of milk.

has, sadly, now gone the same way as Aztec and Glees, ousted by the blue. Originally just a temporary guest edition, like many a lodger it proved so seductive that it's now moved in for good.

Two years later Jerusalem joined the anti-Smarties backlash after erythrosine, a dye used to colour pink and violet Smarties, was banned by Whitehall's Food Additives Commission. It could be used in glacé cherries, but for sweets a substitute had to be found. Rowntree's opted for that old stand-by, cochineal. Problem solved: Smarties really did have the answer, after all. But not for the folks down in Golders Green. According to London's Beth Din, the Jewish watchdogs, these retinted Smarties were definitely not kosher – Leviticus Chapter 11, verses 20–26 was cited as authority – and Orthodox Jews were instructed to steer well clear. Also on the blacklist, for some reason, was Crunchie. Secrecy being the rule, Beth Din refused to say why. One can only wonder in what way the cheerful honeycomb offended against the word of God.

Looking around in the middle of the 1980s, it slowly dawned, on some of us at least, how much we'd lost. Lemfizz cubes, Jubblies, Arrow bars, candy tobacco – all gone – along with all the hundreds of little shops that had once sold them. No retailer could now survive with such a specialized trade.

Still we have a drowning man's grip on the sweetshop. It's a place we seem reluctant to let go. The past is not a foreign country, but a turn-off on a motorway, a road which leads to museums at Beamish and the Black Country. Here it is: the Jubilee sweetshop, where a jolly lady in mob cap and apron hands out striped sticks of rock, or pours a cascade of liquorice comfits into the gleaming brass pan of some old-fashioned scales.

But what kind of hypocrisy is this? Why are we so desperate to feign loyalty to this past – the places where our grandads bought their aniseed balls – but were simply not prepared to support the shops ourselves? No one (apart from militant trainspotters) could have prevented diesel replacing steam, but the sweetshop might have been saved. Instead, people bought their sweets from Menzies along with their fags and newspapers, dropped chocolate bars in their Sainsbury's trolleys, or topped up at the petrol station along with the 4-star. They'd been moaning about their lot for a hundred years, but those grumpy old shopkeepers were proved right in the end.

1985 TOP TWENTY-FOUR

1. Mars	13 = Maltesers
2. Kit-Kat	13 = Fruit Pastilles
3. Twix	15. After Eight
4. Dairy Milk	16. Black Magic
5. Marathon	17. Extra Strong Mints
6. Aero	18. All Gold
7. Milk Tray	19 = Topic
8. Polos	19 = Minstrels
9. Flake	21. Roses
10. Wispa	22. Milk Tray
11. Bounty	23. Smarties
12. Double Decker	24. Milky Way

Yet if the ting-a-ling shop bell may have sounded its last, the variety of sweets got no smaller. Quite the opposite. Rather like books, which consistently defied doom-mongers, sweets refused to die. Old-fashioned sweetshops may have been as rare as travelling knife-sharpeners, but kids had more spending power than ever. Under-10s had an average 20p per day pocket money – but when their annual spend added up to over £840 million it was a case of give 'em what they want, bless 'em. Even the old penny tray was alive and well. Apart from advice to fit a sneeze guard, there were few rules. Kids seemed happy enough to eat each other's fingerprints. The high sugar content of these sweets was bad for their teeth – shopkeepers bravely admitted that – but that same sugar also lessened the risks of infection.

Apart from a few spoilt brats who slunked off to a corner to scoff a whole box of chocolates, what kids wanted most of all was fun. Gimmicks were as important as taste. There were Hologrems (candy sticks with monster holograms); Streemers, which hung down like fly-strips from a shop's ceiling; Giant Pixy Stix gobstoppers, with five colour changes; Daredevils, which tasted alternately hot and cold; packets of candy floss; a bubblegum hamburger in a tiny box. Britain was good at gimmicks.

But the best gimmick of all was insurrection, scandal, sheer bloody-minded annoyance. Just as kids had a sneaking admiration for the class clown, any sweets that caused trouble always found a ready clientele. The *succès de scandale* for 1986 was Pint Pots: beer-flavoured chews – 'the hottest new line since Skullcrushers!' Some children, according to one Aberdeen shopkeeper, were buying fifty Pint Pots in one go. Protests were inevitable from various teetotal spoilsports, but Alma shrugged it off: 'The more controversy the better,' they warbled.

Close behind with Boozy Bottles and Yobbos – cola-flavoured bovver boots – Anglo-Bellamy looked as if they were trying to make nanny-baiting a sport. And considering none of these sweets contained an atom of alcohol, how nonsensical the fuss was. The kids who were buying Pint Pots and Boozy Bottles were not apprentice alkies but the same juniors who, in 1984, spent an estimated £6 million solely on white chocolate mice.

Wispa's syntax may have been misleading, but perhaps confectioners really ought to be applauded for stimulating the word sectors of kids' brains. While our major players agonized over every nuance in every brand name, the sugar magicians produced a lexicography entirely of their own, a positive flurry of candied nonsense words. Sweets slang was wild, conjuring up a bizarre nursery world, day-glo, stickle-bricked, populated by pimpled characters most adults had never heard of – and would have been extremely wary of if they had. One can only feel sorry for adults stuck with formal requests for bars of Dairy Milk and packs of Murraymints when kids could storm their newsagent's and demand a handful of Zegazoids (liquorice and lime chew bars), described by their makers, McCowan's, as 'frightening'. (And why wouldn't you believe it?)

What kid could resist munching through a packet of Galactic Garbage, Silly Asps, Jelly Gators, Fizz Bangs, Gummy Nuts or Horror Heads? Krr-unchy Coal sounds brilliant, as do Twistiz, Fire Sticks and Gorgo, another chew bar from McCowan's, 'with black meteorite pieces'. And here I crave indulgence for a list: Garbage Can-dy, Krypton Bombs, Gob Bombs, Dinosaurs, Smackers, Nutty Licksticks, Liquorice Kang-A-Rus, Meeces, Red Laces, Pirate Tattoo Bubblegum, Bodies, Big Softee, Supas, Space Fings, Crazy Fings. I could go on and on. Pointless cataloguing, really – but it seems such a shame to let all these gems of nonsense drop into oblivion without a mention.

Although Pez arrived in the USA during the 1950s, it took an age to reach Britain. It wasn't exactly new, having been invented in Austria in 1927. Its inventor, Edmund Haas (like Wrigley, another baking-powder magnate), had been selling his mints for a while. Noting their popularity among those who wished to give up cigarettes, he came up with the dispenser idea as an aid – a mechanism that replicated the comforting action of a cigarette lighter but popped up a harmless mint instead – to take away the craving. The word itself, Pez, is simply a contraction of Pfefferminz.

But the real seller, year in, year out, was Horror. Voodoo Teeth, Dead Men's Fingers, Eyeballs – was this the local newsagent's or the lair of a serial killer? Another list: Duckula Suckula, Terror Eyes, Ugly Bug Balls, Freaky Foot, Storm Dogs, Bones, Blood Bugs, Frogs Legs, Munchy Maggots, Jelly Sharks, Slimy Slurps Wormy Wriggles, Sour Slugs, Fangs, Square Balls, Smelly Feet, Barratt's Transplanters – ears, feet, noses, hands, feet in rhubarb or sour-apple flavour. Trebor brought out a whole range of

Crawlies – spiders, grasshoppers, beetles, moths, bees, ladybirds; and, for apprentice witches, Terror Curses, each packet being printed with one of a series of seventy curses. Trebor Mummies – ' the taste from the tomb' – and Horror Lollies, Evil Eric Lollies and Black Hole, a frothy sherbet dip. Nite Bites, a coffin and body – 'aimed at youngsters reared on horror videos'. One might baulk at such cynical marketing, but it was an old idea – a rehash of Kelly In A Coffin.

Another welcome boost to sales came with the 'sick stickers' scandal of 1986. Garbage Pail Kids – supposedly 'the biggest thing since the Hula Hoop' – had stickers which featured the classmates from hell: Dead Ted, Boney Joanie and Nervy Nigel, along with Bugsy Betty with her hideous fly head, Fryin' Brian, who was clamped in an electric chair, and Mean Dean, a punk with a stick of dynamite strapped to his head.

'Nauseating!' was the verdict from many grown-ups.

Packs also included a Liars Licence or a Pain In The Neck Licence which, among other suggestions, encouraged kids to eat spaghetti with their hands. 'The Garbage Pail Kids told me to do it,' pleaded a 9-year-old Yorkshire tyke who had his collection confiscated after he'd stamped on a dinner lady's foot. The 'licences' were condemned by the Campaign for Law and Order, who drew worrying parallels with recent advice in a gay magazine on ways for pupils to sabotage school routines. Questions were asked in the House of Commons but nothing much came of it. All the same, it seemed as if kids had travelled a long way since queueing at a bubblegum machine to get kings and queens of England cards.

Yet, when it comes to tastelessness, Garbage Pail Kids were mere runners-up. The first prize must go, not to bones, bugs and eyes, nor even to Fryin' Brian and his pals, but to Snotty Slurps: 'Pick up the new snot sensation now!' Pauline Picknose, Mick Mucous and Nigel Nostril were ten times more tasteless than any Garbage Pail Kid. The makers claimed that Snotty Slurps had undergone extensive test-marketing. 'We're confident we're on to a winner. Kids like things which are ghoulish, slimy and revolting' – adjectives their parents might just as easily apply to the button-collared whizz kids who intended to build careers by prising every last hot and sweaty penny from a gullible kid's chubby fingers, stooping to whatever depths were deemed necessary.

Space seemed old-fashioned and traditional by comparison. It was usurping cowboys and Indians as the establishment kids' play theme. Even the Milky Bar Kid (fourth in a series of wholesome sprogs) had gone cosmic, no longer riding into town to lay down the law, but rescuing a comely princess from Zartan, an evil robot king with a neat line in poetic taunts: 'I'm robot king from planet Zar, I'll beam away your Milky Bars.' Zartan didn't look like the kind of alien who'd be frightened by a kid in specs (designer now, not NHS) but the MBK was as handy with a laser sword as he had been with a six-shooter. But now that millions of kids had lost their stetson-hatted role model, there was certainly no future for cowboys and Indians.

During the free-market scramble of the Thatcher years, old boundaries became blurred. Golden Wonder brought out Crunchy Frootz, a rice snack with fruity flavours. And what on earth were Cadbury's doing making Criss Cross: potato snacks with a cheesy filling? Old certainties vanished. As if anxious not to miss a single chance, sweets took on multi-functional roles. Cola-flavoured chews had been around for decades, admittedly, but now there were Irn-Bru and Tizer chews, too, deliberately marketed in the hope of stimulating sales of the corresponding drinks. Even jelly babies might taste of bubblegum flavour, but they didn't blow.

But this jostling for territory didn't go unchallenged. Mars 'Cool 'em' campaign – which encouraged shopkeepers to put chocolate bars in the drinks chiller – really got up the nose of Coca-Cola. Reps were instructed to remove Mars products from Coke chillers. The next move was inevitable: Mars Ice-Cream, code named Ice-Cream Mars, was firmly pitched against Wall's Bonanza but had the massive advantage of pre-packed brand loyalty. It all seems so obvious now, but at the beginning Mars Ice-Cream was not much more than a gimmick.

With health an obsession in the 1980s, cereal bars appeared by the handful – Husky, Jump, Tracker and Harvest Crunch. Cadbury's brought out Go, and from Mars came Applause. Payne's even coated their peanuts and raisins in yogurt instead of chocolate in the hope of enticing the Ski brigade. KP introduced lower-fat crisps while Smiths did Jackets, with the hazy notion that leaving the brown bits on was a health bonus. For real *aficionados,* there were even Kelp Crunchies – seaweed crisps in blue cheese, prawn or garlic flavour (though one imagines that seaweed would have enough flavour to start with) – and Vitacrisps, the first ever to be vitamin-enriched. There were also sweets with added vitamins: Vitamints, Vita Fruits, Vita Soothe.

Royal Wedding editions of sweets and chocolates were nothing new and in 1981 Newberry Fruits, Milk Tray and Quality Street all appeared in special packs for Charles and Di's nuptials. Still – in a choice of cheese 'n' onion, salt 'n' vinegar, Bovril or ready-salted – Golden Wonder's Royal Wedding crisps must have been a first. Somewhere there's a daytripper to London, sitting on the steps of St Paul's, staving off the hunger pangs with a bag of crisps as they remember that long-ago day, someone who can't taste Bovril now without bursting into tears ...

There's an unavoidable downside to crisps, Ringos, Skips, Monster Munch, *et al.* – the bad smell of salt 'n' vinegar, toasted cheese, pickled onion, spicy poppadom. Not to mention a kitchenful of pungent aromas – cock-a-leekie crisps, spicy sausage, chilli, curry, sour cream and onion, gammon and pineapple. At least the old bags had breathed, but the new ones – metallicized now for added glamour – merely sealed in the smell, so that it positively burst out, as if kept under pressure. It was no accident, surely, that Skips were advertised by wrestler Giant Haystacks, a man indisputably associated with ripe and spicy aromas after going eight rounds with somebody called Krazy Keef or Mad Mick.

While anti-sugar lobbies managed to get supermarkets to remove sweets from their checkout areas, some manufacturers actually boasted of their indifference: Tip Tops Totem Poles – '10 per cent more sugar!' Sugar confectionery sales were demonstrably falling, though it seems ironic because, with greater awareness, more attention to brushing and better dental care than ever, such dangers were more easily contained.

'Schools can discourage or even forbid children to eat sweets or sugary snacks during lessons,' suggested the GLC's dental adviser. Such softly-softly tactics appalled old-timers, led by the head of Highbury Grove Comprehensive, who apparently advocated the lash for eating in class. 'It seems extraordinary to me to assume there should be anything other than a total embargo on sweets in lessons. What will they tell us next? That children shouldn't eat hot dogs or smoke pot?'

Camric, the campaign for real ice-cream, from the Milk Marketing Board, invested £1 million to make its symbol known and remembered. Wall's joined in the conspiracy with their Jolly Scooper 'original' cornets, while Lyons relaunched their Pola Maid, a 1935 brand that had offered the public their first taste of extruded ice-cream portions. But some things had a genuine feel of the old days. While Wall's ice-cream came under attack for its artificial flavours – vanilla made with piperohal, an ingredient of lice killer; banana synthesized with amyl acetate, used in dry cleaning – consumer mag *Which?* reported unacceptable levels of bacteria in 37 out of 47 ice-creams. Nearly all these instances were traced back to the sellers, to scoops that were left for ages in a jugful of dirty water, developing a nice film of e.coli and listeria.

British shops were full of Euro upstarts no one had ever heard of before – Ferrero Rocher, Werther's Originals, Sula, Dime – but they tried to kid us these sweets had been with us all along. Toffifee was German. Even the kids' lollipops – Chupa Chups – came from Spain where they proudly whirled out 3 million a day.

Dime was launched in 1983 with a £750,000 campaign from Barker & Dobson. Dime came from Swedish confectioners Marabou, famous (at least in the sweetshops of Stockholm and Uppsala) for those other yummy bestsellers: Skotte, Bugg, Piggy and Figaro. Dime was part of a Scandinavian invasion. From Finland came Daily, a nougat/caramel bar; while Payne's elected to take on the British marketing of the Yankee Bar, whose wrapper carried the irresistible endorsement, 'By appointment to the Royal Danish Court!'

But exporting is a tricky business. Our Norse invaders were clever enough to seduce us with words we could understand and relate to – Dime, Daily, Yankee – but Italians weren't half so good at the game. Carletti might have tempted us with their Lunch Bar, but even cursory research would have stopped them trying to sell us a bar called Skum Banana.

We were happy enough to buy their sweets – but then they turned on us, calling British chocolate rubbish. How dare they say such things! Cherished brands in the firing line were Kit-Kat and Flake, both threatened by an EU ban because of the 5 per cent vegetable fat in their recipes. All sorts of rumours flew. We'd have to call it vegolate or something. National pride was at stake. But confectioners won a moral victory when a majority at a blind tasting expressed a preference for the British recipe and said it had every right to be regarded as chocolate.

It was also rumoured that the EU intended to ban wine gums since they demonstrably included not a drip of Chablis or Rioja. Ridiculous literalism, justifiably rubbished by our gung-ho tabloids. Yet the misnomer was enough for one Muslim, owner of a Holborn sweetshop, who took one look at the packets and refused to stock them, despite assurances that the most potent ingredient was nothing stronger than acetic acid.

Once confectionery became big business it could not avoid getting dragged into politics ... The Animal Liberation Front had already threatened to smash the windows of shops selling Mars' products – accusing them of funding experiments in which monkeys were fed a high-sugar diet – but sabotaged Mars Bars indicated a serious escalation. Dozens had been poisoned, said the ALF, and randomly placed in shops in York, Leeds and Coventry. Others, marked with an X and containing a tiny six-paragraph leaflet, were found in Manchester, Leeds and (obscurely) Lytchett Minster. One woman shared two bars with her daughter and her pet dogs before discovering the leaflet. 'Chantle was petrified,' she said angrily, 'standing shaking with fear, waiting for something to happen.' A cruel hoax, as it turned out, but it didn't stop politicians acting as if hundreds had been slain. 'It beggars belief', said David Mellor, 'that these people are prepared to sacrifice children on the altar of their own fanaticism.'

Desperate to show the younger generation just how kind, decent and concerned they really were, other companies showered money on animals. Kids who collected wrappers from Nestlé Animal Bars could help raise ten thousand pounds for the Worldwide Fund for Nature.

In 1985, following Rowntree's refusal to answer a council questionnaire about employment of blacks, women and the disabled, Kit-Kat was banned by London's 'Loony Left' GLC. Henceforth, went the decree, no Kit-Kats or Fruit Pastilles would be sold in youth clubs, schools or GLC offices – an action reckoned to cost Rowntree's seventy thousand pounds.

But these all seem like tiffs compared to the Japanese experience. It started when the boss of a Tokyo confectionery firm was kidnapped from his bath and held to ransom for £4 million and 100kg of gold. Eventually he managed to escape. Soon afterwards, well timed to ruin everyone's St Valentine's Day, came a chilling announcement from 'the man with 21 faces'. Poisoned chocolates had been planted in several Tokyo stores. Of twelve boxes handed in to police, six were proved to contain cyanide. To be fair, though, they were labelled 'Contains Poison'.

Nor was the sabotage limited to chocolate. To Sanetsugu Tsuboi, the extra bottle of pop from a vending machine looked like a lucky bonus. Then he drank it. He was the seventh person to be poisoned, and since the other six had since died he was understandably worried.

The cat and mouse game went on into a second year, causing £25 million of lost sales, bankrupting five firms and resulting in the laying off of thousands of workers. Identikits of the gang leader – a cross between Mao and Carlos the Jackal – were issued, but despite two thousand officers working full time, no arrests were made. 'Even Sherlock Holmes couldn't catch us', taunted the gang. In honourable Japanese style, the policeman in charge of the case set fire to himself rather than face the shame of failure.

In Britain, when Nerds were withdrawn because of a 'dangerous alien substance', it looked as if events might take a similarly sinister turn. Nerds were meant to be colourful and sharp – but not with glass. Cut lips and stomach pains were the main effects, but things could have been worse. With tampering so much in the news, many jumped to the conclusion that it was sabotage, but no evidence could be found of it. It could have been consumer terrorism, or just a few kids larking about. One teenage girl had already been in court for writing 'these sweets are poisoned' on some boxes in her local supermarket.

All these experiences made companies paranoid. With production-line employees viewed as prime suspects whenever there was tampering or sabotage, the vigilance of the foreman was increasingly replaced by the silent all-seeing eye of CCTV.

There were worries of another kind, too. Increasingly fussy about their image, firms began to find out that hitherto uncomplicated deals could blow up in their faces, as when Cadbury's had to scrap its £2 million Fruit & Nut campaign following the *Sun*'s splash about Elton John's involvement in a gay orgy. Despite the singer winning his libel action against the tabloid, Cadbury's campaign was never revived.

But political awareness also encouraged firms to exploit current events. Photo-opportunities could be found all over the place. During the 1988 strike at Dover Docks, disgruntled truckers were showered with largesse – not just 'Sun birds' handing out free copies of the paper, but bars of Yorkie to sustain their energy.

1988 TOP THIRTY

1. Mars	16. Milky Way
2. Kit-Kat	17. Topic
3. Marathon	18. Dairy Milk
4. Wispa	19. Toffee Crisp
5. Polo	20. Caramel
6. Trebor Extra Strong Mints	21. Maltesers
7. Fruit Pastilles	22. Minstrels
8. Flake	23. Buttons
9. Rolo	24. Yorkie
10. Double Decker	25. Aero
11. Bounty	26. Fudge
12. Smarties	27. Turkish Delight
13. Boost	28. Treets
14. Mars King Size	29. Novo
15. Crunchie	30. Trebor XXX Mints

With eight products in this Top Thirty, Rowntree's was obviously a major player; and a happy one until the Swiss kid walked into the playground and started his bullying games. Nestlé (was its pathetic showing in those same charts the cause of a giant chip on the shoulder?) had a good look round, spoiling for a fight. Who should it be? Cadbury's looked a bit too muscular, and that Mars was a Yankee smartarse. How about the Rowntree's wimp in the corner, happily counting his Smarties? He'd do.

That's the colourful version. The real story of the takeover is made up of percentages, shareholdings and wheeler-dealing. Nestlé's first bid was £8.90 a share, including a staggering £1.5 billion for goodwill. Nestlé already owned 6.7 per cent of the York company, but Rowntree's were unwilling to sell. At first they had the backing of friendly shareholders – Prudential, Norwich Union and Jacob-Suchard, who'd recently increased their share of Rowntree's to 24 per cent.

Nestlé were determined. There was talk of Rowntree's making a defensive merger with Cadbury's, but the Bournville giants were themselves under threat from Nestlé. With hostile US shareholders who'd have been quite happy to sell out to Nestlé, Cadbury's threatened to sell themselves to Jacobs.

Nationalism played no small part in it all. Cadbury's and Rowntree's were both as British as Rolls-Royce or British Railways, part of the national psyche. Selling them off to foreigners was unthinkable. Yet there would have been some poetic justice. British firms weren't as sweet and innocent as they liked to make out. After their 1919 takeover, Cadbury's had allowed Fry's the dignity of their own name, but even Cadbury's finally succumbed to the all-important influence of brand in the mid-1980s. The remaining Fry's brands became Cadbury's brands (with Turkish Delight only keeping its Fry's tag to differentiate it from the bigger Cadbury's version). Rowntree-Mackintosh, who dropped the second half of their name and adopted a naff 'round tree' logo, were quite happy to bid for French firm Candice-Martial, which, for all we knew, could well have been as dear to the French as any of our firms were to us.

Rowntree's lobbied Parliament to have the Nestlé takeover bid referred to the Monopolies and Mergers Commission. In the end it all came down to whether Jacob-Suchard could resist Nestlé's increasingly generous offers. Nestlé got what they wanted in the end, for £2.55 billion, a final bid £10.75 per share: far too tempting for even the most loyal shareholders to resist. Rowntree's tasty 21 per cent of the British market was combined with Nestlé's paltry 2 per cent to give the foreign giant a virtual quarter of a deliciously profitable cake.

This looked like the shape of things to come – multinationalism, global brands, the essential sweetness of sweets no more important to the new barons than the romance of gold. But two of the old guard were still able to join forces – Needler's and Blue Bird – selling themselves, rather predictably perhaps, as the champions of 'Great British sweets'.

At the end of the 1980s a £250,000 survey to change Liquorice Allsort shapes heralded the arrival of a little Bertie Bassett one. Bertie B has been around since 1926. Looking for a trade mark, and noting the popularity of the Michelin Man at that time, Bassett's created something remarkably similar, an amiable Frankenstein's Monster of Liquorice Allsorts. In his first incarnation he resembled nothing so much as an animated petrol pump. Over the years he loosened up and could be seen boxing, playing football, swinging on a trapeze, even riding a motorbike in the Isle of Man TT. 'Never a dull moment with Bertie Bassett!' chuckled the ads. But a 1954 advert – 'Bertie's grand around the house!' – shows him looking vaguely sinister to my mind, more like a robot meddling with the electric wiring than the jolly mascot we know today.

It wasn't until the 1980s that Mr B acquired colour, along with such essentials as a hat and a walking stick, and finally, not before time, a face. Destined to become a TV favourite, too, Bertie seemed to have reached the pinnacle of his career. What more could anyone want? Well, the actor inside the rubbery suit went off to play Mr Blobby on *Noel's House Party*. Soon, given Bertie B's age, a Stannah stairlift and an OAP's bus pass will be essential accessories.[7]

---

7 Bertie lives on, you will be pleased to know, as a screensaver that brings cheer to even the glummest writer.

Magnum Force

1990s

Why is it always the same chocolates that are left over on Boxing Day? Do manufacturers still have the Victorian attitude that something nice must always come with something nasty? Or is it just that they've never bothered to find out that some centres are so boring no one likes them?

Times letter[1]

With chocolate ecus on sale at Rococo's, the posh sweet-shop in Chelsea's Kings Road, some people must have believed that monetary union had come a little closer. But no, for now, cocoa coinage would be as serious as it got. And the idea wasn't even that original: way back in 1970 Cadbury's brought out Decimal Coins – sticky bribes to help nervous citizens accept the penny's surrender to the pee. But for sweet-toothed Sloanies these edible ecus were the perfect novelty. Old money, Euro money, chocolate money – they were bound to have oodles, whatever form it took.

Not to be outdone, their poor relations up north invented a novelty of their own – the battered Mars Bar. A symbol of redneck pride, this crispy-coated chocolate turd

---

1 Another correspondent wrote in two days later with a simple, if heartless, suggestion: 'Give the hard centres to your kids.'

was a two-fingered response to all those lettuce-nibbling cissies down south. Reputed to have originated in Scotland, battered Mars Bar and chips – a reasonable 99p and fried in just thirty seconds – was the perfect after-pub supper. Also on this menu of defiance: deep-fried Yorkies, Snickers, Crunchies and – a sweet parallel to bite-sized scampi – battered Chewits.

As if to prove itself as serious food, not just a fast fix for boozers with the munchies, the BMB has since become a fixture on chip shop menus. To fans, it is as unremarkable as curry sauce or battered sausage – themselves looked on askance when first offered for sale. BMB could even be claimed as a regional speciality, like Perigord truffles or Black Forest gateau. Maybe Britain's chip shops really are at the cutting edge of hoi-polloi cuisine: additives aplenty, but guaranteed irony-free. All the same, it's worth asking how many chippie customers could stomach a BMB served up on the same polystyrene tray as a pickled egg or a splattering of mushy peas.

As the first confectionery to be offered in both deep-fried and frozen formats (as well as standard tepid), Mars had achieved a queer double. Mars Ice-Cream, introduced in 1989, claimed to be the first choc ice made with genuine milk chocolate instead of a flavoured coating. For whatever reasons, the public loved it and by 1993 first-year sales of £35 million had increased tenfold. But – and there was a big but – Mars was playing the cuckoo again. Just as Coca-Cola had objected to ordinary Mars Bars chilling out in the same coolers as their cans, so Wall's got awfully shirty about the ice-cream version rubbing frost with Feast and Dream in the freezers they had spent £20 million installing in fifty thousand shops. From now on, all rival ices would be banned. Any shopkeepers found stocking Mars Ice-Creams would have to forfeit their freezers.

The Mars Bar – celebrating its sixty-fifth anniversary in 1997 – has always had a knack of getting itself in the news. In the 1960s, following a drugs bust at the mansion of

Rolling Stone Keith Richards, unchivalrous rumours began to circulate about Marianne Faithfull and a Mars Bar. Barely worth repeating, this was one urban myth that proved nothing about Marianne but plenty about the smutty obsessions of Sunday newspaper readers. Celebrity endorsement was always welcome, even from bad boys like the Rolling Stones, but Ms Faithfull's Mars Bar was one plug unlikely to be found in the company's official book of press cuttings. Nor, from thirty years later, the stories about a schoolteacher who caused a ruckus after allegedly using a Mars Bar to demonstrate certain oral sex techniques to a class of baffled 10-year-olds. Yet, in both cases, one is left with an impression that it was the *misuse* of a Mars Bar that upset people far more than any alleged improprieties; sin being a dozen times magnified by using such a venerable and blameless item as an accessory. It was as sick as swigging Special Brew from a chalice, as monstrous as strapping a hamster to a Catherine wheel.

Rock stars and randy teachers notwithstanding, even at snobby Ascot the Mars Bar curse was at work. In 1987 a winning horse, Tied Cottage, was disqualified after someone grassed on his jockey for giving him a pre-race Mars Bar to chomp. Theobromine gave a magical buzz, so chocophiles believed, and these claims were taken seriously enough for the Jockey Club to include chocolate on their list of prohibited stimulants. Because of the extra energy? Or due to its alleged aphrodisiac qualities? Maybe they feared that Tied Cottage would get so worked up he would veer off the racetrack and head straight for the nearest stud farm.

Fearsome magic indeed. Some sports fans even credited the bar with mind-altering properties. After his defection to Spurs, self-confessed Mars fan Gazza was bombarded by Mars Bars – one of which had a small rock inside, no doubt in the hope of knocking some sense into the lad.

Though Mars, for better or worse, had become part of British culture, there were plenty who challenged its hallowed status. That 'Mars a Day …' slogan for a start. Having learned the words by rote, most people happily accepted them as fact, but it was a blatant lie according to a group styling itself Action and Information on Sugars. They demanded it be changed. Work or play might be helped along by its carbohydrates, they grudgingly admitted – but no way could anyone prove that a Mars Bar aided rest. In response, the company coolly pointed out that their bar complied with all official guidelines and, after fourteen months weighing up the opposing claims, the Advertising Standards Authority finally reapproved the slogan.[2]

Hostilities between the USA and USSR had been replaced by continuing battles between industry and consumer groups. And, as in the Cold War, many shadowy organizations were involved in the spread of propaganda and disinformation. The augustly named Princeton Dental Resource Center, for instance, publishers of *Dental News*, a magazine aimed at patients caught in dentists' waiting rooms – though how many of them wanted to swot up on gory dental details while they awaited fillings and drillings is anyone's guess. Those who did were told, on the best scientific authority, that consumption of cocoa could actually slow down the build-up of plaque and inhibit development of cavities. *Dental News* was never going to be a big seller, but since the magazine was generously subsidized by Mars someone must have believed that, in the long term, publication would more than repay the funding.

Adverts for a 32lb Mars Bar, far from making people wary, only had them rushing to the shops to buy one.[3] Revealed as an April Fool joke, there were thousands who wished it

---

2 A year later, despite more protests from AIS and the Health Education Authority, Mars were also allowed to carry on with their 'sweet you can eat between meals' claim for Milky Way. With a modest 116 calories in it, a Milky Way would be burned up within ninety minutes by any averagely active child.
3 *Daily Telegraph* 16 April 1992.

hadn't been … Greed, a yuppie pose in the 1980s, had become part of everyday life. Though we had some way to go to rival our American cousins in the fat-arse department, we were getting noticeably weightier. Our fondness for confectionery had to take part of the blame. In 1993 the Department of Health, under the auspices of Virginia Bottomley, issued guidelines for a healthier, slimline lifestyle – including a recommended maximum of three boiled sweets per week. Those who thought they'd seen the last of rationing in the 1950s could scarcely believe it. That civil liberties could be threatened in such a way was bad enough – but three sweets a week was plain ridiculous. Some people ate three a minute. Schoolkids ate three at a time. Adherence to the guidelines might have eased strains on the NHS budget, but thousands would have been thrown on the dole.

Supermarkets played a significant part in the industry's expansionism. With more people shopping in bulk, it made sense that confectionery purchases were correspondingly bigger. Down the confectionery aisle, Rolos were rarely sold by the roll, but in five-packs. Tenpenny Chomp Bars were a rare sight, but there were whole racks of £1.50 bars of Lindt. To save shamed-faces at the checkout, these giant nine-inch blocks of chocolate were euphemistically labelled 'family-size' – but they were, for many, selfish pleasures, part of the new pornography of confectionery. Parallels are easily made: a guarded guilty purchase, followed by a personal act. Pleasant enough, granted, but one which leaves a sense of something missing, pleasures unshared. At the end of the day, one person disposing of a giant Yorkie or unshared chocolate orange is nothing more than sweet onanism.

Yet, as fast as things move, it remains important to keep a grip on the past. While Spangles, Polos, Munchies and Aztecs have been prized by accountants as valuable assets, the rest of us cherish them as part of our heritage. Nothing bugs us more than seeing these favourites tampered with. In

March 1998 Opal Fruits became Starburst. Mars had done it before, changing Marathon to Snickers and Treets to M&Ms, so though howls of protest (and even a leader in *The Times*) were inevitable, the noise was half-hearted, already muted by weary acceptance. Big business could do what it wanted. If Mars were willing to spend millions on PR magicians and rebrand merchants, what chance did a bunch of sentimentalists stand? Nostalgia had no place in the global marketplace. We'd get used to Starburst, just as we did to Snickers, and in a year no one would think twice about it. Starburst[4] would still be Opal Fruits, and if Mars wanted us to think we shared our taste for them with a bunch of slitty-eyed aliens, doubtless they had reasons. All the same, it seemed a long way from the day out in the family saloon, Dad at the wheel, hot and bothered kids, and Mum handing round the sweets that were made to make our mouths water.

1997 TOP THIRTY

1. *Kit-Kat*		16. *Crunchie*	
2. *Mars Bar*		17. *Time Out*	
3. *Dairy Milk*		18. *Orbit*	
4. *Roses*		19. *Fuse*	
5. *Twix*		20. *Cadbury's Fruit & Nut*	
6. *Wrigley's Extra*		21. *Bounty*	
7. *Quality Street*		22. *Trebor Extra Strong Mints*	
8. *Snickers*		23. *Milky Bar*	
9. *Maltesers*		24. *Trebor Soft Mints*	
10. *Galaxy*		25. *Milk Tray*	
11. *Aero*		26. *Whole Nut*	
12. *Milky Way*		27. *Fruit Pastilles*	
13. *Polo Mints*		28. *After Eight*	
14. *Wispa*		29. *Cadbury's Caramel*	
15. *Smarties*		30. *Maynard's Wine Gums*	

---

4 No matter how much Mars tried to distance itself from the world of outer space and UFOs – it was only the founder's name for heaven's sake – they kept coming back with these subliminal references.

A hundred years back new products arrived in the shops every week. Someone, somewhere, an unknown man with a long white apron and sugar-scalded fingers, had the job of inventing sweet surprises for children. No Santa Claus, he might even have hated kids, but their pennies paid his wages and his livelihood depended on keeping them amused. Really, it was not kindliness, but the beginning of the commercialization of childhood. As soon as men learned they could make money from kids (without the need to enslave them as chimney sweeps) childhood could never again be the same land. It was a colonized country. From toffee strips to England team strips, the rest was inevitable. Children furnish too many riches to be allowed to stop being consumers ...

In 1912, it took a very large hall to house all the treasures of the confectionery industry. Today it would all fit on a long counter. Choice is a buzzword, but choice is relative. Compared with the thousands of lines even thirty years ago, today's world of confectionery looks standardized. Yet, we have to ask, how could so many lines have co-existed anyway? When dozens of new sweets and choc bars were hitting the counters every month, how could any shop have found room to stock them all? It was just down to a Darwinian survival of the fittest. But, if that were strictly true, why have so many good ideas and delicious tastes been allowed to go extinct?

Having looked at a century's worth of press cuttings, it was easy to work out that, as far as some firms were concerned, I knew more about their past than many of their own directors did. Confectionery's history has always been a shallow one. Snobs might say that confectionery is a shallow subject itself, but that is not the reason. An ephemeral nature is is vastly useful in the world of marketing. Short memories and ignorance help gloss over the embarrassing fact that nothing is new. It's all been done before. Repeats are as common on the sweet counter as they are on the TV. No one minds too much, even if they know. But it's never done openly. Manufacturers would love us all to admire them as smart, streetwise and endlessly creative.

We loved Polos, because they were so English. Who else but a national of lovable eccentrics could have thought of a mint with a hole? But its uniqueness was illusory, another rewrite of history. Cribbed from the American Lifesavers, Polo was just one of several such copies – Ring Mints and Swizzel's Navy Mints being just two. Despite having no great edge on them tastewise, Polo can at least congratulate itself on seeing off these rivals. But, despite the arrival of Sugar-free Polos in 1993, Polo's minty pre-eminence could no longer be taken for granted.[5] In that same year Trebor Extra Strong took over the number one spot from the Holey One, with Softmints in third place. In desperation Nestlé launched spearmint and extra-strong Polos. If part of Polo's charm had been its uniqueness, now there were so many varieties you didn't know which was which.

'Limited editions' are similarly manipulative. Much publicity is extracted from items like Mint Crunchie – yet Mint Crunchies can be dated back to 1971. People can't be blamed for not remembering the sweets of the 1920s, but Rowntree's Body Parts – which Nestlé have the nerve to crow about being original in June 1998 – appear to be little different from Barratt's Transplanters which kids were cannibalistically nibbling in the mid-1980s.

Though the principles are alarmingly simple, few people have ever bothered making confectionery at home.

---

5 Actor Sir John Mills was among several victims of a cowboy asphalting gang who went from house to house offering to resurface driveways. When one customer complained that he'd requested white flecks in his asphalt, one of the gang was dispatched to the nearest newsagent's to buy a dozen packets of Polos. Smashed into small pieces, these were tossed down and rolled into the asphalt. The effect was apparently pleasing and the customer, unaware of the unorthodox artistry, happily handed over a cheque for work done. Happy, that is, until it rained and the Polos dissolved into a sticky white mess.

Cookery programmes, of which nineties folk seem obsessively fond, rarely touch on the subject of confectionery, as if scared of challenging the sugar wizards in case they take offence and withdraw their favours. Perhaps such practices would be seen as a mark of poverty, rather like making one's own clothes. We feel rich enough to pay for our confectionery, for the convenience of it, rather than waste our time making misshapen attempts at wine gums or marshmallows. Or is it more complicated than that, more deep-seated, tangled in psychological imperatives? We expect (were always brought up to expect) confectionery to be provided. Whether from parents, friends or lovers, it has to be a gift, a sign of affection. Even when we buy it for ourselves, as a self-indulgent treat, we expect it to be handy, pre-packed, a pre-chosen recipe.

Though many would say that creativity in confectionery peaked decades ago, it would be foolish to predict that it's come to a dead end. In their heyday Fry's, Cadbury's and Rowntree's might have launched about twenty or thirty new lines each and every year – profligacy which is now viewed with disdain. Big business, serious money, negotiable shares – confectionery employs fifty thousand people, from factory girls to grown men who sweat it out in hotel conference suites (no pun intended), pencil at the ready, trying to look serious as they discuss the thickness of chocolate bars and the thickness of those willing to pay through the nose for them. Compromise is the key word. The most recent examples, Cadbury's Fuse and Nestlé's Maverick, are perfect examples of design by committee. Every minority group must have its say – the crunchers, the suckers, the nibblers, the fruit freaks and nut fans, not to mention the human pelicans who can swallow a Fuse in one mouthful. Willy Wonka's team this isn't: the talk is not of sweeties and love, but of units, couvertures and sales throughput. Never mind convincing the kids; first you have to sell the idea to bankers and shareholders and for that kind of high-level salesmanship fancy language is a prerequisite. Strollers is not just a packet of sweets. Oh no, it has been designed to offer adults a 'functional eat'. Nineteenth-century language, though quaint and elaborate by today's standards, did at least possess some degree of clarity. Modern marketing speak, on analysis, is virtually meaningless.

Non-melting chocolate may not seem like one of the military machine's most pressing needs, but today's soldiers are a great deal more fussy than their predecessors.[6] Invented by scientists from Geneva and designed specially for US troops during the Gulf War, this chocolate was designed to resist drooping at temperatures up to 140°. Were that an end of it, but the technology excited those marketers who loved to promote food as playthings. So, after peelable cheese and aerosol cream, kids are to get chocolate that bends into any number of shapes.

Can it go on for ever? There are only so many flavours, a limited number of textures, and so many combinations of each. Doubtless the future will yield sweet horrors of its own. With genetic manipulation we may yet get flavours that don't even exist in nature but which will have our mouths watering preternaturally ... The possibilities are endless and, with all the profits at stake, food and confectionery scientists are no doubt already busy with their test-tubes and microscopes.

The 1881 recipe for Rowntree's Fruit Pastilles was, like so many winning formulae, the result of trial and error ... and a few words of advice from a passing Frenchman. In 1996, not content with this succulent serendipity, an unholy alliance of Nestlé, the Ministry of Agriculture and scientists from the Applied Biology Department of York

---

6 Most of the chocolate sent by Queen Victoria to Boer War soldiers melted, but they were probably too loyal to complain. Small wonder, perhaps, that so much of it found its way back to the UK to be unearthed by proud relatives in later years.

University set about uncovering the secrets. Nuclear magnetic resonance, capillary electrophoresis and microsampling were just some of the indignities to which the poor sweetie was subjected in an attempt to reduce its tastiness to a pageful of boring chemical annotations. Who were these white-coated men muttering about the pastille's biopolymer mixture and its pleasurable oral reception? No self-respecting scientist would write, 'Tastes nice,' because two words would never fill a research paper.

Fruit Pastilles, after a largely fuss-free century, seemed to be hitting the headlines far too often for comfort. And, as if suffering from Mars syndrome by proxy, none of it was anything to be proud of. In Hull, during the Scottish Ballet's performance of *Sleeping Beauty*, a Fruit Pastille lobbed from the balcony nearly brought the show to a halt. A violinist in the trajectory was enraged by the damage caused to his instrument. Mere japes, though, compared with what was to come ...

After twenty-eight years, Myra Hindley left prison on day release. The first thing she stopped to buy were two packs of sweets: Magic Mints and Fruit Pastilles. Oh, if only the Fruit Pastille fan had been Michael Jackson or Posh Spice or Madonna, PR folk would have broken out the champers. But 'Moors Murderer Picks Pastilles!' was one endorsement no manufacturer welcomed.

Could it get any worse? How about a drugs 'n' religion scandal? Halfway through a droning recital from Exodus, a Bristol RE teacher suddenly went doo-lally, flinging books around the classroom and climbing up the walls. Sir, who had a reputation for cadging sweets from pupils, had been given a Fruit Pastille spiked with LSD – an end-of-term treat from one of the girls in his class. He was rushed to hospital and given charcoal to counteract the effects. 'Did you have a nice trip, sir?' they asked on his return, no doubt laughing at their neat subversion of the old saw about schoolgirls taking sweets from strange men.

Before health concerns nudged Wrigley's sugar-free Extra to the number one spot, Fruit Pastilles had been Britain's top-selling sweets. Until the mad cow scare of 1996 few people had ever considered the animal content of their sweeties. Gelatine – made from cows' bones – had provided the chewiness in everything from jelly babies to fruit pastilles and dozens of penny-tray novelties like wriggly snakes and imitation fried eggs. Kids had been eating it by the ton for decades. Companies had made fortunes from it. In the 1920s the gelatine works of T.M. Duche – end of the line for thousands of knackered farm animals every year – was another of those marvellous palaces of confectionery, a small city state with railway sidings and quayside. But, now we'd all yucked at news pictures of gelatine being extruded, any gelatine company would be staring ruin in the face. That poisoned gunk had been in our children's sweets all this time?

In the USA, Smarties, Dolly Mixtures, Fruit Pastilles and Refreshers were all banned because of their dyes – E104 quinoline yellow and E122 carmoisine. Smarties may still have believed they had the answer – but America's Surgeon-General had the diagnosis – skin rashes and asthma – just a couple of Smarties' alleged side-effects. The ban came as quite a shock for the hundreds of ex-pats who relied on a weekly ration of Smarties for a comforting taste of home. Rowntree's defended themselves by saying the seized sweets had to be imports from a third country. 'It's an emotional reaction,' said one champion of the British favourites. 'It's not a toxicological problem.'

Canada joined in by banishing Fruit Pastilles – not because of nastiness in any of the ingredients but because the wrapping failed to list them in French; an ironic oversight, considering the company's new masters ...

British firms had learned many of the secrets of sweet- and chocolate-making from foreigners. During the 1880s, for instance, Cadbury's and Rowntree's both hired Frenchmen as pastille supremos and, right until the outbreak of World War Two, itinerant confectioners still came to Britain looking for work. But where a Frenchman's advice on fruit pastilles or chocolate might once have been welcome, today such comment is angrily spurned. In the Sweetie '94 trade fair a Bruges firm exhibiting its marzipan potatoes lost no opportunity to slag off the low standards of British marzipan – just the kind of criticism that invokes tabloid wrath. With that easy-going entente long gone, replaced by international brand rivalries and trade hostilities, patriotism has been co-opted in the service of corporate PR. Most steeped in chauvinism, the one subject that causes more squabbling than anything else is chocolate. And, where friendly joshing fails, legal action becomes the only option left to put the British in their place.

In 1997 Chocosuisse began legal action to stop Cadbury's selling a bar called Swiss Chalet.[7] Though the name implied that the chocolate was 'Continental', it was, in fact, made in Britain and had too high a percentage of vegetable fats to conform to European standards. Chocosuisse were understandably resentful of this 'passing off', especially since Cadbury's had previously given a solemn undertaking not to use the word Swiss in any of their products.[8] 'Would we launch a whisky and call it Scottish Castle?' asked a Chocosuisse spokesman.

Cadbury's game was hard to understand. They'd spent years trying to create chocolate as good as the Swiss and French versions, and had come up with a good enough version to please the British palate. Why, then, when Dairy Milk was vigorously defended as delicious, was it necessary to resort to low tricks? Why the need to pretend it was Swiss? Because, while patriots defended British chocolate merely

---

7 Lindt UK had already marketed a British-made Easter egg called Swiss Chalet. No one mentioned that Swiss Chalet is a stupid name for a chocolate bar, and even stupider for an Easter Egg. Swiss Hen Coop might have been more apt.
8 *Daily Mail* 3 December 1995.

because it was British and they'd grown up with it, those who deemed themselves arbiters of taste (Fifth Columnists, others might say) dismissed Dairy Milk as a so-so substitute and were increasingly successful in converting the masses to the Continental version. Swiss Chalet was Cadbury's bid to win them back.

Had things got out of hand, it might have turned into Chocolate Wars, as exciting for Little Englanders as the Falklands or 1973's Cod War. Switzerland v. Britain? We'd smash 'em! And once we might have done just that, but it was just a gung-ho fantasy. Now such tiffs were all sorted out by a posse of Euro-lawyers. Anyway, how could we have got our gunboats stationed off Switzerland?

It doesn't seem so long ago that anyone of school-leaving age might have regarded sweets and ice-lollies as uncool. Fine for kids and grannies, but not for those enjoying post-GCE days, rites of passage times that were pre-booked long ago for an orgy of beer, ciggies and sex. Those who clung to childish habits would be ragged mercilessly. What was the point of wearing shades and Levi's if girls could catch you unawares dipping into a bag of sherbet? Or sucking on a fruit gum for comfort?

Whether it's down to slick marketing or an extension of dependence is debatable, but the whole cultural axis of confectionery has undoubtedly shifted in the last twenty years. Calippo, an ice-lolly that twenty years ago would have been a between-times treat for trainspotters is now aimed directly at style-conscious youth. Before sophisticated irony became *à la mode*, manufacturers would probably just have reworked a line from those old Pontefract cake ads:

CALIPPO!
STUDENTS LOVE 'EM!
THEY ARE THE TEENAGER'S LOLLY!

But it doesn't work that way any more. Mars, Snickers, Topic, a range of otherwise unremarkable choc bars and biscuits come pre-loaded with notions. Their appeal, for young people at least, is less to do with taste than how they define you as a person. Twix, a regular in my snack box when I worked in a wellington-boot factory, now sells itself as 'a break from the norm' – with Norm cleverly personified as a teenager's nightmare of grey conformity, and those who buy Twix as carefree rebels. Twix? We are talking about a choc biscuit, remember, a bit of granny's shortcake, enhanced by a strip of caramel goo that sticks to the chin like congealed gravy. Levi's as a symbol of rebellion I can live with, but Twix as a badge of streetwise nonconformity?

Ice-lollies like Magnum and Solero, if not part of the sexual act itself (and TV ads can only go so far), are suggested as part of foreplay. Tongues dart out to catch flakes of chocolate, the lolly is slipped between the lips with lascivious pleasure. But they're still just ice-lollies. Official marketing terminology may have fancy words for it, but Magnum and Feast are little different in their basic format to Woppa, Fab or Luv. Delicious and sexy as it is, what is Solero but an updated version of the old Cornish Mivvi?

But PMT (post-modern trickery) wasn't used only on the young. Maltesers, which had always targeted their 'less-fattening centres' at women, now turned their attentions to the increasingly vain male market. A TV ad featured a team of footballers finding a box in a team-mate's locker – a discovery which sixty years previously might have led a man to enlisting in the Foreign Legion to escape the shame.

Even fizz has a cool image these days. Ever since Daley Thompson swigged Lucozade on telly it's been associated with speed and energy.[9] Not just sporty, but *isotonic*. Lucozade, sporty? To those of a certain age it must appear as convincing as a pensioner sticking go-faster stripes on his Zimmer. For us, steadfast against revisionism, Lucozade

---

9 Lucozade's NRG is a neat name, but far from original. Barratt's thought of it forty years ago for use on a range of boiled sweets.

will forever be associated with sodden tissues, Beecham's Powders and the smell of hot-water bottles. The only fun thing about it was the crackly yellow cellophane the bottle came wrapped in. Peer through it and it made your mum look like she'd just come in from a hard day at the nuclear reprocessing plant.

Today's Lucozade lovers would surely pooh-pooh the idea that cocoa was once pushed as the sportsman's favourite tipple – 'Increased muscular strength, staying power and sustenance against fatigue' being among its benefits – claims that would be hard to get past the tough guys at today's Advertising Standards Agency.[10]

Even an old favourite like Dandelion and Burdock could be reinvented, though with less success. Seeing it fall from favour during the 1970s, Barr's relaunched it in 1982, updated and repackaged as the trendy but slightly less imaginative D&B. 'It's a matter of taste,' said their adverts, challenging a new generation to adopt it, but perhaps forgetting that half of the pop's appeal came from its peculiar name. Dandelion and Burdock – crazy name, crazy pop – smacked of *Just William* adventures, sitting on level-crossing gates watching steam trains or having a dog named Bongo. D&B sounded like nothing so much as a very small advertising agency.

Even the most expensive facelift always ends with a dismaying snap. In time Lucozade will revert to being old fashioned and fashionable tin-swiggers will switch their allegiances to something else.

Dandelion and Burdock survives, as a nod towards a nostalgia market, but there are no dandelions or burdock in it; were there ever? Confectionery had a gloriously eccentric history, but the ingredients have now been sanitized. Cayenne, pine tar, chlorodyne – all gone the

---

10 Though they were quite happy to go along with the laughable fiction that Lucozade was a favourite tipple of those 1960s mods who scootered down to Brighton on bank-holiday weekends.

same way as paraffin wax, wiped out by all kinds of rules and regulations. Sweets are as good and wholesomely sterile as it is possible to be. Though I have heard that colts-foot rock lingers on, we'd never go for anything as oddly named as Horehound Tablets. Splintery liquorice sticks are only a memory, as are chlorodyne pastilles, banned as far back as the 1960s.

Apart from a few old stand-bys like Tunes, Hacks and Hall's Mentho-Lyptus, the connection between confectionery and medication seems to have been severed. Medicinal claims would never get past the Advertising Standards people. Who but a few OAPs would give credence to quaint-sounding nostrums like Old Mother Betty's Herbal Balls or Uncle Jack's Klorodyne Koffers when they have slickly marketed cures like Beecham's Hot Lemon or Night Nurse?

Yet, though banned from the packaging, wild claims still do the rounds on a regular basis. Liquorice, at least according to a 1997 survey in Chicago, is one of the top turn-on smells for women. Bertie Bassett needs no help from Paco Rabanne, he only has to walk down Main Street, Pittsburgh, and women faint with desire. Catching a whiff of liquorice – and again this is according to scientists who endorsed the survey – increased blood flow to 'sexual areas' by 14 per cent (how did they measure?). Since an extra 10 per cent would be regarded as exceptionally randy, 14 per cent is going some. But really, the idea is tacky enough for the plot of a porno film – a woman driven mad by desire, rolling naked on a squeaking carpet of Liquorice Allsorts. If such claims were true, would these innocuous sweeties be sold in the Canterbury Cathedral gift shop?

Dangerous myths. According to research by a team of Kiwi doctors, regular consumption of liquorice, far from stimulating the parts Viagra cannot reach, causes drastic chemical changes. Swollen ankles and weight increase were just the start for volunteers who agreed to eat four to eight ounces a day for several weeks. Their potassium levels dropped, they had an imbalance of sodium, and hormonal control of body fluids fluctuated wildly. Some threw in the towel, complaining of soreness, headaches and loss of energy. Whew! If Bertie is seen in Out Patients we'll know why.

Even more curious myths occasionally surface, such as one that suggested blackcurrant and liquorice sweets as a cure for Parkinson's disease.

Following the end of East–West tension, various governments opened up their secret bunkers for the media to have a nose. As well showing us the sad steel bedsteads our rulers would have slept in, it was revealed that Britain's command centres had stockpiles of sweets and chocolates. Since they could hardly be planning a kiddies' party with Boo-Boo the Clown, one can only assume this confectionery was intended for adult comfort. Perhaps some civil servant had a hazy notion that Victory V lozenges would be perfect in all kinds of winter, nuclear or merely frosty. Atomic war was always going to be a no-win situation, but the idea of seeing out the final days of human history while nibbling Turkish Delights and Double Deckers is so mad it looks quite logical. Would mankind's last picnic really have been a Cadbury's one?

The idea of sweets as an Armageddon treat isn't so far fetched. Sweets have always had a sinister dimension. A hundred years ago kids were regularly poisoned by rogue traders and, despite a century of warnings, children will still take them from strangers. Like the 12-year-old lured from Croydon station who ended up being kidnapped and bundled into a trunk, found by police only in the luckiest of circumstances.

Sweets can break your heart, too. Hounded by the Child Support Agency, a desperate father who'd decided to end it all handed out sweets to his four children before connecting a hosepipe to the car exhaust and taking them all to a place where no civil servants live. A young mum was murdered as she went to buy sweets for her child. Two little girls were knocked and killed down by a hit-and-run driver on their way home from the sweetshop. To hear of anyone dying on such innocent errands is more than we can bear. And to hear of an old lady robbed of her 81p sweets money while visiting her husband's grave angers us more than any Brinks-Mat job.[11]

Luckily it's not all grim. There are touching moments that help to mend the heart: a boy with a two thousand-pound bionic arm learning to unwrap sweets for the first time. And incidents that just make us smile: a housewife and mother of four in court accused of seducing a 12-year-old boy was alleged to have secured his co-operation with an offer of sweets. One can only wonder about the necessity for a bribe. Either the lady was decidedly unattractive, or the boy was exceedingly slow-witted and hardly typical.

Confectionery's top fifty brands account for 60 per cent of confectionery sales. To this old socialist, it is strangely reminiscent of the old one about 5 per cent of the population owning 95 per cent of its wealth. But Cadbury's, despite its mammoth size, can still trade on its past and secure itself a place in national affections. Its sponsorship of *Coronation Street* was an inspired stroke. Despite us quickly accepting this kind of sponsorship as inevitable, it is ironic that no character in *Coronation Street* would ever be allowed to go into the Kabin and say anything as ordinary as, 'A packet of Polos, please, Rita.'

And all because ... the lady loves her flat too much to move out. Ousted Milk Tray Man, actor Graham Rogers, appeared in court on a charge of harassing the female tenant of his flat, which he was desperate to sell in order to clear his sixty-thousand-pound debts. As if getting sinisterly unsigned letterheads from 'The Concrete Company'

---

11 Most recently, Dutch soldiers in Bosnia, charged with uncovering landmines, were accused of tossing sweets into suspect areas and telling local kids to go in and fetch them.

wasn't enough to put the wind up her, he broke in and trashed the bath, lavatory and washbasin. During the night, in classic Milk Tray Man style, he climbed up on the roof – but then spoiled the image by shouting abuse through the skylight. Finally, while his tenant was out shopping, he dumped her furniture on the pavement and boarded up the windows.

As punishment, Rogers received a hundred hours' community service, with two thousand pounds costs. His thirty-thousand-pound contract with Cadbury's went out of the window – in much the same way as he had once done so dramatically. 'I'm happy with the verdict,' he said stoically. 'Community service is all the rage now.'

It was all spookily prescient. After some twenty-six years of habitual risk-taking, Milk Tray Man had become out of date. Women now preferred a caring Nineties man, at least according to yet another survey. Speedboating, helicoptering, abseiling – all were frowned on. And, at the end of the day, wasn't there something rather unsettling about a man in a black jumper climbing through a woman's bedroom window and leaving things. What else might he do? Rummage through the underwear drawer? Rightly suspicious, Nineties woman wanted more eye contact, more commitment, more presence. Out went the black polo neck and in came a fluffy white jumper. A new actor – RSC and Cambridge Blue – was hired, one who was awarded top marks in an attractiveness test.

Until they take on sponsorship of a fluffy programme like *Children's Hospital* or *Vets In Practice*, Nestlé will never secure itself a place in our affections. Despite 'owning' priceless brands like Milky Bar, Fruit Gums and Yorkie, Nestlé have always come across as a faceless multinational: distant, icy and secretive, as fondly regarded as the CIA or Swiss bankers. At some point during the 1990s Nestlé began to insist that Britain treat them with the respect they deserved, complete with accent. To generations of kids and

– more tellingly – even in its own TV ads it had always been 'Nessles'. Now they'd done away with Rowntree's and Mackintosh's they could get their own back for those decades of pretending to be British.

By 1993 the Rowntree-Mackintosh name had all but been abandoned. Just as Burton's once promised to retain the MacDonald's by-line on Penguins, so Nestlé quietly sidelined the once proud sweet-makers' names. Rowntree's? 'It's just a division of Nestlé,' said a spokesman airily. Our old favourites have become Nestlé Kit-Kat, Nestlé Polo, Nestlé Aero and Nestlé Smarties. To be fair, they have retained the names on Rowntree's Fruit Pastilles and Fox's Glacier Mints – but only because the brands are too entrenched in our minds to risk change and controversy.

Poor Nestlé, the target of more hyperspace hatred than any other firm. Tap the letters into Infoseek and it almost snarls back at you – 1799 sites, and half of them derogatory. Even in Magyar and Finnish, peppered with dashes and circumflexes, you can sense the anger. Why didn't Nestlé stick to selling Milky Bars instead of enticing kids from their mother's breasts with baby-milk formula?

In 1994 Nathan Brandy, a black boy from Nottingham, was barred from becoming the Milky Bar Kid. Racism! shouted Equity. 'A kid is a kid, irrespective of pigment,' protested the city's mayor. 'Why invite all-comers to the audition if you're going to be so choosy? It's time something was done to change these stereotypes.'

Nestlé were unrepentant, even bolshy. 'That's what the Milky Bar Kid looks like and there's no reason to change it. Just as Mickey Mouse looks like Mickey Mouse, you can't go around changing a brand character who's been around for thirty years.'

They may have had a point, but if mascots had to be portrayed as literal embodiments, cynics wanted to know why Black Magic had never been advertised by anyone of Afro-Caribbean origin. Were Nestlé really guilty of racism?

They'd certainly had no qualms about using black folk in Milky Bar promotions of the past. 'Has yo enough stocks of Milky Bar, Mistah Retailah?' asks a top-hatted minstrel in one of their 1950s adverts.

The Internet has brought a whole new dimension to confectionery. You can't actually learn much, of course, but you can dip into a global pick 'n' mix of PR hype, useless statistics and corporate pride masquerading as information. Who cares that 73 per cent of Maltesers are shared with others? How did they arrive at such a precise figure? And why do firms always fall back on useless facts like, '47 Milky Bar Buttons are eaten in the UK per second', or that each day's production of Mars Bars, laid end to end, would stretch from Henley-on-Thames to Aix-en-Provence. (I made that one up, but it's no more odd than the rest of the hundred or so variations on the same formula.)

A wacky story is always *de rigueur*, like Mars' claim that Maltesers were used to replace lost marbles during the world championships. Possible – but a World Marble Championships without any spare marbles seems, at the least, badly organized. And surely such improvisation would be against the rules. Would Tim Henman be allowed to use a Terry's Chocolate Orange if he lost his balls during Wimbledon? Mars also proudly point to their eponymous bar being used as part of British Rail's emergency packs. But since BR is no longer with us and there is no centralized control, that one must be out-of-date. Perhaps privatized companies have made similar arrangements. Do Virgin Cross Country give their accident victims Walnut Whips, or Great Western put their faith in the restorative properties of Crunchie?

There's a Smarties Tarot, accompanied with a thoughtful warning that the black ones don't really signify death, as if the blue ones do really signify a romance in the offing! More fun is the Payne's Poppets website, where my kids can run up massive phone bills while they play confectionery's equivalent of Space Invaders – trying to gobble up a veritable meteor shower of delicious Poppets. Meanwhile, the Science Museum of Minnesota website hosts a game along the lines of Name That Bar – with a series of brown-hued cross-sections that look rather too much like specimens fished from the Paris sewers.

We've been eating sweets for six centuries now. In 1317, during a pilgrimage to Canterbury, Princess Mary consoled herself with five and a half pounds of sugar tablets and eight and a half pounds of rose sugar of honey. Other sweetmeats she might have availed herself of included preserved ginger, citronade candy and penydes (made from pine cones). She would have been one of the select few to enjoy such delicacies, though, as, back then, sugar was expensive stuff, hardly for peasants. The hoi-polloi had to wait a few more centuries to acquire the taste.

But, despite the long history – the developments, invention and innovation – despite the marketing trickery, changing social attitudes and corporate takeovers, when you get right down to it, though the form may have changed in essence, it is the same stuff and our relationship to it has hardly altered. Style changes but function remains the same. We are still feeding our faces, bribing our children, saying sorry to our spouses, making ourselves feel better.

Nothing changes. Having considered rounding off the book with some sort of sociological flourish, I eventually decided against it. Far more interesting to end with a few recent stories, for readers to make of what they will ...

Nothing changes. 'Gum-chewing gives an impression of mindlessness,' said oracle Drusilla Beyfus, author of *Good Manners*. Watching the bovine expressions of many gum-chewers, you can see her point. Doesn't continual chewing lead to some kind of RSI? Marketing men disagree: gum stimulates the brain. Though allegedly the chosen chew of smart airline pilots and daring rally drivers, it's hard to imagine poets or philosophers chewing gum. Nor does it fit in with the composing of ballet scores. No, the only brains stimulated by gum-chewing are those of joyriders and burglars. It's part of the kit, a ready-made mould in which to press stolen keys.[12] Even our youngest are not immune – like the lad caught cheating in his school's egg-and-spoon race by using gum to stick the egg to the spoon.

Nothing changes. To prevent spluttering during quiet passages, the Hallé Orchestra issued cough sweets to its audiences.[13] They even found one with the least rustling paper. It's a problem that typifies the unchanging dynamics of confectionery. In the 1930s, in an effort to stop Bradford churchgoers coughing their way through the vicar's best sermons, they were offered free lozenges and humbugs. Wardens, hovering with a tray, rushed in at the first sign of an attack. The practice was stopped after a couple of weeks due to scroungers. Amazingly, some of the congregation were coughing just to get themselves a free sweet.

Nothing changes. Though few confectionery workers now take early retirement with mouldy fingernails or blue faces, occasional dramas still occur at the coal-face. Tapping out the headline 'Death by Aero' would make a sub-editor's day, even if it was hardly much fun for the deceased. Rowntree's worker Alex Smith narrowly escaped a literally sticky end after falling into an eight-foot-deep mixing vat at the York factory. Spun repeatedly in a revolving drum, spanked by rotating paddles, poor Alex would certainly have copped it if his workmates hadn't formed a human

---

12 Yet let's not become too snobbish: the habit has never been confined to the lower orders. Addicts with eighty pounds to spare can buy a leather gum dispenser from Hermes.
13 In a 1953 talk entitled 'Going to the Theatre' Dame Sybil Thorndike claimed that London audiences were the worst in the world. 'Sometimes I feel like spitting at them because of all the rustling and coughing. It's so terrible some nights I can practically tell which chocolate has been taken from the box.'

chain to pull him clear just as a cataract of very hot, very green, peppermint filling poured into the vat.

Nothing changes. Picture, if you will, a house on a neat council estate, with a front garden that would eclipse the glories of the Chelsea Flower Show – and a back garden little more than a private scrapyard. Among the assorted wrecks and engine parts, and the inevitable moth-eaten mongrel left on barking duty, was an old ice-cream van. Rusted, smooth tyred, its glass panes were in desperate need of emergency Windowlene treatment. Bleached by several summers, the once gaily painted pictures of ice-cream cones and lollies were now almost invisible. Imagine our surprise, one day when the weather turned fine, to see the van backing out of the front gate and setting off in search of customers. But far more incredible than that rusted engine being sparked into life once more was what came next. It began with a sound like nothing we'd ever heard before – glockenspiel therapy for the learning impaired, perhaps – but no, it was the van's chimes being awoken from their dormancy. After half a minute it started to sound normal and, as we heard it repeated that after-noon, each time further and further away, the off-tune tinkling seemed like an essential part of British life.

Not long afterwards I got into conversation with the van's owner and asked if he was a professional ice-cream seller. No, and nor was he Italian, he hastened to add, seeing me glance at his black curls. He and his wife had made a modest living from it once but no longer. However, they'd had a stock of ice-lollies in the freezer for some three years and were determined to get their money back on them. Even now they had a few orange ones left, if our kids would like them …

Acknowledgements

This book required making contact with many sources. Some wanted to help, but couldn't; others could have helped, but wouldn't. But I never expected it to be easy and I *was* warned before I started. I used very few books hence the absence of a bibliography. There weren't many I could have referred to anyway, and besides I wanted a book that would be something of my own rather than a cut-and-paste job from other people's works. My sources came, in the main, from old newspapers and trade journals, and so my first round of applause must go the staff of the Newspaper Library in Colindale, always cheerful, helpful and ready with a suggestion when things occasionally went awry.

Grateful thanks also to Mr Raymond Needler, for a free copy of his informative book about the early days of confectionery in his grandfather's firm – invaluable in forming an impression of how things were – and his kind letter offering help if required.

Thanks also to Tony Bilsborough at Cadbury's, Mrs Kay Nichols at Mars, Carolyn Stirk at Lion Confectionery, Tracey Saunders at Bird's-Eye-Wall's, and to the various PR people at Nestlé, Askeys, Blue Bird Confectionery (who invited me to see their collection of toffee tins), Walkers Toffee, CPC, Swizzels-Matlow, Suchard/Terry's of York, Haribo/Dunhills, Walkers Crisps, Barrs, Golden Wonder,

Shirley Robinson, Wrigley's, and Mrs Christine Coates at the TUC library. If I've left anyone out, please accept my apologies.

Last, but not least, to Mrs Webster and Mr Elliott who wrote to me about the penny pop machine, not so much for the information, but for verifying that it hadn't all been a dream!